THE HARMONIZATION OF EUROPEAN PUBLIC POLICY

Recent Titles in Contributions in Political Science
Series Editor: Bernard K. Johnpoll

Global Mini-Nationalisms: Autonomy or Independence?
Louis L. Snyder

Socialism of a Different Kind: Reshaping the Left in France
Bernard E. Brown

Influence, Change, and the Legislative Process
Janet Miller Grenzke

Coherent Variety: The Idea of Diversity in British and American Conservative Thought
Michael D. Clark

The Social and Political Thought of Michael Bakunin
Richard B. Saltman

From Dictatorship to Democracy: Coping with the Legacies of Authoritarianism and Totalitarianism
Edited by John H. Herz

United States Foreign Policy at the Crossroads
Edited by George Schwab

Managing Crisis Cities: The New Black Leadership and the Politics of Resource Allocation
Bette Woody

National Conventions in an Age of Party Reform
James W. Davis

Neighbors Across the Pacific: The Development of Economic and Political Relations Between Canada and Japan
Klaus H. Pringsheim

International Dynamics of Technology
Ralph Sanders

Party Politics in Israel and the Occupied Territories
Gershon R. Kieval

The Strange Career of Marihuana: Politics and Ideology of Drug Control in America
Jerome L. Himmelstein

French Communism in the Era of Stalin: The Quest for Unity and Integration, 1945-1962
Irwin M. Wall

North Korea in Transition: From Dictatorship to Dynasty
Tai Sung An

THE HARMONIZATION OF EUROPEAN PUBLIC POLICY

Regional Responses to Transnational Challenges

EDITED BY LEON HURWITZ

CONTRIBUTIONS IN POLITICAL SCIENCE, NUMBER 98

Greenwood Press
WESTPORT, CONNECTICUT • LONDON, ENGLAND

Library of Congress Cataloging in Publication Data

Main entry under title:

The Harmonization of European public policy.

(Contributions in political science, ISSN 0147-1066 ; no. 98)
Bibliography: p.
Includes index.
Contents: The harmonization of European public policy: regional responses to transnational challenges / Leon Hurwitz – The harmonization of the European Community's external policy / Werner J. Feld – Aerospatial cooperation: the European Space Agency / Roy Gibson – [etc.]
1. European communities–Addresses, essays, lectures.
2. European federation–Addresses, essays, lectures.
I. Hurwitz, Leon. II. Series.
JN15.H335 1983 341.24'2 82-21063
ISBN 0-313-23119-2 (lib. bdg.)

Library of Congress Catalog Card Number: 82-21063
ISBN: 0-313-23119-2
ISSN: 0147-1066

First published in 1983

Greenwood Press
A division of Congressional Information Service, Inc.
88 Post Road West
Westport, Connecticut 06881

Printed in the United States of America

10 9 8 7 6 5 4 3 2 1

To my children,
Elise Jennifer and Jonathan Steven

CONTENTS

FIGURES

TABLES

PREFACE

The goal of this book is to present in one volume a collection of perspectives on the harmonization of European public policy, both within the European Community and within areas that transcend the Community (the European Space Agency, the European Science Foundation, the Council of Europe). Some of the essays have been contributed by the leading scholars in the field; others have been written by the practitioners themselves. All the essays are original and were written expressly for this volume. Several of the contributors have had direct experience with the European Community or with other intergovernmental international organizations, and although the disclaimer is offered that the views expressed by the authors do not necessarily represent those of any organization, these essays have the advantage of personal experience and information.

The essays reflect a balance among theoretical overviews on the nature of the policy harmonization process, empirical data analyses, and descriptive-narrative case studies. There is also a balance between American and European perspectives, since several of the essays have been contributed by my European colleagues: Roy Gibson (the European Space Agency's first Director-General); John Goormaghtigh (the current Secretary-General of the Strasbourg-based European Science Foundation); Harmen Lehment (a research associate at the Institut für Weltwirtschaft in Kiel); Jonathan Miller (a lecturer in law at the Polytechnic of Central London); and J. A. Albert Verreydt (the current Secretary-General of the Pharmaceutical Group of the European Community in Brussels). Other than myself, the American contributors include Werner J. Feld (University of New Orleans); Rodger Govea (Cleveland State University); Joseph Rallo (U.S. Air Force Academy); and David M. Wood (University of Missouri at Columbia).

This collection of essays is a collaborative and cooperative effort, and I would like to acknowledge the help I received. Most important, I am indebted to all the contributors noted above for graciously providing the essays and suffering through my editing. Several people rendered specific assistance, and each will know what I am thanking him for: John Klineberg at NASA-Lewis, Jean-Marc Mascaro in Grenoble, Sidney Metzger at COMSAT, Michel Pineri at CRN-Grenoble, John Nagle at Syracuse University, Wilfried Prewo at the Institut für Weltwirtschaft-Kiel, J.-P. Roth at the ESF-Strasbourg, and Roger Vaissière in Grenoble.

For most efficient secretarial services, my thanks go to Charles Urbancic and the Word Processing Center of the College of Arts and Sciences at Cleveland State University. I also want to thank the editorial and production staff at Greenwood Press for their professional assistance, especially Margaret M. Brezicki, Bernard K. Johnpoll, Maureen Melino, James T. Sabin, and Mildred Vasan. Additionally, the understanding of my wife Fran and my children Elise and Jonathan was appreciated.

Finally, whatever merit the reader may see in this book rightly belongs to my colleagues who wrote the essays; any shortcomings belong to the editor.

ABBREVIATIONS/ACRONYMS

AFC	Administrative and Finance Committee
BENELUX	Belgium, The Netherlands, Luxembourg
BIPM	International Bureau of Weights and Measures
BMG	Baader-Meinhof Group
CAP	Common Agricultural Policy
CBI	Confederation of British Industry
CCPU	Standing Conference on University Problems
CCTS	Comité de Coodination de Télécommunications par Satellites
CEA	Commissariat à l'Energie Atomique
CEPT	Conférence Européenne des Postes et Télécommunications
CERD	European Research and Development Committee
CERN	European Organization for Nuclear Research
CET	Common External Tariff
CETS	European Conference of Telecommunications
CFDT	Confédération Française Démocratique du Travail
CNES	Centre National des Etudes Spatiales
CNRS	Centre National de la Recherche Scientifique
COPERS	Commission Préparatoire Européenne de Recherche Spatiale
CPR/COREPER	Committee of Permanent Representatives
CREST	Scientific and Technical Research Committee
CSCE	Conference on Security and Cooperation in Europe
DG	Directorate-General
DM	Deutschmark
DNA	Deoxyribonucleic Acid
EC	European Community

ECA	European Communities Act
ECHR	European Convention on Human Rights
ECJ	European Court of Justice
ECS	European Communications Satellite
ECSC	European Coal and Steel Community
ECU	European Currency Unit
EEB	European Export Bank
EEC	European Economic Community
EIB	European Investment Bank
ELDO	European Launcher Development Organization
EMBC	European Molecular Biology Conference
EMBO	European Molecular Biology Organization
EMCF	European Monetary Cooperation Fund
EMF	European Monetary Fund
EMRC	European Medical Research Councils
EMS	European Monetary System
EMU	Economic and Monetary Union
ENA	Ecole Nationale d'Administration
EP	European Parliament
EPC	European Political Cooperation
ESA	European Space Agency
ESC	European Space Conference
ESDAC	European Space Computer Center
ESF	European Science Foundation
ESO	European Southern Observatory
ESRANGE	European Space Sounding Rocket Range
ESRC	European Science Research Councils
ESRF	European Synchrotron Radiation Facility
ESRIN	European Space Research Institute
ESRO	European Space Research Organization
ESTEC	European Space Technical Center
ETPBBR	ESF Training Program in Brain and Behavior Research
EUA	European Unit of Account
EURATOM	European Atomic Energy Community
EURONET	European Data Network
EXIM	Export-Import Bank
FAST	Forecasting and Assessment in Science and Technology
FF	French Franc
FRG	Federal Republic of Germany
GATT	General Agreement on Tariffs and Trade
GNP	Gross National Product
IATA	International Air Transport Association

IGO	International Intergovernmental Organization
IHES	Institut des Hautes Etudes Scientifiques
ILL	Institut Laue-Langevin
IMF	International Monetary Fund
INMARSAT	International Maritime Satellite Telecommunications Organization
INSERM	Institut National de la Santé et de la Recherche Médicale
INTELSAT	International Satellite Organization
ISR	Intersecting Storage Rings
ISRO	Indian Space Research Organization
IT. L.	Italian Lira
IVC	Index of Voting Cohesion
IVL	Index of Voting Likeness
JET	Joint European Torus
JRC	Joint Research Center
LDCs	Less Developed Countries
LEP	Large Electron Positron
MEP	Member European Parliament
MNE	Multinational Enterprise
MPLA	Popular Movement for the Liberation of Angola
MRCA	Multi-Role Combat Aircraft
MTA	Multilateral Trade Agreement
MTN	Multilateral Trade Negotiations
NASA	National Aeronautics and Space Administration
NATO	North Atlantic Treaty Organization
NGO	Non-Governmental Organization
NORDITA	Nordic Institute for Theoretical Atomic Physics
OECD	Organization for Economic Cooperation and Development
OEEC	Organization for European Economic Cooperation
OTS	Orbital Test Satellite
PFLP	Popular Front for the Liberation of Palestine
PIRA	Provisional Irish Republican Army
PLO	Palestine Liberation Organization
PS	Proton Synchrotron
R&D	Research and Development
SC	Synchrotron-Cyclotron
SDR	Special Drawing Rights
SDS	Space Documentation Retrieval System
SE	European Company
S. FR.	Swiss Franc
SPS	Super Proton Synchrotron

STC	Scientific and Technical Committee
TNO	Nederlandse Organisatie voor Toegepast-Naturwetenschappelijk Onderzoek
UA	Unit of Account
UDR	Union des Démocrates pour la Ve République
UK	United Kingdom
UN	United Nations
UNESCO	UN Educational, Scientific, and Cultural Organization
UNICE	Union of Industries in the European Community
US	United States
USSR	Union of Soviet Socialist Republics
ZWO	Nederlandse Organisatie voor Zuiver-Wetenschappelijk Onderzoek

THE HARMONIZATION OF EUROPEAN PUBLIC POLICY

Leon Hurwitz 1

THE HARMONIZATION OF EUROPEAN PUBLIC POLICY: REGIONAL RESPONSES TO TRANSNATIONAL CHALLENGES

The basis for the management of cooperation, the harmonization of public policy across national frontiers, and the existence of regional interdependence is the differential distribution of needs, aspirations, and capabilities of states and their people. These differences have played an important role in the establishment of intergovernmental organizations (IGOs – organizations whose members are nation-states) and of international nongovernmental organizations (NGOs – organizations composed of nongovernmental entities). Examples of IGOs are the United Nations (UN) and the European Community (EC); examples of NGOs are the International Chamber of Commerce (ICC) and the World Confederation of Labor (WCL). In some instances mixed units have been formed – the members are nation-states and nongovernmental units; for example, large business corporations (COMSAT – Communications Satellite Corporation). Showing a remarkable growth in the post-World War II era, both IGOs and NGOs have become increasingly significant factors in world politics.

IGOs are established in order to attain the common objectives of the member-states. These objectives reflect common or converging national interests and thus are normally long-range in nature, and the achievement of these objectives is theoretically carried out with the equal participation of all states, although this is not often the case in practice.

This section borrows heavily from Werner J. Feld, Robert S. Jordan, and Leon Hurwitz, *International Organizations* (New York: Praeger Publishers, 1983), esp. Chapter 1, "Changing Conceptualizations," and Chapter 2, "The Creation of International Organizations." Used with the permission of the authors and Praeger Publishers.

These common/converging interests can be varied, but the enhancement of a country's security and the hoped-for assurance that international peace can be maintained are major interests. Another set of interests may be advancing the level of economic development, raising the economic well-being of a country's citizens, managing economic interdependence in the world, and, in conjunction with national policy, participating in and perhaps controlling the exploration, marketing, and pricing of raw materials. Another important interest pursued through IGOs may be the strengthening of the political power of states. Finally, a major set of interests can be served by utilizing IGOs to search for solutions arising from science and technology problems emanating from worldwide communications and transportation as well as for environmental problems such as the spread of pollution and nuclear issues. Appropriate solutions may be increased border-crossing cooperation to enhance the technological capabilities of the individual states.

Although the above discussion of nation-states' interests reflects a variety of motivations for the establishment of IGOs, a determination must be made under what conditions a national government will resort to the instrument of intergovernmental organization to satisfy these and other interests. It is fair to assume that, under normal circumstances, a government will employ *national* means to meet the security, political, economic, scientific, and technological needs because, if it does decide to become involved in setting up an IGO for whatever purpose or to join an existing IGO, its independence and freedom of action will be impaired to some degree, even if the management authority conferred upon the IGO is very low. Moreover, the relations with other member countries of the IGO impose differing restraints on the actions and behavior of all participating governments.

The governmental decision whether to organize multilaterally for the pursuit and satisfaction of particular interests depends to a large extent on a country's political, economic, security, and technological capabilities and resources. If these are perceived to be sufficient to ensure the successful implementation of appropriate domestic and foreign policies, then international organization through establishing or joining IGOs may not be desirable. If, on the other hand, national capabilities are not regarded as adequate while IGOs appear to offer a more likely path to assuring the satisfaction of important national interests, then a state may be more inclined to encourage the performance of the necessary tasks multilaterally through the creation of appropriate IGOs. These are basically the circumstances forming the background for what John Ruggie calls a state's "propensity for international organization."[1]

Several propositions formulated by Ruggie seem to characterize the basic decision of governments to set up or join IGOs for the enhancement of national interests in various policy areas:

1. The propensity for international organization is determined by the interplay between the need to become dependent upon others for the performance of specific tasks, and the general desire to keep such dependence to the minimum level necessary.
2. There exists an inverse relationship between the ratio of international to national task performance and the total level of national resources a state possesses. In other words, from the perspective of the state, the greater its resources, the lower the number and scope of tasks assigned to IGOs for performance and the more of its resources that can be assigned to national task performance.
3. The propensity for international organization decreases over time as national capabilities increase and become sufficient to perform a given task.
4. A process of encapsulation built into the international performance of any given task tends toward limiting further commitments to, or further increase in the scope or capacity of, the collective arrangements.[2]

The general loss of independence or the loss of control over a state's own activities resulting from the accumulation of collective restraints caused by the creation and behavior of IGOs is termed by Ruggie "interdependence" costs. There is a large amount of literature on this concept of "interdependence," and the following presents a brief description of interdependence and its effects on national governments and upon IGOs.

William Coplin and Michael O'Leary describe interdependence as the existence of conditions in which the perceived needs of some individual groups in one state are satisfied by resources or capabilities that exist in at least one other state. The patterns of transnational interdependence thus are a product of the interface between needs and capabilities across national boundaries.[3] Such capabilities—military forces, economic and financial means, industrial and technological proficiency—can be translated into international power and influence while their absence may signal serious vulnerability. Small states are usually more modest in their policy goals than the big powers because of more limited resources although the skillful exploitation of a larger country's weaknesses may compensate for the limitations in resources.

Another view of interdependence has been put forth by Oran Young, who defines it as "the extent to which events occurring in any given part or within any given component of a world system affect (either physically or perceptually) events taking place in each of the other parts or component units of the system."[4] Directed primarily to economics, Richard Cooper suggests that interdependence is present when there is an increased "sensitivity" to external economic developments.[5] Robert Keohane and Joseph Nye also emphasize sensitivity as a dimension of interdependence. According to them it "involves degrees of responsiveness within a policy framework—how quickly do changes in one country bring costly changes in another, and how great are the costly effects?"[6] A second dimension of interdependence stressed by Keohane and Nye is "vulnerability" which "rests on the relative availability and costliness of the alternatives that various actors face."[7] Vulnerability reflects a country's or IGO's or a private actor's varying inability to accept and cope with economic, political, and social costs imposed by external events even if policies have been or will be changed.

It is the inequality of capabilities within interdependence relationships which at times evokes fears of dependence on the part of the governments and nongovernmental entities. Instead of producing perceptions of *reciprocal* dependence that might induce governments to treat the acts of other governments or IGOs as though they were events within their own borders and might be seen within the context of converging — if not identical — interests, *unequal* capabilities among states are likely to lead to suspicion, envy, and tensions.[8] Hence, governmental leaders may feel called upon to resort to national means and solutions as a countervailing force against the real or imagined threat of dependence on other countries or private entities. Such actions harm the prospects of useful collaboration among states and are likely to undermine, if not destroy, the benefits which interdependence networks may produce. Perceptions of this dependence have aggravated all the other problems that many leaders of the developing countries have faced in their priority task of nation building and their consequent preoccupation with sovereignty and autonomy of choice.

During recent years, United States foreign policy regarded growing interdependence as not only inevitable, but also desirable in producing consensus and restraining unacceptable conduct. It was viewed as a positive value, and the State Department promoted the idea of purposefully pursuing a strategy of interdependence which included the deliberate support of larger entities such as the European Community.[9] These views are not shared in all quarters, however. Many Third World — as well as a number of Western — intellectuals look at interdependence as creating undesirable dependence, and some think it is a code word for economic bondage.[10] They see a widening economic gap between affluent and poor societies. For these observers, the process of interdependence escalates tensions over the restrictions of national or societal autonomy, threatens the achievement of national economic, social, and political objectives, and may produce violent nationalist and interstate conflict.

This brings the discussion back to IGO organizational tasks, which include the management of cooperation through coordination and harmonization measures, the achievement of compromise, the selection of appropriate goal-attaining strategies, and the resolution of conflicts. The effective execution of all these tasks can produce or maintain beneficial interdependent relationships, accomplish a more adequate distribution of costs, resolve perceptions of dependency, and initiate new interdependent arrangements which maximally promote the interests of all participants.

It is in Western Europe that one finds the best examples of regional-interdependence enhancement through the management of cooperation and the harmonization of certain public policies by various IGOs and NGOs. Although there have been many management failures, several European organizations have played an important role in the management of cooperation and policy coordination-harmonization. Some past attempts—with varying levels of success—have included the harmonization of agricultural policy through the EC's Common Agricultural Policy, the coordination and common interpretation of antitrust legislation, the European energy policy; certain areas of foreign policy decision making, fiscal harmonization in relation to the value-added tax, and the coordination of certain health and social security policies.[11]

This book is concerned with some additional attempts by various European organizations—the European Community, the European Space Agency, the Council of Europe, the European Science Foundation—to produce or maintain beneficial interdependence relationships through the harmonization of certain public policies and thus promote the interests of all the participants.

There are ten essays in this book. Werner J. Feld, a political scientist at the University of New Orleans, writes on the harmonization of the EC's external policy. Roy Gibson, the first Director-General of the European Space Agency, reviews European aerospatial cooperation. Rodger Govea, a political scientist at Cleveland State University, discusses the European response to terrorism. David M. Wood, a political scientist at the University of Missouri-Columbia, analyzes the EC's higher civil service. John Goormaghtigh, the current Secretary-General of the European Science Foundation, reviews scientific cooperation in Europe. Joseph Rallo, the U.S. political scientist at Air Force Academy, discusses the EC's approach to the multinational enterprise. Harmen Lehment, a research associate at the Institute für Weltwirtschaft, writes on the European Monetary System. Leon Hurwitz, a political scientist at Cleveland State University, analyzes the voting behavior of the European Parliament. Jonathan Miller, an attorney on the faculty of the Polytechnic of Central London, writes on the harmonization of civil rights and civil liberties legislation. And J.-Albert Verreydt, the current Secretary-General of the EC's Pharmaceutical Group, discusses coordination of the pharmaceutical profession.

The harmonization of European public policy remains one of the primary methods by which the objectives of regional integration may be approached. Harmonization suggests the gradual evolution of a unified system without the disruptions occasioned by the imposition of more direct means of integration policy. The ability to propose and implement such measures is relective of the status accorded EC institutions by the governing instruments which also outline the scope and pace of such integrating efforts. This combination of institutional responsibility within defined operational parameters suggests that harmonization will be actively pursued in the future. Part of this optimism for the future of harmonization measures stems from the potential of a semi-insular region to shield itself from many of the effects generated by a less stable international system.

In "The Harmonization of the European Community's External Policy," Werner J. Feld writes that the coordination and harmonization of the EC's external policy is a complex process. The formulation of this policy is based not only on the constituent treaties of the three Communities (the ECSC, Euratom, and especially the EEC), but also emanates from a policy-coordinating mechanism which was established by the EC member states and evolved in the 1970s. This coordinating mechanism is now generally known as European Political Cooperation (EPC).

Feld comments that EPC, as a mechanism for the coordination of the EC member states' foreign policies, must be considered against a background of often divergent national foreign policy goals which the member governments seek to attain and the relationship of the pursuit of these goals to the formulation of Community policies toward third countries. In analyzing this relationship, Feld discusses several important factors. First, the establishment of the EEC represents in itself the realization of certain convergent economic foreign policy goals of the member governments. Second, in the field of external relations for which the Community organs are competent, the EC represents a centralized effort of the member states for the formulation and implementation of selected facets of their economic foreign policy, especially commercial policy.

A third factor complicating the formulation and implementation of common policies has been the reemergence of nationalism in the member states, and this has tended to accentuate what is conceived of as the national interest. Evidence of strong nationalistic feelings has been observed during the last few years in all of the member states, and the view that each government must serve foremost the interests of its own people before worrying about the Community interest is frequently put forth. Such sentiments strengthen the resolve of national governments to employ national instruments in the pursuit of their foreign policy goals rather than to submit to a joint approach under Community auspices.

The last factor to be considered is the views and attitudes of the national civil service in the member states concerned with Community affairs. These attitudes have a significant bearing on the effectiveness of external policy making in the EC. Sentiments of opposition against a "takover" of their functions by Community civil servants may express themselves in the use of subtle means to boycott the objectives of the EC treaties to turn over gradually the formulation and direction of certain economic foreign policies to the Community institutions.

How much success has EPC enjoyed? Feld writes that the results are mixed. Although EPC has been involved in a number of important international issues during the 1970s, clear-cut successful accomplishments have been rare. The most significant achievement of the EPC has been the coordination of policies leading to a common position during the preparatory phase of negotiations with respect to the Conference on Security and Cooperation in Europe (CSCE) from 1973 to 1979 and the follow-up evaluation meetings in Belgrade (1977-78) and Madrid (1980-81). The EC Commission participated vigorously and effectively in the deliberation on economic issues and contributed materially to shaping the common stand ultimately taken by the Nine. This was a clear example of effective policy harmonization of both the member states and the Community proper, although the specific competences of the latter were not directly involved. EPC has been involved in a number of other international issues, and Feld also discusses the Euro-Arab Dialogue, the Cyprus issue, relations with Spain and Portugal within the EC's Mediterranean policy, and the more recent attempts to evolve acceptable proposals to induce the Soviet Union to withdraw its forces occupying Afghanistan.

Feld concludes his essay by writing that regardless of how effective the EPC is as an external policy-harmonizing agent for the EC member states, it must be recognized that the EPC is basically a *national* instrument for foreign policy formulation and implementation, and its utilization is effectuated in accordance with what is perceived as best for the national interest. In addition, the EPC offers a number of special advantages to the member governments that are useful for domestic political purposes.

The first advantage is that EPC provides an alibi when member governments are faced with hard choices such as support for Arab or Israeli positions or whether to favor Greece or Turkey in the Cyprus dispute. Under such circumstances, the EPC is a highly useful framework to divert conflicting pressures and to transfer them to an "anonymous" body where the blame can be put on the "group" or on other parties. Second, the EPC can have a legitimating effect on foreign policies of member states vis-à-vis public opinion and, thereby, may give the government more freedom of action in relation to opposition forces. Third, the EPC is apt to increase the influence and power of all member states and especially of the smaller EC countries in international affairs. Clearly, the quantitative and qualitative weight of all Community countries as reflected by harmonized EPC policy action is stronger than the voice of any individual member government.

Roy Gibson's essay, "Aerospatial Cooperation: The European Space Agency," is written as a firsthand account. Gibson served as a staff member first of the European Space Research Organization (ESRO) and subsequently of the European Space Agency (ESA) from February 1967 to May 1980, the last five years as Director General. His service gives an insight into the subject matter, but it also undeniably increases the risk of personal bias. It is obvious that Gibson's thirteen years of service created passions and prejudices, but it is also obvious that Gibson has not written a polemic. His biases and prejudices are almost nonexistent, and, where this proved impossible, he identified them in order that the reader may more easily form a dispassionate opinion. Gibson makes no attempt to name scapegoats or to award personal praise; he is all too aware that he is still too close to the events to be able to make such judgments, and he is conscious that there are many differing interpretations of the happenings of the last twenty years.

One—probably the major—of Gibson's prejudices is stated explicitly at the outset of his essay: he has been unashamedly a European throughout his professional life. European here of course means more than the geographical meaning; it is a mind-set. He writes that his experience with ESRO and ESA put his faith in the European idea under considerable stress but that he emerged from his experience more convinced than ever that full European cooperation is the only sensible way to proceed. He is also convinced that the disadvantages of, and the frequent discomfort caused by, this cooperation can be attributed more to the inadequacies of individuals or groups of individuals, rather than to any innate flaw in the concept of European cooperation itself.

Gibson's essay traces the creation and development of the European space effort and examines in some detail some of its successes and failures. A common strand throughout the process was the desire to seek measures to prevent a further widening of the technological gap between the United States (and the USSR) and Europe. The challenges of space research and exploration were beyond the capabilities of any one individual European government; the cooperation within ESRO and ESA allowed technological and scientific advances for Europe.

The US National Aeronautics and Space Administration (NASA) is described as being responsible for Europe's entry into space. One of ESRO's first international agreements was a cooperation agreement with NASA; this served as the cover for a whole series of specific agreements subsequently covering projects on which NASA worked together with ESRO and then with ESA. In some cases NASA provided the launcher free of charge and ESRO/ESA accommodated a US experiment on board or supplied data acquired by its satellite. For some projects, ESRO/ESA simply purchased the launcher and launch services from NASA.

In Gibson's view, the European space successes are in a large measure due to the generous help and encouragement received from NASA, which went far beyond any purely commercial arrangement. From the outset, the senior staff at NASA were even more enthusiastic about European space cooperation than many Europeans. Some commentators have remarked that this

American generosity was forthcoming because the technological gap was so large that competition from Europe was difficult to envisage. Be that as it may, NASA most certainly aided the European space effort, as did several US aerospace firms who had formed valuable and sometimes lasting links with the European industrial aerospatial consortia.

As an IGO engaged in the management of cooperation, ESA tested the waters of external relations, but the sensitivity of ESA's member states was quite evident in this area. There were several opportunities for Europe to benefit from the reputation of its space agency, but the concerned governments were, in general, very reticent. Gibson thinks it was a reaction against any desire ESA might have to develop into a real supranational authority. Closer relations with Africa and the Middle East were particularly discouraged.

Gibson leaves little doubt that Europe missed several interesting opportunities because of the reluctance to play the ESA card. Non-Europeans with whom ESA officials came into contact were sometimes mystified by the attitude of member states, and the Director-General himself at times had difficulty in finding an explanation which was acceptable even given habitual diplomatic tolerance. Most member states were more interested in improving their own individual relations with developing countries by the provision of training courses and advice in the hope of an immediate commercial advantage for their own industry. That some overseas countries preferred a European approach to assistance and advice, and saw in ESA a firm guarantee of impartiality, was never really understood by some member states.

Nevertheless, ESA did have relations with many countries all over the world and concluded agreements with NASA, the Academy of Sciences of the USSR, the Indian and Japanese Space Research Organizations, and the corresponding authorities in the People's Republic of China. ESRO and ESA from the outset had close relations with the Council of Europe, but ESA-EC relations leave something to be desired. It is Gibson's view that the EC Commission was never really interested by ESA or by space affairs in general, but he hopes that a time will come when the Community can better exploit what ESA has to offer.

Gibson concludes his essay on a very optimistic note: there are ample indications that ESA's member states have every intention of continuing to cooperate together in space programs and even to extend their cooperation to new areas. European cooperation may cause member states periods of disillusionment and profound irritation, but progress is being made and will continue to be made as long as a minimum of goodwill is present. The cooperation and harmonization have been successful, and this success is of extreme importance for the making of Europe as a whole and not solely for aerospace.

In "The European Response to Terrorism," Rodger Govea discusses the recent attempts to achieve a regional anti-terrorist policy in Europe. The Council of Europe's 1977 Convention on the Suppression of Terrorism, as well as various resolutions passed by the European Parliament, are analyzed in terms of their contribution to a regionally harmonized policy.

The Council of Europe's Convention allows any country to reserve the right to refuse extradition in any offense which it considers to be "political" in nature, but the Convention defines away the political dimension of any terrorist activity. States are thus asked to accept the premise that insurgent terrorist behavior is unacceptable under any circumstances, and it is not surprising that only seven of the Council of Europe's twenty-one member states have given unconditional approval of the Convention. There are reservations to the effect that a state reserves the right to refuse extradition in any case involving a "political" offense, for offenses punishable by death in the requesting state (Portugal), and for "anyone persecuted on account of his action for the cause of liberty" (France).

The European Parliament resolutions clearly illustrate the differences and divisions among Western Europeans on the issue of a coordinated response to terrorism. One motion came from the socialist group; the other from a combination of the Christian Democrats, Progressive Democrats, and the Liberal and Democratic Group. While both motions condemned terrorism as an act and called upon member governments to harmonize policy, several differences in emphasis were evident.

The centrists' motion emphasized the dangers of terrorism itself; the socialists' emphasized the dangers of counter-terrorist policy. Moreover, the socialists seem to believe that governments share some of the blame for terrorist activity. The idea that the causes of terrorism should be eliminated implies that terrorism is a result of social and political conditions; nation states which experience terrorism may therefore be inducing these actions. In contrast, the centrist coalition places blame squarely on the terrorists themselves and sees terrorism as completely unjustifiable. No mention is made of restraints on governmental counter-terror actions.

Govea concludes that, overall, it is clear that there has been little real progress in a unified European—Council of Europe and/or European Community—response to terrorism. In addition, it appears that the prospects for a concerted Western European response are not particularly bright.

Some suggestions by the European Parliament for an international body of jurisdiction and enforcement within the EC require a ceding of sovereignty by the member states. But when terrorism is directed against a single government, that government will necessarily insist on directing countermeasures because it has been challenged. It is inconceivable that governments faced with a threat to their own internal security will allow another political body to decide its fate. The very sensitivity of the terrorism issue is an additional obstacle to increased cooperation and harmonization. There is a natural tendency for countries to avoid dealing with terrorism outside their borders, partly because of a reluctance to encroach on the domestic politics of another country but more so out of a desire to avoid the difficult political problems caused by a sustained terrorist campaign. Western European countries outside of Britain are relieved that they do not also have a Northern Ireland. It is understandable that they do not adopt the conflict as their own; by similar logic other terrorist campaigns are avoided whenever possible.

The European response to terrorism has been composed primarily of symbolic gestures assuring nation-state cooperation. Undoubtedly, the biggest effect of the European response is to have provided symbolic reassurance to those citizens who are aware of the activities of the Council of Europe and the European Community. Since true security against terrorism is impossible, perhaps the nations of Western Europe, in posturing against terrorism, have done virtually all that can be done.

David M. Wood's essay, "Future Technocrats? Recruits to the Higher Civil Service of the European Community," is based upon research and extensive interviews at the EC Commission in Brussels. As Wood writes, the EC Commission is a bureaucracy that is located at the conjunction of political and administrative functions. As the executive organ of a truly transnational organization, it is charged with the responsibility of taking policy-making initiatives and seeking to reconcile the conflicting interests of member states as well as implementing policies made by its political superiors, the Council of Ministers.

The staff of the Commission is an international civil service whose members must wed their perspectives as nationals of their native countries to their commitments to the international (European) mission with which the Commission is entrusted. A considerable amount of the work of the Commission is of a technical, specialized nature, reflecting largely the economic policy/administration role of the organization. Thus, in addition to political sensitivity and administrative skill, the job description for the European civil servant often includes technical competence in professional/academic disciplines whose skills are in demand for employment at the national, as well as the international level, in the private sector as well as the public. Wood's essay examines the sorts of professional specialities the EC Commission has sought in recruiting European civil servants.

Two related but conceptually distinct types of recruitment approaches are established by Wood: the "technocratic" pattern and the "Eurocratic" pattern. The technocratic civil servant, when compared to the Eurocrat, prefers policies promoting material progress rather than other values such as social justice or environmental protection; is incrementalist rather than fashioning policy to serve utopian ends or slavishly adhering to bureaucratic routines; makes policy that is insensitive to those group demands or anticipated political consequences that the civil servant does not recognize as legitimate; and shows a preference for centralized control over the implementation of policy.

The findings of Wood's analysis are mixed: there are several results that would support the technocratic pattern if they were not accompanied by counter-findings. The results drawn from national profiles make it impossible to affirm the technocratic hypothesis because different academic disciplines and professional mixes appear for different countries, each with its own explanation.

The EC Commission has made a substantial effort to upgrade the professional quality of its personnel practices, including the recruitment process. Recruitment is handled in a highly professional fashion, with every effort made to ensure that new entrants will be of superior quality. One indication of this is that the Commission has not adhered rigidly to national quotas but has in fact discriminated in favor of some nationalities over others ("discrimination" in a technical sense and not implying willfull intent). Another indication is that recruitment has not been one-sidedly technocratic or juridical. Efforts seem to have been made to adjust to differences in the mixes of talent most readily available from different countries.

Another indicator is the preference for candidates with superior language skills, other factors being equal. Finally, Wood's data have shown that the EC Commission tends to reward European experience when it finds it, suggesting that the intention to instill an institutional loyalty in its employees has not seriously diminished.

John Goormaghtigh's essay, "Scientific Cooperation: The European Science Foundation," is written from the viewpoint of a long-term international organization administrator. Goormaghtigh is currently the Secretary-General of the Strasbourg-based European Science Foundation, and the same caveats that were offered with Gibson's essay are also offered here: his service gives an insight into the subject matter, but it also undeniably increases the risk of personal bias. However, his biases are almost nonexistent, and his essay is a most balanced account of scientific cooperation in Europe and the European Science Foundation.

The European Science Foundation (ESF) legally came into existence when its draft statutes were approved by an assembly of representatives of 42 academies and research councils from 15 different countries in November 1974. The statute stipulates that the ESF is an international nongovernmental nonprofit association of organizations devoted to the promotion of basic research. It is really not a "foundation"—it is an "association" of organizations and it has no capital endowment or independent income with which to make grants for research projects (the ESF is funded by contributions from the member organizations).

The principal objectives of the ESF are to advance cooperation in basic research; to promote mobility of research workers; to assist in the free flow of information and ideas; and to facilitate the harmonization of the basic research activities of the member organizations. Additional objectives are to facilitate cooperation in assessing and executing appropriate projects of major importance; to facilitate cooperation in the provision of expensive specialized services; and to make grants for the support of concerted actions and collaborative schemes. The ESF statute defines "science" in the broadest sense of the term so as to include the humanities, the social sciences and jurisprudence, and natural, medical, and technical sciences. This is a very broad mandate, and Goormaghtigh remarks that it should not be surprising that the ESF in its short existence has been able to progress on such a wide front.

The ESF is flexible and adaptable in spite of its somewhat complicated bureaucratic structure. It is clearly neither a European research council nor primarily an establishment carrying out its own research. It has neither the funds nor the necessary national support to aspire to the first function, and it could not possibly consider becoming a European research facility dealing with so many disciplines. Goormaghtigh writes that the ESF fulfills essentially a "forum" function: it constitutes a link and a means of intra-European communication between scientists. But however well-intentioned and well-equipped an international organization may be, the institution will never be recognized as a legitimate forum where ideas can be exchanged, cooperation initiated, conflicts ameliorated, joint projects planned, and policies harmonized, if it merely offers an infrastructure of conference facilities and a secretariat. To play the role effectively, an institution has to enjoy the full confidence and respect of the community or communities it was set up to serve—in the case of the ESF, essentially the scientists, the member organizations, and also to some extent the governments. To acquire the necessary reputation and confidence, an organization cannot just sit back and wait for projects to be submitted; it has to be active, take initiatives, run a program—of course, with the backing of its clientele—to prove its capability and its standards.

Goormaghtigh writes that the ESF has become a recognized instrument of scientific collaboration in Europe. It enjoys the confidence and respect of scientists and scholars, and it is an acknowledged forum for contacts and communication among them and among the science funding agencies. It has conducted a series of worthwhile projects. However, its full potential as a tool for harmonizing European science policies and organizing cooperative projects is far from being fully exploited. What is lacking is not an efficient institutional framework (the machinery is there), but the political will of governments to pool their resources.

Why has science, which by essence is international, not become one of the dynamic forces pressing for greater European cooperation, particularly when the scientists themselves and public opinion in general seem to be in favor of closer cooperation in this field? Goormaghtigh writes that in spite of the proliferation of international institutions which have come into being since 1945, in spite of all the efforts toward European unification and the achievement of the EC, there is so far no organization which has as its main or principal objective to work toward an overall European R&D policy or even to attempt to harmonize effectively national science policies. One can only conclude from this that the political will to do so does not exist.

This hesitation is no doubt largely attributable to perceived national economic and security interests. At a time when scientific innovation constitutes more than ever before a determining factor in the economic potential and the military security status of a state, no government is prepared to run the risk of losing a possible advantage gained from research to its neighbors or competitors. For this reason governments—and to a large extent government-funded R&D agencies—wish to keep strict control over their own science policy. And in many cases where national and private interests coincide, powerful pressure groups just reinforce the restrictive attitudes of governments.

Goormaghtigh concludes his essay by writing that international cooperation in science, as in other areas, demands an institutional infrastructure. The effectiveness of these organizations depends mainly on the political will of the member governments. The organizations cannot by themselves create consensus, but they are an indispensable forum for consensus formation and for its implementation.

In "The European Community and the Multinational Enterprise," Joseph Rallo discusses the relationship between the multinational enterprise (MNE) and the state. The threat posed by the MNE's mobility and operating practices directly affects a state's ability to pursue its independent economic policy objectives. Of particular concern is the demonstrated ability of the foreign MNE to dominate domestic industrial potential in vital areas of technological research and development. Individual state responses to such MNE activity differ in approach but not in objective. National regulation of the MNE is viewed as the key to future relations between the state and the foreign MNE. The question that remains is the manner in which such national objectives can be harmonized, given the transnational nature of MNE activities.

Rallo emphasizes the policy responses to the problem of MNE activity proposed by the members and institutions of the European Community. As a major global economic actor engaged in the pursuit of harmonized industrial policies for their region, the EC and its members are in an advantageous position to establish a regulatory system for MNE activities.

Several themes overlap in the discussion of such a regional regulatory policy. First is the gradual loss of member support for the objectives of regional political and economic integration. Second is the shift of policy responsibility from the Community-oriented Commission to the member-controlled Council of Ministers. Third is the undeniable fact that few of the Community's proposals in this area have ever been fully implemented.

Finally, there is a close connection between the development of internal community proposals and EC participation in the work of extraregional international organizations, especially the Organization for Economic Cooperation and Development (OECD), in the area of MNE regulation.

The Commission-sponsored proposals, covering the spectrum of international corporations' activities, have met with more opposition than most other harmonization attempts. The main reason for such lack of success is that the issue of MNE regulation cannot be achieved by measures whose scope is limited only to the area of the Community itself. By their very nature, MNEs operate transnationally, and thus any attempts to address certain excesses in their operating style must similarly be transnational in scope. Commission harmonization proposals must therefore be responsive to these externally generated consequences of MNE activity as well as being sympathetic to the changing internal definition and objectives of Community integration policy. It is an unfortunate aspect of the duality that those measures most successful in addressing the externally generated consequences of MNE activity are also those very same proposals which require the greatest amount of integrative commitment on the part of the Community's member states.

Two conclusions are suggested by Rallo for the future of integration theory and for the potential role of the region in international affairs. First, since internal measures alone cannot adequately resolve the issue of MNE regulation, one must seriously question the future capability of a region to address problems whose solutions require the participation of extraregional actors (both individual states and IGOs). Second, regulation of the MNE will evolve from the increasingly similar international economic objectives of certain states pursued through intergovernmental cooperation within regional organizations. Organizational membership does not require the political commitment, as do integrating regions, and will therefore tend to reinforce rather than mitigate economic differences between groups of nations. Resultant inequalities in the ability of regional organizations to control MNE operations will also serve to perpetuate inequities in the present international division of technological capabilities and resources. Care must therefore be taken to balance the advantages of regional regulation of the multinational economic stratification that such action can produce.

The recently established (1979) European Monetary System (EMS) is discussed by Harmen Lehment. The decisive event for the creation of the EMS was the so-called dollar crisis that started in autumn 1977. The substantial depreciation of the dollar and a weakening confidence in the ability of the Carter administration to protect the internal and external value of the US currency caused the political heads of France and Germany to start an initiative for a European "zone of exchange-rate stability."

An additional French consideration was that France, as a leading EC country, should also be a member of the exchange-rate arrangement that already existed among several EC countries. One driving force behind the

German initiative for the EMS had been the intent to dampen the revaluation pressure on the German mark.

Lehment writes that a common motive for the initiative may also have been that the EMS was regarded as a step toward a currency union in the EC, the final stage being "one money for Europe." The outline of the EMS was presented and discussed at the meeting of the European Council of Heads of State or Government in Bremen in July 1978. After some revisions and supplements, the main lines of the system were adopted by the European Council in Brussels in 1978 and the EMS was formally introduced on March 13, 1979.

There are three main elements of the EMS: (1) an adjustable peg system for most EC currencies; (2) an extension of credit facilities through the European Monetary Cooperation Fund; and (3) the introduction of a European Currency Unit. The main element of the EMS is the introduction of an adjustable peg system for all EC currencies except the United Kingdom. The UK did not join the exchange-rate arrangement and continues with an independent floating of its currency. Greece, which only joined the EC in January 1981, is also not a participant in the exchange-rate arrangement. Exchange rates in the EMS are not completely fixed but are allowed to fluctuate around a margin of 2.25 percent on both sides of the central rate; for Italy the respective margin is 6 percent in order to account for the fact that the relatively high Italian inflation rate tends to require more exchange-rate flexibility. In addition to these elements, the Brussels resolution provided for the potential participation on non-EC countries in the EMS and the coordination of exchange rate policies vis-à-vis third countries.

Lehment writes that the EMS has several economic problems. One such problem is that a system of exchange rates runs into difficulties, not because the member countries cannot defend the exchange rates, but rather because governments are not willing to defend exchange rates. They are unwilling because the required measures would run counter to domestic policy targets. Also, compared to the previous "snake" system, the EMS provides less favorable conditions for a further step toward a currency union. The main reason is that the EMS comprises both a larger and a less homogeneous group of countries. Attempts to narrow the margins for exchange-rate fluctuations among the member currencies—considered as a future task in the Brussels agreement—will be more difficult to realize than in the "snake," where national inflation rates of the remaining member countries did not differ as widely as inflation rates in the EMS. A centralization of monetary policy and the introduction of a common currency, two central elements of a currency union, are not even mentioned in the EMS agreement.

Lehment concludes his essay with the comment that the few exchange-rate adjustments in the first years of the EMS have not been sufficient to offset the inflation differentials in the member countries. One can, therefore, expect that future exchange-rate realignments have to be stronger than those which have been observed. The question is: Can the EMS react to the increased exchange-rate pressure with sufficient flexibility? Or will it share the fate of its predecessors: the Bretton Woods system (which finally had collapsed) and the "snake" (where countries with a relatively high rate of inflation left the exchange-rate arrangement)? The real test of the EMS is still to come.

The transnational political party groupings in the European Parliament are examined through roll-call analysis by Leon Hurwitz in "Partisan Ideology or National Interest: An Analysis of the Members of the European Parliament." The European integrative process attained a milestone in June 1979 when approximately 112 million voters went to the polls across the nine-country EC and elected 410 (24 Greek members were added subsequently) representatives to the first directly elected supranational Parliament in history.

These 434 representatives are from ten separate, sovereign states—each with its own culture, national identity, and political values—but they have formed six major transnational party "groups" in the Parliament. Prior to 1979, the representatives were chosen by and from, and were responsible to, their respective national parliaments. The new Parliament, directly responsible to the EC's population and voter constituencies, possesses a political legitimacy that the former appointed Parliament never had. This does not by itself give the Parliament any more real effective power vis-à-vis the Commission and the Council of Ministers (its real power, in fact, is quite low—most of the EP's "decisions" are only statements of intent without any force in community law), but it at least strengthens the Parliament's potential to have more influence at the European level in the future.

Employing the techniques of roll-call analysis, Hurwitz identifies the general level of conflict/consensus in the EP as a whole, notes the degree of voting cohesiveness within each of the delegations and the transnational party groups, and identifies the degree to which the members of the EP vote along partisan ideological lines compared to national interest lines. The fact that some beginnings have been made to formulate transnational party platforms across the EC and that the groupings have been established in the Parliament leads to the view that transnational party affiliation will be a stronger explanatory variable for the observed voting differences than will national identity.

Strong transnational party groups with coordinated and harmonized policy positions may encourage the various community interest groups to use their electoral weight to bargain for changes. A more balanced representation of interests at the European level might then be secured, for, until now, the most influencial interest groups have been producers and employers. Cohesive parties in Parliament—at least those on the Left—may be more sympathetic to trade unions and consumer and environmental groups. Hurwitz also offers some comments on the scope of the erosion of long-held national mind-sets by Europeans and the emergence of truly coordinated transnational political attitudes. This would hint that nationalism is breaking down, and, while not necessarily decreasing levels of conflict in the short run (ideological conflict would be simply substituted for nationalism), elite consensus and cooperation appear to be more readily attainable when based upon explicit and bargainable political goals rather than when based upon the subconsciousness of national identity.

Although the transnational political groups in the EP do attempt to work out coordinated positions, the roll-call analysis shows that the degree of internal cohesiveness—although higher for the political groups than for the country delegations—does not reach significant levels. The very fact of direct elections may contribute to this comparative independence of the individual member of the EP; no longer responsible to the party hierarchy in the home parliament, the member has much more leeway when he is now responsible to an amorphous electorate.

The transnational political *groups* in the European Parliament may develop into transnational *parties* with a truly coordinated and harmonized position, but, in order to do so, they will first have to present candidates for the EP across the 10 members under a single label and with a single, common platform. At present, there are three parties linked at the European level—the Socialists, the European Peoples Party, and the Liberals. These federations attempted to coordinate the 1979 campaign and they try to maintain links between the EP groups and the national political parties. But these federations cannot be called transnational political parties—there is an attempt at coordination, but they are not yet truly harmonized.

Jonathan Miller's essay, "A European Bill of Rights?," discusses the effect and impact of the European Convention on Human Rights and EC Treaty provisions upon domestic law, especially UK domestic law. Miller writes that not only is Community law superior to national law and liable to prevail over inconsistent subsequent national law; it is also part of the national legal systems, bestowing in certain circumstances rights and obligations upon individuals. A statement by the European Court of Justice is cited to this effect: "Every national court must, in a case within its jurisdiction, apply Community law in its entirety and protect rights which the latter confers on individuals and must accordingly set aside any provisions of national law which may conflict with it, whether prior or subsequent to the Community rule."

In the initial period after the establishment of the EC, the European Court of Justice failed to deal with the issue of the protection of human rights, but with the growth in the activities of the Community and the unequivocal endorsement of the supremacy of Community law, apprehensions were aroused in the member states about the impact of the EC law on the rights of individual citizens, even though the Community has neither a specific charter of fundamental rights nor any guarantee that individual rights would be protected as contained in the European Convention on Human Rights. The European Court nonetheless held that "... respect of our fundamental rights has an integral part in the general principles of law which the Court of Justice ensures respect. The protection of such rights, while inspired by the constitutional principles common to the member states, must be ensured within the framework of the Community's structure and objective."

Although the EC as an entity has not acceded to the European Convention on Human Rights in any formal sense, the Community institutions have endorsed the view that fundamental human rights and their protection are part of the objectives of the Community. Miller discusses an April 1977 joint declaration issued by the European Parliament, the Commission, and the Council of Ministers on the relationship between the EC and the ECHR. The joint declaration stated that the European Parliament, the Council, and the Commission stress the prime importance they attach to the protection of fundamental rights as derived in particular from the constitutions of the member states and the European Convention for the Protection of Human Rights and Fundamental Freedoms. In addition, the Community organs stated that in the exercise of their powers and in pursuance of the aims of the Communities, they would respect these rights.

Miller concludes his essay with the view that, looking over the past some twenty-five years since the establishment of the EC, the EC has felt confident enough to pronounce on issues other than economic ones. The European Court of Justice, by making the first cautious steps toward establishing a human rights philosophy as part of its jurisprudential arsenal, has helped in the development of the final goal of the Community: that of political union and perhaps with it a European Bill of Rights.

The last essay in this volume is by J.-Albert Verreydt who presents a brief discussion on "The Evolution of the European Pharmaceutical Profession." Verreydt begins his essay with a discussion of the European pharmaceutical industry. Created from the individual pharmacist's workbench in the 1800s, the pharmaceutical industry evolved rapidly into major corporations with a high degree of technical expertise in synthetic chemistry. The vast advances made by medical and pharmaceutical research provided dazzling benefits for the maintenance of public health and the general standard of living. But since this particular area of industrial activity was—and still is—so closely linked to the public interest, the national government authorities were obliged to institute certain legislative controls and restrictions.

The (sometimes) conflicting national legislation, in turn, necessitated that the EC institutions issue various harmonizing directives concerning pharmacological, toxicological, and analytical controls; the marketing of pharmaceutical products; and the periodic inspection of the laboratory facilities and the manufacturing plants. The obvious first task was to reach an agreement on a "European" definition of medicine, and this was achieved in a 1965 Council of Ministers Directive.

One of the principle objectives of the EC is to achieve among the member states the full and free circulation of people, goods, and capital. The Rome Treaty anticipates the right of establishment for the liberal (self-employed) professions. As of the time of writing, however, the only professionals that have yet to receive "European" status are self-employed physicians; pharmacists have yet to benefit from the free-circulation clause. But, as Verreydt writes, the free circulation of pharmacists should be relatively easy to achieve because the European pharmacy profession is approaching a standardized curriculum across Europe.

A 1981 directive dealt with this curriculum, but, in order to avoid as much as possible upsetting national traditions, the directive was limited to coordination: a program of minimum study of at least five years after which a professional training stage of six to twelve months was required. The directive defined the course of study's general content and listed the required areas but did not fix a specific duration within any area. The same directive also was concerned with some coordination of the areas of pharmacist activity after receipt of the diploma. Here again the EC was faced with national traditions and diversity, and the EC opted to identify some general directions rather than to attempt a more determined coordination.

Verreydt concludes his essay by writing that although the pharmaceutical profession is relatively harmonized across Europe, the various directives do not anticipate a standardization of the curriculum or a complete coordination of all the pharmacy-related activities across the EC member states. This hesitancy is the consequence of the very real differences that have evolved within the profession in each member state. The directives respect the differences in national cultures and traditions as well as the differences which exist from university to university even within the same country. Verreydt, as the Secretary-General of the EC Pharmaceutical Group, believes that it is obvious to all that a more rational coordination must be achieved in the future; but too much coordination too fast will lead to turmoil in many member states.

NOTES

1. John Ruggie, "Collective Goods and Future International Collaboration," *American Political Science Review* 66 (September 1972): 874-893.

2. Ibid., p. 882.

3. William D. Coplin and Michael K. O'Leary, "A Policy Analysis Framework for Research, Education and Policy-Making in International Relations," paper delivered to the 1974 International Studies Association Convention, St. Louis, Missouri.

4. Oran Young, "Interdependence in World Politics," *International Journal* 24 (Autumn 1969): 726.

5. Richard N. Cooper, *The Economics of Interdependence* (New York: McGraw-Hill, 1968), pp. 3-8.

6. Robert O. Keohane and Joseph S. Nye, *Power and Interdependence: World Politics in Transition* (Boston: Little Brown, 1977), p. 12.

7. Ibid., p. 13.

8. An extensive literature on the issue of Third World dependency has evolved during the last few years. For example, the entire issue of *International Organization* 32 (Winter 1978) is devoted to dependency and dependence with five articles focusing on theoretical aspects and four dealing with regional problems. See also Richard B. Fagan, "Studying Latin American Politics: Some Implications of a Dependence Approach," *Latin American Research Review* 12 (1977): 3-26; Robert R. Kaufman, Harry I. Chermotsky, and Daniel S. Geller, "A Preliminary Test of the Theory of Dependence," *Comparative Politics* 7 (April 1975): 303-30; Benjamin Cohen, *The Question of Imperialism* (New York: Basic Books, 1973); and Thomas Moran, *Multinational Corporations and the Politics of Dependence* (Princeton, N.J.: Princeton University Press, 1974).

9. United States Department of State, *Toward a Strategy of Interdependence*, Bureau of Public Affairs, no. 17 (July 1975).

10. See Hayward R. Alker, Lincoln P. Bloomfield, and Nazli Choucri, *Analyzing Global Interdependence*, vol. 2 (Cambridge, Mass.: Center for International Studies, M.I.T., 1974), p. 3.

11. For a discussion of some of these policy-coordination attempts, see the essays by Werner J. Feld, Stephen D. Kon, Robert J. Lieber, Corrado Pirzio-Biroli, Donald J. Puchala, and Roger Vaissière and Jean-Marc Mascaro in Leon Hurwitz, ed., *Contemporary Perspectives on European Integration: Attitudes, Nongovernmental Behavior, and Collective Decision Making* (Westport, Conn.: Greenwood Press, 1980).

Werner J. Feld — 2

THE HARMONIZATION OF THE EUROPEAN COMMUNITY'S EXTERNAL POLICY

Harmonizing the European Community's (EC) external policy is a complex process because the formulation of this policy not only is based on the constituent treaties of the three Communities, and especially the EEC Treaty, but also emanates from a policy-coordinating mechanism established by the EC member states which evolved during the 1970s. This coordinating mechanism is now generally known as European Political Cooperation (EPC). This chapter will first examine the Community instruments and processes for the formulation and, to a lesser degree, the implementation of external policies; and then proceed to a discussion and evaluation of EPC. The last part of the chapter briefly reviews the substance of major policies developed by both processes.

EC TREATY COMPETENCES

The Common Commercial Policy

The main clause providing the Community institutions with the authority to engage in foreign economic policy is Article 113 of the EEC Treaty. It stipulates that after the transitional period (1958-69) had expired, a common commercial policy toward third countries based on uniform principles was to be instituted "particularly in regard to tariff amendments, the conclusion of tariff or trade agreements, the alignment of measures of liberalization, export policy and protective commercial measures including measures to be taken in cases of dumping and subsidies." The enumeration of activities in Article 113 is not exhaustive. Therefore, measures such as the regulation of export and import prices, the establishment of import and export quotas, the stipulation of conditions for export transactions, the issuance of currency regulations for commercial transactions with nonmember states, matters concerned with tourist trade, and perhaps others also seem to fall under the competence of the Community organs. Not covered, however, are such matters as exchange rates for the currencies of the member states, balance-of-payments problems, and policies regarding economic trends because special provisions of the EC Treaties govern these subjects.

It was anticipated by the Treaty framers that the implementation of the common commercial policy toward third countries could at times cause economic difficulties for the Common Market members when disparities in the execution of commercial policy measures by the various member governments arose or diversions of trade were produced. If such difficulties should appear in the economy of one or more member states, the Commission may, according to Article 115, recommend methods whereby the other states provide the necessary cooperative assistance. In the event that these methods fail to remedy the problem, the Commission may authorize the states involved to take specified protective measures such as temporary changes in tariff rates or interim restrictions of imports. The member states have made extensive use of these protection measures, especially with respect to products coming from countries with very low wages or state-operated foreign trade, the usual method in communist states.

Another unfortunate consequence of the implementation of the Community commercial policy might be difficulties in a member state's balance of payments. If such difficulties are likely to prejudice the functioning of the Common Market or the progressive establishment of the common commercial policy, Article 108 requires the Community organs to organize "mutual assistance" operations in the form of concerted action in international organizations, the provision of limited credits, or special trade measures. The member states have also taken advantage of these provisions on several occasions.

The Common External Tariff (CET)

An essential ingredient for the creation of a customs union, upon which the Community is based, is the erection of a common external tariff toward the outside world. It has become a fundamental instrument of trade and external policies of the Community.

The original schedule specified by the treaty for the introduction of the CET set January 1, 1962 (the end of the first stage of the transition period) as the target date for the completion of the tariff. But the CET was 97 percent completed nearly two years before this date when in March 1960 agreement was reached in the Council on most tariff items.

The completion of the CET did not signify that its duties were to apply immediately for all imports into the Community; rather, the CET was to be used as a guideline toward which the four individual tariffs were to be either lowered or increased in three stages beginning on January 1, 1962. By the end of the transition period in 1970, the CET was to be applied exclusively.

Several reasons, such as charges of protectionism and discrimination against the Community's tariff policy and the prospect of a speeded-up reduction of internal tariffs within the Community, induced the Community authorities to begin the progressive adjustments of the four individual tariff schedules toward the CET in January 1961, a year earlier than that specified in the EEC Treaty. The second alignment was made two-and-a-half years ahead of schedule, on July 1, 1963, and the full implementation of the CET took place on July 1, 1968, the date when all internal tariffs were eliminated.

Treaty-Making Power

Several provisions of the EEC Treaty (among them the authority for the negotiation and conclusion of agreements to implement the common commercial policy) explicitly bestow treaty-making powers on the Community organizations. This power is one of the most important instruments for the implementation of foreign policy.

The negotiations for a tariff agreement with nonmember states are conducted by the Commission, which requires an authorization or mandate from the Council to begin negotiations. The Commission may submit recommendations regarding the opening and substance of negotiations, but the Council can also act on its own and ask the Commission to commence the negotiation of an agreement. The Commission is not legally obligated to comply with such a request, but for political reasons the Commission is well advised to follow the wishes of the Council.

In the conduct of negotiations, the Commission must follow the directives issued by the Council and consult with a special Committee appointed by the Council, called "Committee 113," because its employment is stipulated in Article 113 of the EEC Treaty.[1] This Committee is composed of national officials of the member states who, depending on the nature of the particular negotiations, may come from the foreign, economic, or agricultural ministries. The Commission is not required to seek the consent of this Committee for specific actions in the negotiations; all it needs to do is to establish rapport with the Committee in order to enable that body to perform its supervising and possible influencing function for the Council. In practice, however, the members of the Committee are quite influential and often are bound by and carry out specific instructions of their governments.

The agreements negotiated by the Commission are concluded by the Council on behalf of the Community, for which a qualified majority vote is sufficient.[2] Properly concluded agreements with third countries bind not only the EC as an intergovernmental organization, but also the member states. In other words, for the member states the effect is the same as if they themselves had concluded the agreement with the third countries.[3]

The exact scope of the treaty-making power of the Community organizations is not specified in the EEC Treaty, but since this authority is contained in the same provisions that apply to the development of a common commercial policy, the assumption seems to be justified that all matters falling within the scope of the common policy may also be the proper subjects for bilateral or multilateral commercial agreements between the EC and nonmember states. Some observers, however, consider this interpretation of the Community's treaty-making powers too broad. They hold that it is primarily the principles of policy that are under the control of the Community organs and that, as a consequence, the conclusion of any concrete and detailed agreements remains in the hands of the member states. Although this interpretation appears to contravene the spirit and purpose of the EEC Treaty, it may well be preferred by the member governments.[4]

The Euratom Treaty also contains provisions conveying authority upon the EC organs for limited treaty-making power. However, in view of the highly technical and specialized nature of the Euratom Treaty, only a relatively small segment of the economic life in the member states is affected by this power. Specifically, under the Euratom Treaty the European Community can conclude agreements for the purpose of exchanging scientific or industrial information on nuclear matters.[5] It can enter into agreements with third countries, international organizations, and nationals of a third country regarding their participation in the financing and management of joint enterprises in the field of nuclear energy.[6] The Community, through its supply agency established under the Treaty, also has the exclusive right of concluding conventions that have as their principal object the importation of fissionable materials and appropriate ores from outside the territory of the member states. Finally, it can make agreements concerning measures of safety and security with respect to fissionable materials and nuclear fuels.[7] Some of these provisions have been used during the 1970s by the EC Community organs.

Association Agreements

In terms of impact on international politics, perhaps the most significant treaty-making power of the Community has been the ability to enter into agreements of association with nonmember states, "unions" of such states, and international organizations. Article 238 of the EEC Treaty, authorizing the creation of associations, stipulates only that they must embody "reciprocal rights and obligations, joint actions and special procedures." There are no geographic limitations for associate countries; in other words, they may be located anywhere in the world. For agreements leading to an association, the Council of Ministers must act unanimously at all times; that is, both during and after the transitional period. As in the case of tariff and commercial agreements, the Commission conducts the negotiations for an association; in the performance of this task, it must follow the directives of the Council and consult with Committee 113. Prior to the conclusion of the agreement, the Council is obligated to consult the European Parliament, but the advice of the Parliament is not binding.[8]

In the most general terms, the objective of an association agreement is the creation of a relationship exceeding that which can be attained by the conclusion of a tariff or commercial accord but falling short of full membership. Although the Treaty does not furnish a definition of the objectives, certain possibilities come to mind. For an association with the Community that is based on the concept of a customs union, a first objective might be the extension of this union to include the associated state or states. For European countries wishing to join the Community as full members, but unable to fulfill the economic conditions for accession, the establishment of a customs union by the association agreement may serve a secondary purpose—preparation for full membership. Greece has already moved from associate status for about twenty years to full membership, which was granted on January 1, 1981. Turkey, also a long-time associate, may also request full accession within the next decade.

Another objective of an association with the Community may be the creation of a free trade area, in which case the customs duties between the Community and the associated country will be abolished but no common external tariff will be established. This has been the pattern of associates with less developed countries (LDCs) in Africa in the Yaoundé and Lomé Conventions.

Under the provisions of the General Agreement on Tariffs and Trade (GATT), both customs unions and free trade areas may qualify under certain conditions for exemptions from the terms of the most-favored-nation clause. Long-range objectives of all association agreements may be the raising of living standards and economic levels in the associated countries.[9]

The central institution of all association agreements concluded so far is the Council of Association. It is the top-level forum for consultation and decision making for the association partners, although the specific competences vary from agreement to agreement. All the EC associations also have an Association Committee, which takes care of all routine matters for the Council. Since the Council meets only infrequently, the Association Committee supplies the continuity necessary for the smooth operation of the association arrangement. When preparing the work of the Council sessions, the details of many important decisions are hammered out in these committees. Additional institutions are parliamentary association bodies consisting of equal numbers of delegates from the European Parliament and from the parliaments of the associated states, and adjudication units—either a special arbitration tribunal or the Court of the European Communities—to settle disputes between the association partners.

Since the association agreements are based on international law treaties concluded by equal partners, the principles of bilateralism and parity must characterize the institutional structure and must be controlling elements in the administration of the associations. At the same time, since the EC as a legal unit is now, and may be in the future, a partner in several associations, the autonomy of the Community decision-making process must be safeguarded, as otherwise the Community's freedom of action would be considerably impeded. By not limiting the decision-making power of the associated countries, association could become tantamount to full membership.

Admission to Full Membership

Admission to Community membership may also constitute an important subject of Community foreign policy. According to Article 23 of the EEC Treaty, any European state may apply for membership in the Community, but the term "European state" is not to be construed in too narrow a geographic sense.[10] As a consequence, Turkey is considered to be a European state, although the greater part of its territory is located in Asia. On the other hand, Israel cannot be regarded as European because it lacks any geographic connection with Europe, although much of its population has European roots.

To ensure the smooth adjustment of the new member state into the existing Community system, important economic and essential political conditions must be met by the applicant country. First, the level of economic development in the prospective member state must be roughly equal to that of the current Community members. Otherwise, the broad, economic equilibrium necessary for continued successful economic integration might be upset and serious problems encountered eventually by the Community as a whole. The lower level of economic development in Italy has cast repeated shadows over the Community's operations. Second, the political system in the applicant state has to be congenial to that prevailing in the Community. This means that applicant countries must be committed in a broad sense to democratic ideals and that their governments follow practices that are ultimately responsive to the wishes of their populations. It implies periodic elections and shifts in governments and their policies in accordance with the wishes of the people as expressed by their votes.

Despite reservations expressed by a number of observers about the differing economic levels between Greece and the other EC member states, Greece was made a full member, in part because it was hoped that accession would encourage the fragile Greek democracy. Therefore, it is somewhat ironic that Greece's recently elected prime minister, Socialist Andrea Papandreou, has conducted his election campaign on the promise to withdraw Greece from the EC.

Spain and Portugal, two other candidates for full membership, also have economies whose levels are appreciably below those of most present EC countries. Moreover, their agricultural products strongly compete with those of France and Italy.[11] Nevertheless, their memberships may well be accepted primarily on political grounds in order to strengthen in these two countries democratic forces whose survival is not entirely assured.

In contrast to association, admission to membership carries with it by definition the assumption of rights and obligations equal to those of the original member states. Nevertheless, it is conceivable that for a limited period the admission agreement may permit a differential treatment for the new member in order to ensure an orderly transition in such critical fields as agriculture and the adjustment of various industries to the common external tariff. However, the eventual full assumption of treaty rights and obligations is imperative, and it is for this reason that a neutral state such as Austria has been reluctant to petition for admission. Admission of new members also requires added seats on the Commission, the European Parliament, and other EC organs, or redistribution of existing seats. The weighted votes in the Council of Ministers must be redistributed, and the annual contributions to the Community budget and Social Fund must be altered.

Relations with International Intergovernmental Organizations

During the last few decades, international intergovernmental organizations (IGOs) have assumed an increasing importance on the world scene. The Community, itself a collective IGO, requires a variety of contacts with other IGOs in order to safeguard and promote its interests. Hence, the EC Treaties contain explicit provisions regarding Community relations with those IGOs with which cooperation is likely to be profitable.

The most specific of the provisions, Article 229 of the EEC Treaty,[12] stipulates that the Commission is responsible for ensuring all "suitable" contacts with the organs of the United Nations, its specialized agencies, and with GATT. Beyond that, the Commission also has the task of engaging in "appropriate" contacts with other IGOs.

"Suitable" contacts are those involving the exchange of information or the dispatch of observers; they are concerned primarily with technical matters. The term "appropriate" contact appears to suggest that it must be useful for the Community. Obviously, organizations of an economic nature fall into this category, but, beyond that, it is not inconceivable that relations with organizations of a general political character may also be beneficial.

Two IGOs have been given special treatment by the EEC Treaty. These are, understandably, the Council of Europe and the Organization for Economic Cooperation and Development (OECD), formerly the Organization for European Economic Cooperation (OEEC). According to Articles 230 and 231 in the EEC Treaty,[13] the Community as a whole, not just the Commission, must establish close collaboration and cooperation with the two organizations. This seems to indicate that the relationship with these organizations is considered to be on a broader basis than that with the United Nations, its specialized agencies, or any other international organization. However, beginning in 1974, the Community began to play a more significant role in UN affairs when the General Assembly approved UN observer status for the EC. Indeed, during the Seventh UN General Assembly Special Session to examine practical approaches to economic aid for the developing countries, the Community representatives assumed a leadership position for the Nine. They put forward common positions for the member states throughout the discussions, sometimes even on questions outside the Community's field of competence.[14] After observer status was received, the Community made a special contribution of $150 million to the UN Special Fund for developing countries hardest hit by rising food and oil prices.

The general obligation of the member states to act in concert with each other and with the EC organs and to refrain from measures likely to jeopardize the attainment of the treaty objectives is given special impetus by treaty provisions governing the actions of the member states in IGOs of an economic nature. According to Article 116 of the EEC Treaty, the member governments can proceed in matters of particular interest to the functioning of the Common Market only by concerted and uniform action. As a consequence, the member governments are deprived of their freedom of action in economic IGOs insofar as such actions may affect the unified market operations of the Community.

How is such common action to be organized? A delegate of one of the member governments may be requested to act as spokesman for the Ten. Usually this delegate would come from the country that occupies the chair in the Council of Ministers, but in exceptional cases where the interests of one member state are particularly affected a delegate from that state may be selected to act as spokesman for the whole group. Another possibility is the selection of a Commission member to act as spokesman for the member governments.

It should be emphasized that although the EC may establish and maintain a variety of relations with other international organizations, it does not become a member of these organizations nor does it act for the collectivity of the member states. Rather, the governments of the member states retain their positions in these organizations, but their activities require close coordination and cooperation.

The Organizational Framework for EC External Policy Operations

The proposals for the formulation of the Community's external policy are worked up in Directorate-General I, which has been given the main responsibility for the conduct of external relations. Other foreign policy proposals come from Directorate-General VIII, concerned primarily with relations to developing countries. The organizational structure of the two Directorates-General is shown in Table 2.1. The personnel of Directorate-General I also maintain the daily contacts with the members of the various diplomatic missions accredited to the Community. These contacts provide much of the information needed to formulate and implement policy. The Council of Ministers must be kept apprised of all important communications by third-country diplomats. More than ninety diplomatic missions from nonmember countries have been established in Brussels, attesting to the importance attributed by the majority of the countries of the world to the activities of the Community.

There has been considerable argument as to whether the Community has the power to establish diplomatic missions in third countries. The principle of such right had been accepted by both the Council of Ministers (as early as 1960) and the European Parliament. In a resolution adopted November 19, 1960, the Parliament declared that "The European Communities by virtue of their international legal personality enjoy the active and passive right of legation," and in view of this it advocated the establishment of permanent missions in London and Washington.[15] In practice, however, the Community has not made use of its active right of legation except in Great Britain, where the European Coal and Steel Community (ECSC) had a representative with ambassadorial rank from 1956 until the end of 1972, when Britain became a member.[16] In 1971 a representative of the Community was appointed in Washington. However, although sometimes addressed as "ambassador," he represents only the Community Commission, not the member states as a collective unit. In order to provide him and his staff with the traditional diplomatic immunity and privileges usually accorded to diplomatic personnel of nation-states, a special law had to be introduced and passed by Congress. In 1975, appointments of EC representatives that followed generally the procedural lines worked out in Washington were made in selected other countries, including Canada and Japan.

PROBLEMS OF THE EC EXTERNAL POLICYMAKING PROCESS

In our examination of the Community competences for the conduct of external relations, we have indicated the functions that the EC Treaties

TABLE 2.1

COMMUNITY EXTERNAL RELATIONS STRUCTURE

Commission of the European Communities

Directorate General I (External Relations)		Directorate General VIII (Development and Cooperation)	
Directorate A	GATT, OECD, Commercial questions regarding agriculture and fisheries, South Africa	Directorate A	General development policy, UNCTAD
Directorate B	North America, Japan, Australia, New Zealand	Directorate B	Coordination of aid policies and programs
Directorate C	Latin America, Asia, Middle East, generalized tariff preferences	Directorate C	Projects
Directorate D	External economic policy, International organizations other than UNCTAD	Directorate D	Operations
Directorate E	Textile agreements, Energy, Hong Kong, Macao, Korea	Directorate E	Finance and Administration
Directorate F	Northern, Central, and Southern Europe		
Directorate F	State Trading Countries (mostly communist)		

Source: Bulletin of the European Communities, Special Supplement, "Directory of the Commission of the European Communities," October 1980.

assign to major Community organs for the formulation of pertinent policies and decisions. On paper, the distribution of functions for this task is clear-cut; in practice, however, the decision-making process is highly complex and intricate. This characterization applies not only to the decision-making process in the area of external relations, but also to the evolvement of any kind of major Community decision. It is a process that involves multilevel interaction and interpenetration among the Community institutions, national governments and administrations, and interest groups — a relationship much more intensive and extensive than that usually prevailing between traditional IGOs and national authorities or professional interest groups. The goals pursued by national economic groups in the member countries, the domestic politics of each member state, and the interstate politics within the Community often play significant roles in the making of external EC policies. Moreover, the general foreign policy goals pursued by the member states and pressures exerted by third countries on both the national and Community level may also materially affect the end product.

An organ hardly mentioned in the EC Treaties, the Committee of Permanent Representatives (CPR or COREPER, following the French title) has exerted increasing influence on the Community's external policymaking. Basically, the CPR has the duty of preparing the sessions and decisions of the Council (which usually meets only a few days each month) and of carrying out any tasks assigned to it by the Council. In addition, its staff is frequently consulted informally by the Commission before it submits a formal proposal to the Council. In order to accomplish its missions, the CPR, composed of the ambassadors from the ten member states and their staffs (totaling more than 400 civil servants) has established a number of working groups, subcommittees, and special ad hoc committees patterned after the administrative structure of the Commission. One of the working groups deals with the Common Market's relations with third countries and concentrates on questions of commercial policy and GATT problems. Another working group is concerned with relations to other international organizations; and two subcommittees deal with problems arising from various associations in Europe, the Middle East, and Africa.

While in view of the CPR's tasks and functions it is not surprising that it is in an excellent position to shape the EC's external policies, the Committee also serves as a harmonizing agent for these policies. It has the appropriate channels to the various relevant ministries in the member states, the necessary contacts with the EC institutions, and the political clout to iron out problems of harmonizing policy developments. However, as we will see later, there are limits to the CPR's influence, particularly on issues involving bureaucratic turf struggles with prominent national foreign service officials and when the national ministries want to retain what they perceive as important prerogatives in the formulation of foreign policy.

The Influence of Economic Interest Groups

The discussion of the Community external policymaking process makes it amply clear that economic interest groups in the member states have many opportunities to express their opinions and press their demands. However, it is equally obvious that, in order to be successful in eliciting favorable Community policies, these groups also require the support of both their national administrations and the Community institutions. It is therefore proper to speak of a two-tier foreign policymaking process in the planning and formulation of Community economic policies toward third countries: policy decisions made by the member governments are essential elements in the final Community-level decisions. Thus, all factors operating in policymaking on the national plane are apt to have their influence, directly or indirectly, on the ultimate Community external policy product.

It is generally recognized that there is a definite interrelationship between a state's domestic politics and the formulation of its foreign policy. The pursuit of domestic political objectives can have an important bearing upon the selection of foreign policy goals and the methods for their implementation. For this reason, when formulating foreign policy, every democratic government must pay some attention to the demands and attitudes of several types of elites and especially those of what Gabriel Almond calls the interest elites,[17] which include the representatives of a vast number of economic, ethnic, religious, and ideological associations.

While acknowledging the influence of these elites, we must guard against overestimating their influence. Certainly, in the formulation of national security policy and the strictly political aspects of foreign policy, their influence is often likely to be minimal. But even in the field of economic foreign policy, this claim may be exaggerated at times. Jean Meynaud, a very knowledgeable student of French and European group activities, stated that "it is impossible to accept without serious reservations the theses which attribute to business a decisive influence upon foreign policy."[18] However, he recognizes that economic interest groups may be moderately effective in influencing economic foreign policies.

The numerous statements made in the publications of both national- and European-level interest groups show the definite concern of these organizations with seeking favorable Community decisions in the field of external policy. However, while they do not disregard the Community institutions, it seems that most industrial and agricultural groups direct the main thrust of their lobbying efforts at their own governments because they regard the national government route as promising greater success.

Most economic interest groups in the member states also seek to enlist the assistance of political parties for the pursuit of their objectives. At a minimum, they seek to keep the channels of communication to the party organizations open. Even in France under deGaulle, where party officials admitted freely that the influence of their parties—including the Gaullist Union des Démocrates pour la Ve République (UDR)—upon governmental policymaking was small, economic groups maintained relations with the political parties. Their hope was that this would ensure the availability of the necessary contacts when the political situation in France had changed.

While it is therefore obvious that national channels for influencing EC external policies are preferred by economic interest groups despite the existence, mostly in Brussels, of approximately 250 European-level interest group federations, opportunities to press demands at the offices of the Commission, the Council, and even the CPR are often pursued with skill and vigor. However, since national economic interest groups also use their political muscle in the member states and frequently pursue different and conflicting objectives, the already complex Community decision-making process is complicated further, and the rules of the treaties suffer additional emasculation. In this connection, we must not overlook that the manifold contacts between Community civil servants and interest group representatives also provide channels through which EC organs may exercise some influence upon the policy formation in the capitals of the member states. Thus, it is conceivable that subtle cooperation between the Commission and some national interest groups in the pursuit of a common external policy objective may lead to the application of concerted pressure on the national governments and perhaps, through them, on the Council, resulting eventually in a favorable decision. On the other hand, no matter how shrewdly interest group efforts are devised for the elicitation of favorable Community decisions in the field of external policy, overriding considerations, stemming from the pursuit of general foreign goals and from perceptions of the national interest, may prompt a member government to protect and promote the economic interests involved exclusively through national foreign policies rather than through common Community policies or, in fact, withhold all protection or promotion. This brings us to the discussion of EPC where the main burden and influence lies with the officials of the foreign ministries of the Ten.

EUROPEAN POLITICAL COOPERATION

European Political Cooperation (EPC) as a mechanism for the coordination of the EC member states' foreign policies must be considered against a background of often divergent national foreign policy goals which the member governments seek to attain and the relationship of the pursuit of these goals to the formulation of Community policies toward third countries. In analyzing this relationship, several important factors must be kept in mind. First, the establishment of the Common Market represents in itself the realization of certain *convergent* economic foreign policy goals of the member governments. Second, in the field of external relations for which, according to the EC Treaties, the Community organs are competent, the Community represents a centralized effort of the member states for the formulation and implementation of selected facets of their economic foreign policies, especially commercial policy. However, economic foreign policy goals cannot always be separated neatly from foreign policy goals concerned with national security or the advancement of a country's political power in general. Indeed, sometimes there is a certain degree of interdependence among the economic, political, and strategic goals of a state, and the attainment of an economic policy objective may be a means for the accomplishment of a political or strategic goal. It is also possible that the attainment of economic goals may be closely intertwined with the simultaneous acquisition of political advantages or be dependent on making certain political or strategic concessions.

On the other hand, the pursuit of economic foreign policy goals may be strongly influenced by assertions of what member states and their governments perceive as their overriding "national interest." Such assertions may render the formulation and execution of a coordinated commercial policy within the framework of the EC highly complicated or entirely impossible. Of course, in some cases the national interest and the foreign policy goals of the member governments are compatible and could be attained through the employment of common EC policies. In fact, the use of joint policy instruments, such as the conclusion of an association agreement, may be the only method available for attaining certain economic, political, and even strategic foreign policy goals, and thereby enlarges the range of foreign policy instruments at the disposal of the member governments. However, significant divergent elements, some potential rather than actual, are also evident in the goals of all ten member states. Hence, it has not been and will not be unusual that a clash of wishes, will, and wiles—highly traditional in interstate relations but dysfunctional and therefore not desirable in the framework of the Community—impedes or obviates the formulation of common external EC policies, although theoretically the member states are not opposed to having such policies.

A third factor complicating the formulation and implementation of common policies has been the reemergence of nationalism in the member states, which has tended to accentuate what is conceived of as "national interest." Although France is the obvious case of the reemerging nationalism, flashes of strong nationalistic feelings have been observed during the last few years of all of the member states. Beliefs that each government must serve foremost the interests of its own people before worrying about the Community interest are heard frequently. Such sentiments strengthen the resolve of national governments to employ national instruments for the pursuit of their foreign policy goals rather than to submit to a joint approach under Community auspices. Since the realities of the power distribution between the central institutions and the national governments continue to strongly favor the latter, it is not surprising that the reemergence of nationalism has severely weakened the position of the Commission as the main guardian of the Community interest.

Lastly, the views and attitudes of the national civil service in the member states concerned with Community affairs have a significant bearing on the effectiveness of external policymaking in the EC. Sentiments of opposition against a "takeover" of their functions by Community civil servants—often called Eurocrats—may express themselves in the use of subtle means to boycott the objectives of EC Treaties to turn over gradually the formulation and direction of certain economic foreign policies to the Community organs.[19]

It is important to stress that the views and attitudes of any civil service play a role in shaping the policies of those who wield political power in a state. These attitudes are likely to affect working papers that may become the basis for policy decisions and tend to influence the implementation of any instructions received. Passive resistance and a lack of enthusiasm often suffice to block a policy. A pertinent example of the influence of the bureaucracy in foreign policy was the lack of sympathy with European integration within the British Foreign Office, which probably was an important factor contributing to British reluctance prior to 1961 to join the Six in their endeavors.[20]

The Evolution of EPC

The problems and complexities which burdened the formulation of EC external policies, as described in the preceding section, and the desire expressed by many West Europeans to see their countries "speak with one voice" in international affairs contributed to a search for other means of evolving common foreign policies on the part of the EC member states. It is fair to assume that national foreign service officials were particularly interested in these efforts to find special methods of foreign policy coordination since this would ensure their continued participation and influence in most phases of foreign policymaking while at the same time retaining as much as possible the prerogatives of the member governments across the whole range of foreign policy formulation. In terms of bureaucratic politics, it would be a convenient means to bar the "intruders" from the Community's Directorate-General I and would assure the vigorous continuance of their carrer patterns and, in fact, their survival as influential administrators.

As a result of these efforts, an alternative structure outside the Community decision-making framework as specified in the three Community treaties was created in 1970 for coordinating the foreign policies of the Community member states. This structure, which became gradually known as EPC, has only very loose, poorly defined ties to the Community system. Its origins were in the so-called Fouchet Plans, which were elaborated in 1961 and 1962 by a committee of diplomats chaired by Christian Fouchet, then the French ambassador to Denmark. The basic idea of the Fouchet Plans (there were two somewhat different proposals made by the committee) was the creation of a Council at the level of heads of state and government, which was to meet every four months and, acting by unanimity, was to coordinate foreign and defense policy. To assist the Council and to prepare policy proposals, an intergovernmental European Political Commission, perhaps in the form of a permanent secretariat, was to be established. This was to be composed of senior officials in the national foreign services and to be located in Paris.[21]

Although a chance for success seemed to exist in the early stages of the negotiations on the essentially Gaullist draft treaty for policy coordination, no synthesis between the divergent positions of France and her EC partners could be evolved. Therefore, the concepts of the Fouchet Plans lay dormant from 1963 to 1969, although some students of European integration felt that the ideas embodied in the two Fouchet Plans should have been given further consideration and study. After the summit meeting of the heads of states and governments of the Six held in The Hague in December 1969, efforts were again initiated to find new paths for the construction of some kind of European Union. One of these efforts was the creation of a committee composed of high foreign ministry officials of the Six under the chairmanship of Vicomte Davignon of the Belgian Foreign Ministry. This group held a number of sessions beginning in April 1970.[22] The results of the deliberations of the Davignon Committee were published on July 20, 1970, in a report of the foreign ministers of the Community member states.[23] In accordance with this report, the foreign ministers of the Six began to schedule joint meetings every six months. In important cases, a conference of chiefs of state and government could also be called when crucial issues justified such a meeting.

To prepare the sessions of the foreign ministers, a committee was created composed of the political directors of the Six foreign ministries, to which were added in 1973 their counterparts of the three new member states, and in 1981 a Greek member. This committee was named the Political Committee and was to meet at least four times a year, but actually has met more often. Subordinate to this committee are various working groups and groups of experts, which have the mission to investigate particular problems and recommend possible solutions. The place for the sessions of the Political Committee is rotated from one member country to the other in accordance with whatever country chairs the Community Council of Ministers, whose presidency changes every six months. In line with the rotation of this presidency, the chairmanship of the Committee also changes every six months.

The major task of the periodic sessions of foreign ministers is the consideration of important questions of foreign policy. The member governments can suggest any issue for consideration that may pertain not only to general foreign policy problems but also to such matters as monetary affairs, energy, and security. Whenever the work of the Political Committee or of the foreign ministers impinges on the competence and activities of the European Community, the Commission is requested to submit its own position on the matter under consideration and is invited to send a representative. It is interesting to note that during the discussion in the Political Committee regarding the preparatory conference on European security and cooperation in Helsinki, it was felt that this subject was likely to deal with problems affecting the activities and competences of the European Community in the international trade field. Therefore, a Community representative was invited and the President of the Commission, then Franco Malfatti, participated in some of the sessions.

The foreign policy coordination activities of the Political Committee are supplemented by periodic sessions of staff members in the embassies of the Ten, located in different capitals. Such meetings had already taken place prior to the creation of this Committee when Community affairs affecting third countries needed to be discussed and coordinated, but their scope has now been expanded.[24] The commercial councillor of the embassy of the member state that holds the presidency in the Council of Ministers of the Community at a particular time prepares a report on these meetings. These reports are addressed to the president of the Council and are also distributed to the Permanent Representatives in Brussels and a number of national governmental agencies. If no objections are raised by a member government within eight days, a copy of this report is furnished to the Commission. When Community affairs are discussed in the embassy meetings, officials of the EC Information Service participate if the Service has an office in a particular capital, such as Washington or Geneva. In such cases, the Community officials make a direct report to the president of the Commission.

Policy coordination meetings have also been held in the United Nations to assure the maximum cohesion in voting and policy positions of the member states. The influence of the Commission staff in these meetings may well have been increased when the EC was granted official observer status by the UN.[25]

An interesting study made by Leon Hurwitz regarding voting cohesion by the member states in 518 roll-call votes in the General Assembly from 1948 to 1973 shows the following results. The variations in cohesion levels are wide: the Netherlands and Luxembourg have the highest level (92 in a 0-100 scale), France-Italy the lowest level (72 in the same scale), the original EEC members have a cohesion level of 84, and Great Britain, Denmark, and Ireland have a cohesion level of about 80.[26]

To strengthen the work of the Political Committee and the foreign ministers, the establishment of a permanent secretariat has been proposed. It would be located in one of the capitals of the Ten or operate on a rotating basis in the capital of the Committee chairman. But, so far, all that has been done is to set up a small team to help the president of EPC, a team composed of officials from the country which just finished holding the presidency and from that which now assumes this task.[27]

Another problem is the relationship between the EPC structure and the CPR. Some kind of liaison arrangements with the staff of the Permanent Representatives of the Ten located in Brussels is now envisioned to be established through ad hoc groups of senior civil servants of the foreign and other ministries so that matters affecting Community policies can be discussed together. So far, the Permanent Missions have not played any role in the coordination activities of the Political Committee. Indeed, the power of the CPR may have suffered from the activities of the Political Committee because the Permanent Representatives have been generally neglected in the foreign policy coordinating process. And when the latter did become involved in this process, their significance was minor and their influence limited. On occasion, the Commission has been able to take advantage of these circumstances and play a more significant role in the EPC process than normally was expected.[28]

The emergence of the Political Committee as an important factor in the formulation of common foreign policies is pitting three organizational and bureaucratic groups against each other. One group consists of the officials of the foreign ministries operating through the Political Committee and perhaps in the future through a permanent secretariat, which will be concerned with the coordination of a wide range of foreign policy issues and thereby may invade the competences of the Community. Second, we have the Community decision-making process with its own group of civil servants striving to produce and implement external policies in accordance with the provisions of the Community Treaties. It is noteworthy that in this process, which originally was to be dominated by the international civil service of the European Community, we find expanding control by a third group of national officials.

These officials operate through the offices of the Permanent Representatives, who have played an increasingly important role in the decision-making process of the Community but have not been able to exert the same kind of influence within the EPC process. Some of these national officials come from the foreign ministries of the member states, and others are assigned by the ministries of economic, agriculture, and finance as technical experts. These experts may be called upon to give advice, not only to working groups of the CPR, but also to those of the Commission, since the major competences of the Community are concentrated on the activities with which these technical experts are concerned. Hence, these national officials play perhaps a more salient part in evolving decisions for the Community than to their colleagues of the foreign ministries.

We therefore see not only a subversion of the original concepts of Community decision making in the field of foreign policy by the national officials, but also competition and interpenetration between two distinct national bureaucratic groups struggling, perhaps subtly, to extend their own competencies and those of their institutions. Indeed, as Helen Wallace reports, the endeavor of different government departments in the member states to stake out their own areas of responsibility for formulating policy has provoked tensions between foreign ministries and domestic departments, as foreign ministries have had to increase their awareness of domestic policy considerations and ministries concerned with domestic problems had to involve themselves more in international negotiations. At the same time, the Permanent Missions have come to enjoy a special status and to acquire a certain solidarity with each other.[29]

For the foreign ministry officials, on the other hand, the Political Committee constitutes their seat of power, which they seek to expand by including within its boundaries every type of foreign policy issue including economic matters, a range of subjects corresponding to the existing set of functional division in their ministries. The rapid expansion in the Committee's activities and increasing frequency of meetings of senior officials and ministers have produced great satisfaction and are seen as signs of effectiveness and progress. The Political Committee, therefore, constitutes a kind of "caucus" in which the participants "understand each other," can engage in trade-offs on policy developments that cause few surprises, and most importantly, can continue to play their traditional roles without being inundated by "innovative" proposals from the Commission experts.

Thrust and Scope of EPC

The basic thrust of EPC is based on two diplomatic agreements concluded among the EC member states and known as the Luxembourg and Copenhagen Reports of 1970 and 1973.[30] Accordingly, the aims in broad substantive and procedural terms are:

1. To ensure a better mutual understanding of the great international problems
2. To strengthen the solidarity of the EC member states by promoting the harmonization of their views, the coordination of their positions, and, where it appears possible, to engage in common actions

Although the undertaking of common action is highly qualified, the range of activities by the staff of the Political Committee that might lead to common action has been impressive. They include:

1. An average of some 100 communications transmitted every week over a common telex-system called COREU.
2. More than 100 sessions of common working groups composed of national diplomats to analyze important international problems.
3. Political Committee meetings are held twice a month to exchange information about the work and operations of the various foreign ministries that are relevant to EPC. A "crisis procedure" is in the planning stage which will assure meetings of the Committee within 48 hours.
4. Representation of the Ten at international conferences and in IGOs is carried out by *one* delegation.
5. Consultation among diplomatic missions of the EC countries has been placed in an institutionalized basis in various third-country capitals to coordinate positions and actions.
6. The heads of government meet three times in the European Council, where discussion of issues before the Political Committee is included.[31]

In spite of the impressive range and intensity of EPC-related activities, there are also some serious weaknesses. The distribution of competences and roles between the EPC mechanism and the EC external relations apparatus has never been clearly set forth, in spite of repeated requests by the European Parliament that appropriate, clear rules should be spelled out.

Therefore, harmonization and coordination between strict EC external policies and those developed through EPC depend on the goodwill of the EPC participants. Even information exchange between the Political Committee and the Commission is haphazard and depends much on who is presiding over EPC at a particular time. The degree of the Commission's participation in EPC deliberations and decision making also is unclear; in some cases, its representative actively participates in the decision making while others the Commission merely plays the role of an observer. Finally, the relationship between EPC and Commission is all the more difficult because the level of confidentiality, with respect to EPC deliberations upon which national foreign ministries insist, is high.[32]

As a result of the EC's particular external policy competences and the EPC mechanism, third countries have become aware that their own foreign policy developments must take into serious consideration both processes and, in order to influence the foreign policies of the Ten, the foreign ministries of third countries should know as much as possible of what is happening in the EPC deliberations on various international issues. The United States has been especially sensitive to this set of problems and was particularly concerned with events and policies during the Yom Kippur War in October 1973 and the initiation of the Euro-Arab Dialogue in 1974, which will be discussed later in this chapter. To satisfy the concerns of the United States, a compromise agreement was concluded among the foreign ministers of the EC countries at Gymnich in West Germany in April 1974. This so-called Gymnich Agreement makes it possible for the United States to participate in EPC deliberations prior to a final decision by the EC foreign ministers if a member state desires consultation with Washington on a particular issue and the remaining member states agree to that procedure. If unanimity about the invitation of such consultation cannot be attained, then contacts and consultations with the United States can only be conducted on a liberal basis.[33] This arrangement has worked well and seems to have satisfied all parties.

EPC OUTPUTS: HOW MUCH SUCCESS?

The success story of EPC is mixed. Although the Political Committee has been involved in a number of important international issues during the 1970s, clear-cut successful accomplishments have been rare.

The Conference on Security and Cooperation in Europe

The most significant achievement of the EPC has been the coordination of policies leading to a common position during the preparatory phase of negotiations with respect to the Conference on Security and Cooperation in Europe (CSCE) from 1973 to 1979 and the follow-up evaluation meetings in Belgrade in 1977-78 and Madrid during 1980-81. The EC Commission participated vigorously and effectively in the deliberations on economic issues and contributed materially to shaping the common stand ultimately taken by the Nine. Consultations between the United States and the EPC members on the CSCE issue were concluded within the framework of NATO: Washington accepted the leading role of the Nine in the preparation of the CSCE negotiations as far as nonmilitary matters were concerned; and, as a consequence, the Final Act of Helsinki carries the imprint of conclusions reached in the EPC deliberations.[34] Clearly, this is an example of effective policy harmonization of both the member states and the Community proper, although the specific competences of the latter were not directly involved.

The Euro-Arab Dialogue

Another major foreign policy effort in which the EPC mechanism is used jointly with the EC external relations system is the Euro-Arab Dialogue which was initiated in 1975 and continues in 1982. The delegation for the Community and its member countries is led by the government chairing the EPC and by the Commission president or his representative.[35] The delegation of the Arab League, the dialogue partner, is led by the country holding the rotating presidency of the League.

The Euro-Arab Dialogue was initiated in Cairo in June 1975 to discuss ways of more fruitful cooperation between the Community and its members on the one hand, and Arab countries in the Middle East and North Africa on the other. Conceivably, the issue of oil deliveries could be included in return for technological and economic assistance. The specific areas of cooperation with which the dialogue has been dealing include industrialization, basic infrastructure, agriculture and rural development, financial cooperation, trade, science, technology, culture, labor, and social questions. Several working groups study these areas of cooperation, identify worthwhile projects, and make proposals for action.

Nine proposals were approved: three agricultural projects including the development of the Juba Valley in Somalia and meat production in Sudan; five projects relating to infrastructures, including the construction of a regional port in Syria; and a symposium on relations between the Arab and European civilizations.[36] Financing of these projects has been delayed, although the principle of allocating their cost to the Arabs and the Community on an approximate ratio of five to one seems to be generally accepted.[37]

A number of conflicts of interest burden the dialogue partners; since so far the council problems of oil prices and guaranteed supplies have been excluded from the dialogue, it is hard to see how other major economic questions can be tackled realistically. Nevertheless, the Arab countries seek support to develop their own refineries and petrochemical industries in order to expand earnings from their oil resources. They also want to establish steel mills and fertilizer plants. However, the West Europeans find it difficult to encourage such ventures in view of already existing excess capacities. Finally, the Arab League countries would like to conclude a comprehensive preferential trade agreement with the EC and to have suspended the "economic assistance" and tariff preferences now extended to Israel. This has been consistently rejected by the EC institutions.[38]

In spite of these economic problems, the Euro-Arab Dialogue has not been without benefits for the EC countries. The framework of contacts and interpersonal relations built up through the dialogue has considerable political value in itself, including on occasion support of West European foreign policy goals. In this connection, it is important to point out that of total EC world trade, the share of the Arab countries is very substantial, amounting to 13.5 percent of EC exports and 20 percent of its imports. Even more impressive is the share of global Arab trade which the EC enjoys: 40 percent of Arab exports go to the EC while imports from the EC amount to 43 percent. The comparative figures for the United States on these four types of trade flows are 12, 16, 9, and 13 percent, respectively.[39] This intensive trade relationship may also offer special advantages and concessions for the EC countries that might be denied other Western industrialized states. However, overall, the concrete economic benefits derived by the EC countries specifically from the dialogue have been meager.

From the political point of view, it is noteworthy that in 1977 the European side felt constrained to reiterate its concern over the continued Israeli occupation of Arab territories since 1967 and to restate that a solution of the Middle East conflict will be possible only "if the legitimate rights of the Palestinian people to give effective expression to its national identity is translated into fact."[40] The Nine's position was expressed again, perhaps more forcefully and to a much wider public, during the meeting of the European Council in London in June 1977. "A Declaration on the Middle East" issued at that time reemphasized the need for Israel to end its territorial occupation and stated that it must be ready to recognize the legitimate rights of the Palestinian people and their need for a "homeland."[41] Although this declaration aroused a very negative reaction in Israel and a vigorous diplomatic protest, it simply confirms and continues a policy line taken by the EC member states individually as well as by the Community as a whole, which became apparent at the Copenhagen summit in December 1973. Even the successful conclusion of the peace treaty between Egypt and Israel in the spring of 1979 received little applause from the Nine, despite efforts in the EPC to produce a more enthusiastic coordinated response.[42] The harshest statement, from an Israel perspective, came in June 1979. It not only reiterated previous declarations regarding Security Council Resolutions 242 and 338 and urged respect for the "legitimate rights" of the Palestinians, but singled out as impediments to peace Israeli settlement policies outside its territory proper and its claim to permanent sovereignty over occupied territory.

These declarations emanating from the EPC process have encouraged de facto and perhaps later de jure recognition of the Palestine Liberation Organization (PLO) in Europe.[43] In addition, despite expressions of displeasure on the part of Washington, a number of initiatives were undertaken in 1981 under the auspices of the PLO by the Dutch foreign minister and the British foreign secretary to find solutions for the peace process by enlisting the aid of Saudi Arabia and other moderate Arab states while somehow circumventing the Camp David Accords.

Other Issues

EPC has been involved in a number of other international issues, but their even brief discussion would exceed the scope of this chapter. Suffice it, therefore, to list some of the major issues. In 1974 the smoldering dispute between Greece and Turkey over Cyprus assumed crisis proportions when Turkish troops invaded that island. The EPC apparatus was called upon to coordinate the policies of the Nine on this issue, but was not able to find a solution to the crisis acceptable to the contending countries, although it contributed to limiting the conflict. It should be noted that the EC Commission assisted in finding a solution to this crisis when it urged negotiations with Cyprus to prolong the Community's association agreement whose first phase expired in 1977. In this endeavor, the Political Committee and the Commission collaborated closely.[44]

The EPC also played a positive role in the democratization of Portugal and Spain inasmuch as it reacted favorably to these developments and encouraged them with declarations, diplomatic actions, and recommendations for loans in the case of Portugal. Again, there was considerable cooperation between EPC activities and the EC Commission,[45] strengthening the basic EC Mediterranean policy consisting of a number of association and other preferential agreements with nearly all countries rimming the Mediterranean except Albania.[46]

In Africa, opportunities also presented themselves for EPC action. Common policy stands were sought regarding the independence of Mozambique in 1975, the civil war in Angola and recognition of the Popular Movement for the Liberation of Angola (MPLA) regime in 1975 and 1976, the problem of Rhodesia, and the continuing difficulty of finding a solution for the achieving of an independent status for Namibia. Finally, a more recent and also continuing initiative is the EPC effort to evolve acceptable proposals to induce the Soviet Union to withdraw its forces occupying Afghanistan. So far, no proposal of the Ten has found approval by the Soviet Union which considers the EPC suggestions as "unrealistic."[47]

POLICY HARMONIZATION BETWEEN THE EC AND EPC

To examine the degree of external policy harmonization that has been possible between the exercise of relevant competences by the EC institutions and the EPC activities requires first a brief survey as to what has been accomplished until 1982 by the Commission and the Council of Ministers. The accomplishments, mostly in the field of foreign economic policy, are indeed impressive.

Most impressive, perhaps, is the Commission's participation in multilateral negotiations and conclusions of three agreements to lower tariffs and eliminate nontariff barriers. They are the so-called Dillon, Kennedy, and Tokyo Rounds of negotiations during the 1960s and 1970s, the last better known in the United States as simply "multilateral trade negotiations" (MTN). In all of these negotiations, the Commission played a leading role. Other multilateral agreements to which the Community is a party in its own name include the International Wheat Agreement (1979), the International Coffee Agreement (1977), the International Natural Rubber Agreement (1980), the Convention on Future Multilateral Cooperation in the North-West Atlantic Fisheries (1979) and forty-one other agreements.[48]

An increasing number of bilateral agreements has also been concluded by the Community with third countries. They include a number of association agreements, for example with Turkey, Malta, other Mediterranean countries, and with more than 50 African, Caribbean, and Pacific countries under the Convention of Lomé, its last version having been signed and ratified in 1981. Preferential agreements aiming at the creation of a free trade area have been concluded with most West European nonmember states and so-called economic cooperation accords have been negotiated with Yugoslavia, Canada, Mexico, Brazil, Bangladesh, India, Pakistan, and Sri Lanka. Regular trade agreements exist with Argentina, Uruguay, and the People's Republic of China. With the United States, Japan, Australia, and New Zealand, the EC has agreements for regularized periodic consultation and the United States also has a special accord with the EC under the Euratom Treaty. Finally, the Community has a number of agreements dealing with special products such as textiles. The third countries which are parties to these agreements are all less developed countries in Asia and Latin America.

While it is obviously in the nature of the EC that its external policies should concentrate mostly on economic issues, it is equally evident that the EPC is mainly concerned with political and selected matters such as Cyprus, Afghanistan, and some aspects of CSCE. Hence, while EPC complements the external activities of the EC, it serves as a harmonizing agent for overall policy only insofar as it draws the Commission into deliberations on a particular issue. But, as we have seen earlier, clear-cut rules on Commission participation have not been promulgated and, therefore, much depends on how individual international issues are perceived by the foreign ministers of the member states and by their political directors who are the permanent top officials in the EPC mechanism. Another influential factor may be the information which the Commission is able to acquire about pending EPC issues and how it can exploit this knowledge to extract an invitation from the Political Committee to become a participant in the discussions of a particular issue.

In this connection, we must not lose sight of the fact that the effectiveness of the EPC varies from international region to region. It has been most effective in the European Mediterranean area and has contributed there to the creation of the impression that Western Europe does now indeed act as a unit. Most recently, the EC foreign ministers have discussed ways of involving Spain and Portugal also in their political cooperation work, perhaps by holding talks with the foreign ministers of these countries after each EPC meeting.[49] It has been less effective in the Middle East and Africa. While the problems of the Middle East have evoked a number of anti-Israeli declarations, the latter have not enhanced peace in the region very much. EPC endeavors in the southern part of Africa (Mozambique, Zimbabwe, Angola, and Namibia) have not had much impact on the solutions finally reached or still outstanding in these countries. With respect to policies vis-à-vis Asian and Latin American countries, the EPC mechanism has been used only sparingly so far; on the other hand, the Commission has used its external competence to good advantage in these regions, although the scope of these relations remains fairly limited. In the relationship of the Community countries to the United States and the Soviet Union, EPC has played a distinctly minor role.

The effectiveness of EPC also depends on the issue area involved. As already pointed out, the EPC was and continues to be a major success in the CSCE policy coordination process. It has been less successful in other security issues such as Cyprus and Afghanistan. Clearly, in security matters the EC member states lack adequate military capabilities or resolve to employ necessary resources, and, therefore, EPC does not possess much leverage.

EPC BENEFITS FOR MEMBER GOVERNMENTS

Regardless of how effective the EPC is as an external policy harmonizing agent for the EC member states, it should be recognized that the EPC is basically a *national* instrument for foreign policy formulation and implementation, and its utilization is effectuated in accordance with what is perceived as best for the national interest. In addition, the EPC offers a number of special advantages to the member governments that are useful for domestic political purposes.

First, it provides an alibi when member governments are faced with hard choices such as support for Arab or Israeli positions or whether to favor Greece or Turkey in the Cyprus dispute. Under such circumstances, the EPC is a highly useful framework to divert conflicting pressures and to transfer them to an "anonymous" body where the blame can be put on the "group" or on other partners.

Second, the EPC can have a legitimating effect on foreign policies of member states vis-à-vis public opinion and, thereby, may give the government more freedom of action in relation to opposition forces.

Third, the EPC is apt to increase the influence and power of all member states and especially of the smaller EC countries in international affairs. In particular, this increase of influence may be felt within the Atlantic Alliance, in relations with less developed countries outside the areas covered by EC associations and preferential agreements, and in the United Nations and its specialized agencies. Clearly, the quantitative and qualitative weight of all Community countries as reflected by EPC policy action is stronger than the voice of any individual member government.

EPC AND POLITICAL INTEGRATION

The question has been raised as to how much the EPC mechanism will contribute to moving forward the political integration process and whether it may perhaps become a major force in the creation of a European union, either on a federal or confederal basis. I am rather skeptical about EPC developing into a significant stimulus to materially enhance progress toward political integration.

Without doubt, EPC has given rise to a policy-coordination reflex in the foreign ministries of the Ten. This means that most foreign policy issues requiring attention by the officials of these ministries will be evaluated in terms of their suitability for the EPC process. There is also no question that both EPC and EC channels in the external policy field are often linked very closely. But because of bureaucratic turf protection reasons discussed earlier, as well as concern with protecting a member state's basic national prerogatives, any strong move toward some sort of "communautarization" or "federalization" would be vigorously opposed. It seems that that member governments are content with the current nature of intergovernmentalism which the EPC mechanism reflects. They may be willing and even interested to extend the scope of this mechanism and rationalize its procedures and methods, but they would resist any attempt at fundamental reform which would eliminate the existing total national control over the collective EPC activities. Indeed, it is not entirely inconceivable that the establishment of the EPC mechanism was seen by some national foreign ministry officials as a counter-strategy against the prospective loss of function in their own field of action as a result of expanding involvement by the EC institutions in external policymaking.[50]

Whatever some of the concealed motivations for setting up the EPC mechanism may have been, it is quite evident that at the present this mechanism and the EC external policymaking process operate side by side in a pragmatic manner. While so far no particular integrative effect by the EPC on the Community system can be observed, and while, in fact, EPC may have strengthened intergovernmentalist trends in the relations between the member states and the EC institutions, seen in longer terms, EPC may become a building stone for developing the necessary preconditions for integrative forward movement.[51] Meanwhile, the aspirations of many West Europeans to see their region "speak with one voice" in international affairs have received a strong boost by the EPC operations during the last decade.

NOTES

1. The Committee used to be called "Committee 111" in accordance with the number of the article governing its operation during the transitional period.

2. During the first eight years of the transition period, a unanimous vote was required for this act (Art. 144). In practice, a unanimous vote is still required if vital interests of a member state are involved.

3. For details see Art. 228.

4. Cf., Werner J. Feld, *The European Common Market and the World* (Englewood Cliffs, N.J.: Prentice-Hall, 1967), p. 13.

5. Euratom Treaty, Arts. 10, 29.

6. Ibid., Arts. 46-47. See also Art. 16(5).

7. Ibid., Arts. 52(b), 64, 77(b).

8. For fuller information see Werner J. Feld, "The Association Agreements of the European Communities: A Comparative Analysis," *International Organization* 19 (Spring 1965): 223-49.

9. Probable objectives of association agreements concluded under the ECSC and Euratom treaties are cooperation and consultation with third countries. These, in fact, were the objectives of the association between the ECSC and the United Kingdom, concluded in 1954. Whereas the Euratom Treaty contains provisions for association agreements identical to those in the EEC Treaty, the legal situation under the ECSC Treaty is more complex. See ibid., 224-25.

10. Similar provisions in the Euratom and ECSC treaties are 205 and 98, respectively.

11. In this connection, see Christian Deubner, "Problems of Community Enlargement: The Accession of Greece, Portugal, and Spain," in *Western Europe's Global Reach*, edited by Werner J. Feld (New York: Pergamon Press, 1980), pp. 30-53.

12. Euratom Treaty, Art. 199.

13. Ibid., Arts. 200, 201.

14. *European Community*, no. 181 (November 1974), p. 22; and *Agence Europe Bulletin*, September 18, 1975.

15. *Amtsblatt der Europaischen Gemeinschaften*, 1960, p. 1496/60; and EEC Commission, *Third General Report*, sec. 390. In this connection it is interesting to note that the German Bund (1815-66) possessed the active and passive right of legation simultaneously with that of the sovereign states that were members of the Bund.

16. Accreditation was to the British government, not the Court of St. James. However, with regard to all diplomatic functions, the ambassador was treated on an equal basis with colleagues accredited to the queen.

17. Gabriel A. Almond, *The American People and Foreign Policy* (New York: Praeger, 1960), pp. 130-43. See also James N. Rosenau, *Public Opinion and Foreign Policy* (New York: Random House, 1961).

18. Jean Meynaud, *Nouvelles Etudes sur les groupes de pression en France* (Paris: Librarie Armand Colin, 1962), p. 391. See also pp. 392-93.

19. See Werner J. Feld, "The National Bureaucracies of the EEC Member States and Political Integration: A Preliminary Inquiry," in *International Administration*, edited by Robert S. Jordan (New York: Oxford University Press, 1971), pp. 218-44; and Werner J. Feld and John K. Wildgen, "National Administrative Elites and European Integration: Saboteurs at Work?" *Journal of Common Market Studies* 13 (March 1975): 244-65.

20. Anthony Nutting, *Europe Will Not Wait* (London: Hollis & Carter, 1960), p. 5.

21. For details see Alessandro Silj, *Europe's Political Puzzle* (Cambridge, Mass.: Harvard University Center for International Affairs, December 1967, Occasional Paper no. 17).

22. Cf., *Agence Europe Bulletin*, March 6 and April 3, 15, 1970.

23. For details see "Bericht der Aussenminister der Mitgliedstaaten der Europäischen Gemeinschaften an die Staats-bzw. Regierungschefs vom 20. Juli 1970, betr. mogliche Fortschritte auf dem Gebiet der politischen Einigung," *Europa Archiv* 25, no. 22 (1970): D520-D524.

24. Cf., Ralf Dahrendorf, "Possibilities and Limits of a European Communities Foreign Policy," *The World Today*, April 1971, p. 161.

25. *Agence Europe Bulletin*, September 18, 1975.

26. See Leon Hurwitz, "The EEC in the United Nations: The Voting Behaviour of Eight Countries, 1948-1973," *Journal of Common Market Studies* 13 (March 1975): 224-45.

27. *Agence Europe Bulletin*, October 15, 1981.

28. G. Bonvicini, "Der Dualismus zwischen EPZ und Gemeinschaft," in *Die Europaische Politische Zusammenarbeit*, edited by Reinhardt Rummel and Wolfgang Wessels (Bonn: Europa Union Verlag, 1978), pp. 89-90.

29. Helen Wallace, *National Governments and the European Communities* (London: Chatham House: PEP, 1973), p. 84.

30. See *First Report of the Foreign Ministers to the Heads of State and Government of the Member States of the European Community*, October 27, 1970 (Luxembourg Report), and the Copenhagen Report, in Press and Information Office (Federal Government) European Political Cooperation (EPC), Bonn 1978, 3rd ed.

31. See for greater details, Wolfgang Wessels, "New Forms of Foreign Policy in Western Europe," in *Western Europe's Global Reach*, edited by Werner J. Feld (New York: Pergamon Press, 1980), pp. 12-29; and *Agence Europe Bulletin* October 16, 1981.

32. Bonvicini, "Der Dualismus zwischen EPZ und Gemeinschaft," pp. 93-95; and *Agence Europe Bulletin*, October 16, 1981.

33. For details see Beate Kohler, "Die Europaisch-Amerikanischen Beziehungen — Die EPZ als Vehikelder Emanzipation?" in *Die Europäische Politische Zusammenarbeit*, edited by Reinhardt Rummel and Wolfgang Wessels (Bonn: Europa Union Verlag, 1978), pp. 178-80.

34. See for details, Goetz von Groll, "The Helsinki Consultations," and "The Geneva Final Act of the CSCE," *Aussenpolitik* 24, No. 2 (1973): 123-29; and vol. 26, no. 3 (1975): 247-69, respectively.

35. EC Commission, *Ninth General Report* (1975), pp. 260-61.

36. *Agence Europe Bulletin*, November 1/3, 1977; January 30/31, 1978; April 13, 1978 provide details.

37. Ibid., May 8/9, 1978; and July 12, 1978.

38. Ibid., October 27, 1977; and November 7/8, 1977.

39. Agence Europe, *Selected Statistics*, June 13, 1977.

40. *Bulletin of the European Community* (2/1977), p. 65.

41. *Agence Europe Bulletin*, July 1, 1977.

42. *Bulletin of the European Communities* (3/1979); and *Agence Europe Bulletin*, March 28 and 29, 1979.

43. For details see Werner J. Feld, "The European Community and the Middle East," *Middle East Contemporary Survey* 3 (1978-79): 38-47.

44. Nicholas van Praag, "Krisenmanagement in Sueden Europas," in *Die Europäische Politische Zusammenarbeit*, edited by Reinhardt Rummel and Wolfgang Wessels (Bonn: Europa Union Verlag, 1978), pp. 191-220.

45. Ibid., pp. 193-99 and 205-10.

46. For more information on this policy see Werner J. Feld, *The European Community in World Affairs* (Port Washington, N.Y.: Alfred, 1976), pp. 131-52.

47. *Agence Europe Bulletin*, July 13/14, 1981.

48. For a complete listing see Reinhardt Rummel, *Das Europa der Zehn in der internationalen Politik* (Ebenhausen, West Germany: Stiftung Wissenschaft und Politik, 1981), pp. 233-34.

49. *Agence Europe Bulletin*, October 28, 1981.

50. See also Rummel, *Das Europa der Zehn*, pp. 136-43.

51. See also the cautious comments by Wessels, "New Forms," pp. 22-23.

Roy Gibson 3

AEROSPATIAL COOPERATION: THE EUROPEAN SPACE AGENCY

The writer served as a staff member first of the European Space Research Organization and subsequently of the European Space Agency from February 1967 to May 1980, the last five years as Director General. This service gives an insight into the subject matter of this article, but it also undeniably increases the risk of personal bias. It would be wrong to deny that these thirteen years of professional activity engendered passions and created prejudices, but in this essay I have done all I can to keep them under control, and, where this proved impossible, I have indicated them in order that the reader may more easily form a dispassionate opinion.

For those who have already decided to read only the first page, let me here declare my basic philosophy. Throughout my professional life I have been unashamedly a European. My experience with ESA put this faith under considerable stress, but I emerged more convinced than ever that full-blooded European cooperation is the only sensible way to proceed, and equally I am persuaded that the disadvantages of, and the frequent discomfort caused by, this cooperation can be attributed more to the inadequacies of individuals or groups of individuals, rather than any innate flaw in the concept of European cooperation itself.

It is the intention here to trace the creation and development of the European space effort and to examine in more detail some of its successes and failures. Although it is part of my belief that the individual plays an extremely important role in this, as in many other areas, there is no attempt to name scapegoats or to award personal praise. We are in any case still too close to the events to be able to make such judgments, and I am conscious that there are many differing interpretations of the happenings of these last twenty years.

BACKGROUND

La Commission Préparatoire Européenne de Recherche Spatiale (COPERS)

The visible start was indeed more than twenty years ago when, on 1 December 1960, a convention was signed in Meyrin, near Geneva in Switzerland, creating the body known as COPERS – la Commission Préparatoire Européenne de Recherche Spatiale (the Preparatory Commission for European Space Research). The convention was signed by twelve European states: Austria, Belgium, Denmark, Federal Republic of Germany, France, Italy, Netherlands, Norway, Spain, Sweden, Switzerland, and the United Kingdom. The Commission thus created was intended within one year to review existing space activities in Europe, to establish a draft development program, and to produce a draft of an international convention creating a European organization capable of carrying out that program. A small secretariat was established in Paris early in 1961, under Professor Auger, and the work began. By the end of that year, after detailed enquiries throughout Europe, the team had produced its report: the so-called Blue Book. It foresaw an initial period of eight years' activity, during which time the new organization was intended to develop and launch 440 sounding rockets and 34 satellites. Whatever those pioneers lacked in realism, they compensated by an enthusiasm that has never since been equaled. The program called for the construction of a technical center and the establishment of a network of ground tracking stations and a computer center for data processing. The total cost of this eight-year plan was initially estimated at 1,411.9 million French francs (FF) – approximately \$282.4 million – but the finance experts increased it to FF 1,614 million (\$323 million), and if one includes a provision for possible cost overrun, the total came to FF 2,107 million (\$421 million).

The European Space Research Organization (ESRO)

With a rapidity which we were later to envy, the twelve signatories examined the Blue Book and on 14 June 1962, the convention was signed bringing into existence the European Space Research Organization (ESRO). ESRO's basic program consisted of 12 satellites and around 400 sounding rockets, with a financial ceiling of FF 1,500 million (\$300 million) for the eight-year period. Ten of the original twelve States signed the Convention and thus became Member States of ESRO; Austria and Norway decided – at a relatively later stage – not to sign. The Convention came into force on 24 March 1964. During the months of intensive discussion at the beginning of 1962, decisions had to be made about the siting of the various establishments with which ESRO was to be endowed. It was quickly agreed that the headquarters of the organization should be in Paris. There was also no opposition to Kiruna in northern Sweden being ESRO's sounding rocket range (ESRANGE, as it became known). The siting of the remaining establishments, however, gave rise to considerable discussion. It was finally agreed that the technical center (to be known as ESTEC) should be located in Holland and the computer centre (ESDAC) at Darmstadt in Germany. The price of this agreement — shades of things to come — was the creation of a research institute (ESRIN) at Frascati, near Rome.

This act merits a short digression from the course of this brief historical recapitulation. ESRIN existed as a research institute with what appeared to be the very minimum of supervision either from the ESRO management or from the Member States until the first real ESRO financial crisis and reorganization in 1971. Although it had attracted excellent scientific staff, its activities became progressively more detached from the main thrust of ESRO's program. In 1971-1972 the institute as such was closed; half of the buildings were transferred to the Italian Research Council and the remainder of the establishment was used to house the space documentation retrieval service (SDS), which was transferred to Frascati from Paris. The SDS has done its best to exploit the possibilities of ESRIN, but this transfer was in many ways unnatural and simply compounded the original error of creating an unnecessary establishment, the continuation of which, of course, became a point of honor for the Italian delegation. The creation of ESRIN — although perhaps it was essential to obtaining Italy's adherence to the ESRO Convention — was an expensive compromise. Investment and annual expenditure at Frascati up to the end of 1981 can be estimated at around $65 million.

The European Launcher Development Organization (ELDO)

Although the 1961 Meyrin Convention was the first public act toward the creation of a European satellite and sounding rocket program, initiative to establish a European launcher organization in fact preceded this. Toward the end of the 1960s the British had started to persuade other European nations to join in the development of a European launch vehicle, using the British Blue Streak as the first stage. The French were quick to accept, on condition that they be given the task of providing the second stage. Austria, Sweden, and Switzerland felt that their neutrality prevented them from joining this program; Denmark and Spain were interested but unable to consent to the necessary financing; and Norway decided that its own state of technical development was not adequate to allow a meaningful industrial participation. The remaining six states who had been participating in the COPERS discussions (Belgium, Federal Republic of Germany, France, Italy, Netherlands, the United Kingdom) plus Australia had by 30 April 1962 signed the Convention giving birth to the European Launcher Development Organization (ELDO). Australia had been invited to participate in the negotiations in order that ELDO might take advantage of an agreement for the provision of a launch and test site already existing between the United Kingdom and Australia in connection with the Blue Streak program.

In this way, Western Europe had by mid-1962 two international organizations: ESRO for the development and exploitation of satellites, and ELDO for the development of launch vehicles. It is important to note that not only were the two communities not the same but that the motivations leading to the creation of the two organizations were quite different. ESRO was created under the pressure of European space scientists who were far-sighted enough to realize that their future needs could not be satisfied by a continued dependence on the (US) National Aeronautics and Space Administration's (NASA) generosity or through national programs. It is easy to see that ESRO's birth was considerably influenced by the success of the European nuclear research center (CERN); indeed many of the ESRO pioneers were involved either as CERN council members of experimenters. ELDO, on the other hand, was basically an industrial initiative. The United Kingdom had developed the Blue Streak rocket under a military program, but by 1960 it had become patently outmoded for its original purpose. The British therefore sought to turn their instrument to some use by offering Blue Streak as the first stage of a European launcher for peaceful purposes. France, too, had developed national rockets which would obviously give it a privileged position in an international venture of this kind. The seeds of future dissent and setbacks were sown by the acceptance of the UK offer and by the decision not to await the ratification of the ELDO Convention before starting work, but to authorize individual governments in the meantime to pass the industrial contracts necessary for the development of the six pieces into which the program had been divided.

Laudable though it was to seek measures to prevent a further widening of the technological gap between the USA (and the USSR) and Europe, the method chosen set the stamp on ELDO as an organization incapable of imposing a systems concept on its program, and condemned it to docilely following the developments in its Member States in the hope that the various pieces would in fact fit together into a launcher which would function. It is difficult to avoid the conclusion that only the relative weakness of the aerospace industry in some of the six Member States spared Europe from the development of a six-stage launcher. The ELDO Convention only came into force in February 1964 through ratification by six of the seven Member States. Italy, the seventh member, finally ratified the convention a year later. Thus, for two years the newly born organization had to operate without a real legal framework, and unanimous approval was necessary for each decision relating to financial commitments and to the recruitment of personnel.

Although for many years in the same building and separated only by one floor from the headquarters of ELDO, relations between the two organizations were so extremely limited that I am frankly not competent to record or comment on the evolution of the launcher organization up to its fusion with ESRO in 1975. I hope that it is fair to all the participants to divide this era into two periods: the first ended, after a series of unsuccessful tests of the Europa rocket, with a radical change of management and management methods. The second was clouded by increasing governmental doubts over the wisdom of investing ever more money in an independent European launcher toward participation in the US Post-Apollo Program.

It is tempting to moralize over the birth, life, and transformation of ELDO, but this might be left to another author. I will restrict myself to two comments which have a relevance to the future development of European space activities. First, it is beyond dispute that the first ELDO period painfully demonstrated the inability of technicians to bring a political project to a successful conclusion. Political bargaining must be kept separate from the actual management of the project, otherwise the politicians (or their representatives, the governmental delegates) begin to meddle in the content of the project and its management, and—equally harmful—project engineers start to fancy themselves as astute politicians. Second, the subsequent development and production of the European Ariane launcher owes a great deal to the financial involvement made and the experience gained during ELDO's lifetime.

The European Space Conference (ESC)

The creation of the two distinct organizations, ELDO and ESRO, with their separate conventions and different membership, put a temporary end to attempts to found a single European space organization, and the two organizations began to develop personalities and objectives of their own. This divergence was to continue until the signing of the European Space Agency Convention in 1975.

The need for some form of overall coordination of European space continued, however, to make itself felt, and this led to the formation in 1966 of the European Space Conference (ESC). It consisted of representatives, nominally at ministerial level, of all the countries of Western Europe. It had no formal terms of reference and unanimity was needed for such decisions as were taken, and even these had subsequently to be passed through a committee of senior officials, known as the Committee of Alternates, and thence to the Councils of ESRO and ELDO before being put into effect. The Conference was serviced by a Secretariat provided by the legal staff of ESRO and ELDO in addition to their other duties and headed in alternate years by the Secretary General of ELDO and the Director General of ESRO. The pipeline was long, and the input at the top did not represent a great head of water; small wonder that at the executive level the tap produced generally no more than a tantalizing drip.

The ESC was at best a clumsy instrument with which to forge a European space policy, but it corresponded well enough with the mixed motives prevailing among the various national participants. As has been seen all too often, Europe hesitates to create effective international instruments which may one day act contrary to national interests or aspirations.

A series of devoted Belgian ministers presided over the ECS, and, with the limited means that the conference provided, they persuaded and bludgeoned their colleagues into taking at least the minimum of decisions necessary to keep the European space ship afloat. Its meetings in 1966 and 1967 were concerned principally with ELDO problems, but thereafter ESRO was able to furnish material for the virtually perpetual crises.

ESRO's First Years

The supreme authority of ESRO was its Council, consisting of two delegates from each of the ten Member States. The principal of "one country, one vote" was applied. Austria and Norway, as associate members, also had delegates in the Council, but without voting rights. From the outset there were two subordinate delegate bodies—the Administrative and Finance Committee (AFC) and the Scientific and Technical Committee (STC).

The AFC was responsible for all financial matters, personnel, and, easily the most contentious area, the award of industrial contracts. The basic philosophy for the funding of ESRO can be summarized as follows: all projects were to be supported by all Member States in proportion to their gross national product; provided, however, that no Member State should contribute more than 25 percent of the budget; and by unanimity, the Council should approve a level of financial resources for a three-year period, following which the individual annual budget would require only the approval of two-thirds of the Member States (irrespective of the size of their contributions).

Voting on the award of industrial contracts was equally straightforward: only a simple majority was required. This led to bargaining, even on occasions blatantly conducted during the meetings of the AFC, whereby delegates tried to ensure what they considered to be an adequate allocation of contracts for their national industries. The Secretariat attempted to achieve some geographical distribution of the technical contracts, but the space-related industries in the various Member States were far from having a uniform capacity. French—and to a lesser extent, British—industries were well advanced, but in some countries there was in the mid-1960s virtually no aerospace industry. The first priority was, as the Secretariat saw it, the completion of its program, and pursuance of this aim led to a serious imbalance in the award of industrial contracts during the first few years of

ESRO's existence. The Secretariat had little inclination and even less time for passing vital contracts with industrial firms eager to cut their teeth on interesting high-technology work, but with little or no previous experience. Moreover, delegates of Member States were rarely willing to have ESRO pay more than necessary except when their own industry was involved. In order to have some yardstick by which to measure the fair return, it was decided around 1969 that each Member State should be entitled to receive industrial contracts equivalent in value to 80 percent of its financial contributions to ESRO, excluding, of course, internal expenditure.

It was in this period, and partly as industry's own response to the need to assure a geographical distribution of industrial work, that the first European industrial consortia were formed. With a few changes, these consortia are still active and have much to their credit. They were the means for European aerospace firms to learn how to work together in fairly large, high-technology programs, often with close interfaces with American industry and NASA. There was much to learn: even the rudiments of project control and management, which these firms now take as axiomatic, had to be invented or adapted from a US model. Each firm had its own internal finance and management organization, and language differences provided an added complexity. It must be admitted that when ESRO first negotiated with these consortia, neither side had a great deal of experience to offer. On the ESRO side were newly appointed international officials, some recently returned from NASA scholarships at US universities, some from national administrations, and a relative few from Europe's embryonic aerospace industry. The battle lines were drawn: ESRO officials in the Paris headquarters were expected to wrest from the delegate bodies the funding and formal approvals necessary for the program; those at ESRO's technical center in Holland (ESTEC) went into battle with industry to obtain quality, prices, and schedules which were acceptable. In the moments of lull on the external fronts, morale was raised by intensive warfare between Paris and Holland.

The work of the STC was relatively calm; after all, many of the delegates were the same influential scientists who had pushed—not to say schemed—for the creation of ESRO. There were, of course, differences of opinions as to the priorities to be accorded to the various areas of space science, but these were largely ironed out in separate working groups. The standing of the scientists involved, and the respect and influence they exerted at home, were such as to ensure the fairly orderly conduct of business. The program consisted principally of an optimistic and not very well-defined program of applied research; a program of sounding rockets to be launched mainly from ESRO's own launch site at Kiruna in the extreme north of Sweden; and scientific satellite programs (originally divided between small and large satellites).

The applied research program was intended to prepare ESRO and European industry in the areas already identified as crucial for future satellite programs, and where Europe was then dependent upon NASA and US industry. During the early years it was not possible to prevent the small budget allocated for this purpose from being diverted to provide financial reinforcements for the ongoing scientific satellite programs. With the clarity that hindsight habitually brings with it, one can see how these budgetary diversions slowed down Europe's technological development in this field, particularly among the smaller Member States. This was clearly predicted at the time, but the temptation to use available money rather than to face unsympathetic treasuries for supplementary budgets was normally too strong for the delegates to resist. In spite of these deprivations, the program stuttered along and produced work which was extremely useful in subsequent programs.

ESRO's sounding rocket program initiated staff, industry, and scientific experimenters in the rigors of working "in space," albeit for journeys which were measured only in seconds. Many of those now engaged in complex space projects graduated through the sounding rocket school. Before the program finished in 1970, ESRO launched over 100 sounding rockets, mostly of French or British manufacture.

The first ESRO satellite to be launched successfully was ESRO II (baptized IRIS) on 17 March 1968, after the first flight model had been lost due to the malfunctioning of the US Scout launch vehicle. IRIS was followed by ESRO I (AURORA) on 3 October 1968, HEOS-AI on 5 December 1968, and ESRO IB (BOREAS) on 1 October 1969. The scientific value of these four small satellites—the largest weighed only 108 kg—has been extensively described in the literature. But it is important here to recall the invigorating effect they had on morale both inside ESRO and among the representatives of the ten Member States. There were complaints: ESRO was too expensive; procedures were complicated and time-consuming; too much work was going to industry in the already technologically advanced Member States; and each Member State could add to this list its own inventory of grievances. But, for the first time, Europe had proved that by working together they could enter the esoteric domain of satellites. Even at that time there were voices protesting that this or that country could have produced the same results quicker, cheaper, and better alone. Happily, the chauvinists who revealed themselves were heavily outnumbered by a combination of European-minded supporters from all the ten Member States, plus the delegates from the seven or eight Member States who at that time most certainly could not have boasted of any similar single-handed ability.

NASA's Contribution

Europe's entry into space was, however, only possible thanks to US launch vehicles. Launchers available in Europe were not adequate for such purpose, and, of course, the European launcher being developed by ELDO was not available then. One of ESRO's first international agreements was in fact a cooperation agreement with NASA, which served as the cover for a whole series of specific agreements subsequently covering projects on which NASA worked together with ESRO and later with its successor the European Space Agency (ESA). For the early launchings there were several different arrangements. In some cases NASA provided the launcher free of charge and ESRO accommodated a US experiment on board or supplied data acquired by its satellite. For some projects ESRO simply purchased the launcher and launch services from NASA. In my view, such success as ESRO achieved is in large measure due to the generous help and encouragement received from NASA, which went far beyond any purely commercial arrangement. It is indeed remarkable that right from the outset the senior staff at NASA were even more enthusiastic about European space cooperation than many Europeans—using this latter word in its strictly geographical sense. Latter-day analysts have explained that this generosity was forthcoming because the technological gap was so large that competition from Europe in this area was difficult to envisage. Be that as it may, anyone connected with ESRO during those formative years cannot fail to testify to the unstinting help which came over the Atlantic, not only from NASA, but also from several US aerospace firms who had formed valuable and sometimes lasting links with the European industrial consortia.

Telecommunications

Although not part of the initially approved program, ESRO had since 1966 become involved in telecommunication satellites. As early as 1963, telecommunication by satellite had been accepted as a reality even by the European telecommunications authorities. In that year, representatives of the telecommunications entities from all the countries of Western Europe, including the Vatican and Monaco, met to form the European Conference of Telecommunications by Satellite—known by its French abbreviation of CETS. With a small secretariat in London, CETS was intended to weld the European countries into a solid alliance capable of defending Europe's interest in the tough negotiations leading to the creation in 1964 of the International Satellite Organization (INTELSAT). Predictably, CETS proved to be inadequate for this heroic task: once again the individual motives were so varied that it was scarcely ever possible to develop, present, and maintain a common European line. CETS did, however, manage to sow the seeds of Europe's own satellite telecommunication program by asking ESRO in 1967 to undertake studies for a satellite system known as CETS-C, sometimes called the Eurafrica project because of its intended coverage.

The 1971 ESRO Package Deal

By 1968, in spite of near universal joy at the satellite successes, there was considerable dissatisfaction with ESRO. The principal overt cause was the increase in the cost of producing the next group of ESRO satellites, but underlying that problem was the growing feeling that the rapid developments in space in the previous five years necessitated changes. In particular, it was obvious that ESRO could not continue to devote its attention almost exclusively to scientific satellites; the era of application satellites had almost arrived. In order to underline the need for change, Denmark and France went so far as to denounce the ESRO Convention, a facility the Convention provided to Member States after the first six years of operation. The notice period of a little more than a year was an incentive to all to negotiate a settlement before the expiration date, for an ESRO without France (although probably easier to manage) could not claim to be truly European.

A great deal of 1971 was devoted to negotiations between the ESRO Member States in an attempt to give the required minimum of satisfaction to all. This was achieved at the ESRO Council meeting in December 1971, and France and Denmark remained members of the European space family. The agreement, in the form of a Council Resolution, provided a level of financial resources for the years 1972-74, and a provisional level for the succeeding three years; for ESRO to undertake an Aeronautical Satellite Program (together with the USA), a Meterological Satellite Program and a Communication Satellite Program; for the continuation of the Scientific Program and the ESRO activities in the fields of technology and the dissemination of information; and for the cessation both of the sounding rocket program and of the scientific activities conducted at ESRIN near Rome.

The ESRO which emerged from these negotiations was completely different from the original organization: the emphasis had moved away from space science toward a range of application programs, and both the internal structure and that of the delegate governing bodies had to be changed. Moreover, it was necessary to draft changes to the ESRO Convention so as to provide legal cover for the enlarged range of activities. For example, it was envisaged that the application satellite programs should be optional rather than mandatory and that the contributions of the Member States should reflect their degree of interest and not simply be calculated on gross national product.

It is important to note that this same fateful Resolution conferred on ESRO "the coordinating and concerting role in respect of all space programmes for peaceful purposes within the Organisation and national agencies." The wording was the product of many hours of argument between national delegates, and its unanimous acceptance has been hailed as a victory for European cooperation. This it undoubtedly was, or could have been, if those same national delegates had on their return home insisted on its observance. After formally receiving this coordination role, ESRO spasmodically received word of national activities, but mainly from the press rather than from the national space agencies. It was always surprising to me that the Secretariat found such tepid support on the occasions when it complained that it received too little input to be able to attempt coordination. The same reluctance was apparent in ESRO's efforts to coordinate its own ground station network with the ground stations already built or planned by Member States. Only those Member States with no ground stations of their own were capable of the objectivity necessary to see that Europe as a whole was overendowed with ground facilities and yet not equipped to handle the oncoming generation of geostationary satellites.

The reorganization continued throughout 1972, and ESRO's reputation— and morale— were enhanced by a further three successful launches of scientific satellites (Heos A2 on 31 January; TD-1, Europe's heaviest and most complex satellite thus far, on 12 March; and ESRO IV on 22 November), and despite evidence that coordination would not be easy or universally welcomed, the trend toward Europeanization continued. The ESC at its meeting in Brussels on 20 December 1972, agreed that a new space organization should be created out of ELDO and ESRO, if possible by 1 January 1974, and that both the Ariane launcher and Spacelab programs should be undertaken.

The Post-Apollo Program

The Spacelab program was the outcome of a visit to Europe in October 1969 by Dr. Paine, then Administrator of NASA, when he addressed a meeting of the Committee of the Alternates and invited Europe to participate in the new American space transportation program—the so-called Post-Apollo Program—which had just been presented to the US president. This visit was destined to lead to the largest ever space cooperation between the USA and Europe and to permit Europe to participate for the first time in a manned space program. The decision process, however, took three years and demonstrated once more the inadequacy of the European Space Conference as a negotiating and decision-making body. In spite of this unsubstantial criticism, it must be admitted that ELDO and ESRO were very rapidly authorized to study Dr. Paine's proposal. Approximately $6 million was allocated for industrial studies, and a liaison office (which later became a permanent ESA antenna) was opened in Washington.

Participation in the US Post-Apollo Program was for many Europeans, however, closely linked to the question whether or not Europe could cease its efforts—and expense—to build its own launcher and more or less permanently rely on US launchings. After six months' reflection, the USA declared that from their side the two matters were not connected: the terms of obtaining US launch services were independent of Europe's decision on participation in the Post-Apollo Program. This answer was subsequently used to reinforce the arguments of those who insisted that it would be imprudent for Europe to continue to rely exclusively on US launchers.

After this clarification, discussions and negotiations went on at two levels: between US and European experts to define what Europe's contribution to the program might be and among civil servants and politicians to determine the appropriate form and conditions for the cooperation. Europe's disarray was this time not the only complicating factor, for technical and financial pressure radically modified the concept of the US programs. The initial concept of a space station was displaced by the prior development of the space shuttle, the design of which also underwent changes. Automatically, the range of choice for European participation in the program shrank, until by mid-1972 it became apparent that only the sortie module, a sort of shuttle-borne manned laboratory, remained available for Europe. NASA pointed out that Europe would need more time to develop the sortie module than if it were to be made by US industry, and, after presidential approval for the whole program was received in January 1972, it became urgent for Europe to make a decision one way or the other.

The attitude of the major European space powers at that time can briefly be described as follows: Germany was the prime mover for participation in the US program. This fitted well with Germany's general tendency to promote closer relations with the USA as well as within her determination to put an end to the ELDO launcher program; Italy, too, was enthusiastic for participation in the US program but willing also to try to find funds for a symbolic participation in the European launcher; France from the start saw that the corollary to European participation in the US Post-Apollo Program would almost inevitably be a reduction in the declining support for the development of any European heavy launcher and thus a perpetuation of the US launch capability monopoly. The United Kingdom pleaded a poverty which in fact thinly masked an indifference both to the US Post-Apollo Program and to future development of the European launcher. Confident that launch services would continue to be made available by the USA, the UK preferred to put its money into the development of the telecommunication satellites.

It was the reconciliation of these four positions which was to lead to the definition of Europe's space program for the next ten or more years. This is not to say that the opinions of the six smaller Member States of ESRO were of no value, but rather that they were in general content to support a majority view and to participate in any sensible European space program within the limits of their financial possibilities. Although occasionally exasperated by the inability of the three or four larger Member States (Italy alternately played the role of the smallest of the larger and the largest of the smaller, according to circumstances) to arrive at a reasonable compromise, the smaller Member States rarely played a decisive role during the multitude of meetings of delegate bodies which characterized the early 1970s. There was, to my knowledge, only one attempt to rally the representatives of the small countries into some form of alliance capable of influencing the large countries whose divergent aims were preventing progress on a European scale. This led to two or three meetings of decreasing fervor, until it was realized that such a separate movement was largely irrelevant to the issues at stake.

Alone of the large Member States, France realized the importance of winning the support of at least some of the smaller members. Sweden became a regular, if undeclared, ally, not through any residual sentiments for Bernadotte, but rather because the growing Swedish space program had the same analytical approach as the French, and because—not less important—the French were willing through their national space agency (Centre National des Etudes Spaciales, CNES) to provide generous support. Belgium, also, was a regular but less constant ally of France. The motive was invariably one of industrial return, for the Belgian aerospace industry had little chance of gaining contracts other than through the good offices of a prime contractor from one of the larger members. It must, however, be stressed that Belgium's principal motive was always to further the work of the ESC, of which their Minister had the chairmanship for nearly a decade. Switzerland, too, almost always acted and voted in favor of European themes and, particularly in the earlier years, was extremely modest in her national demands.

The Role of the Delegate

The influence of the various Member States was—and indeed still is—to some extent a product of the size of their participation in the different space programs, but this is by no means the whole story: the importance of the individual delegate is not to be underestimated. The delegate normally arrives at a meeting with some form of instructions, which in some cases he has himself formulated in whole or in part, and on his return he is expected to report on the meeting and to explain how far the national point of view has prevailed. In order to explain his country's position to his colleagues, the delegate must be capable of expressing himself clearly (and preferably concisely) in one of the languages officially permitted at the meeting. It is obviously an advantage to be able to continue this missionary work outside the formal sessions and without the aid of simultaneous translation. A knowledge of languages is therefore helpful, but strangely enough, some of the most successful delegates to ESRO and ELDO were not great linguists. They had, however, the all-important quality of sincerity and—both at home and in international meetings—presented national requirements within a European framework. One felt immediately that they were seeking an acceptable international agreement rather than attempting to force through their own national wishes. Of course, the most successful delegates were those who achieved the latter while leaving others with the impression of the former, but they were few. Apart from personal qualities—some national civil servants are simply not suited to an international atmosphere ("not for export")—it is important for the delegate to be adequately graded in the home hierarchy. During the early COPERS meetings, most countries produced rather senior representatives, but this level was unfortunately not uniformly maintained. It is understandable that senior officials could not spare the time to attend the scores of meetings which the ESRO crisis management demanded, but all too frequently the junior officials who replaced them could do little more than keep the debate going and fix the date of the next meeting. It would, in my view, have been possible to reduce the number of meetings and the volume of official papers if a higher standard of national representation had been possible and if these senior officials could each have received a clear and realistic mandate from national authorities.

However, even the very identification of these national authorities was not always simple. No country had a Minister of Space Affairs and so each had to find an organizational solution appropriate to its own internal division of responsibilities (there were scarcely two alike). The United Kingdom suffered from a fundamental dichotomy in financial responsibility: the Science Research Council was wholly responsible for the funding of the ESRO scientific program, whereas the Department of Industry's budget carried all other ERSO programs. Naturally, both organizations required a delegate in the ESRO Council. But which one should vote on the general issues? There was an added complication in the insistence of the Foreign Office to be present at, and to take active interest in, all debates with policy implications. In general, the UK delegation achieved an adequate coordination through an interdepartmental committee, and the same formula was used by others. Some countries were, however, not quite so fortunate, and the Council was on occasion treated to the unedifying spectacle of two national delegates struggling for the microphone in order to present the "authorized" point of view of their country.

National delegates, with an unusual display of modesty, showed unfailingly that they believed it more important to have one of their nationals in a key post within ESRO than to have the right man in the delegation. I believe this to be a mistaken view. Perhaps in the very early days, the first twenty or so ESRO officials tended to look to their homelands for reinforcements and to place industrial work. But this was certainly more because of the absence of a machinery to provide a timely, international solution. As the organization became more sophisticated, it became virtually impossible for even the most highly placed ESRO official systematically to favor his own country's industry or recruits. Nevertheless, some of the most bitter delegate struggles occurred in the selection of senior staff, and it is hard to believe that the prestige value of the post alone justified the effort. Delegates were not, however, always quite so rigorous about the qualifications of the candidates they offered and whose cause they supported sometimes up to ministerial level. The ESRO Secretariat was, however, resistant to the off-loading of these "diplomatic passengers," as they were known, and very few penetrated the portals. This double judgment standards is a feature of life in an international organization: too many delegates are capable of criticizing the level of efficiency of the staff, while at the same time they are trying to find a home somewhere in the organization for a civil servant who has outlived his usefulness at home.

THE CREATION OF THE EUROPEAN SPACE AGENCY

It was against this background that the Ministers in the ESC meeting on 20 December 1972 passed their forward-looking resolution.

On the following day, the Committee of Alternates appointed a Working Group to study the modifications needed to transform the newly drafted, revised ESRO Convention into a vehicle to pursue the ESC's objective of a single space organization. The ESC resolved that both the Ariane launcher and the Spacelab program should be undertaken. The Group was also asked to examine the financial and other means needed as well as the structure. A further charge was to examine the staff problems.

The working Group held its first meeting on 11 January 1973. The European Space Agency (ESA) actually came into being on 30 May 1975 at a Conference of Plenipotentiaries held in Paris. These twenty-eight months were again packed with meetings of delegates and experts at every conceivable level. The strain, both on national participants and members of the Secretariat, for all of whom this was a supplementary task, was considerable. It is not appropriate here to attempt a chronological account of the negotiations, but it is relevant to the general theme of this book to identify some of the points which provoked the most discussion and where the European fervor collided with national interests.

Surprisingly, the designation of official languages for the new agency became a difficult point. ESRO used French and English for all its official documents and as working languages in the Council and delegate bodies. It had also become accepted custom for the German delegation in the Council to speak in German and to have simultaneous translation into the two working languages. During the early discussions on this subject, two conflicting tendencies emerged: most delegates favored the use of a single language for the Agency, while others—perhaps basically believing that the single-language solution could never win acceptance—saw no reason to favor English and French over German and Italian. Seeing the imminent spectre of an agency using nine or ten different languages, one brave British delegate proposed—in French—that French be the single official language, but the proposal is remembered mainly for the good humor it engendered among the delegates than for its chances of success.

The compromise which was eventually engineered promoted German to be the third working language of the Council and delegate bodies (with a tacit recognition that the translation of the documents into that language could not be produced with the same rapidity as for French and English), and, because of Italy's significant financial contribution to that program, Italian was accepted as an official language for all Spacelab program matters. Provision was also made whereby a delegation might require arrangements to be made for the use of yet another language, but this was mainly at the request of the Scandinavians and was in order to demonstrate that they had for more than a decade been working in a foreign language. The facility has, thankfully, not so far been invoked. The whole was enshrined in one of the ten resolutions which accompanied the Final Act of the Plenipotentiaries for the establishment of the European Space Agency. It represents a clumsy and expensive solution to what many consider to be an outdated problem, but no one has since had the stomach to reopen the question.

More substantial was the debate over the relationship between the space facilities owned by the national space agencies and those of the Agency. The insipid wording of the relevant resolution does less than justice to the hearty nature of the exchange between delegations on this subject. Expressed bluntly, France, and to a lesser degree, Germany, had been steadily increasing investment in ground facilities (satellite tracking stations, computer, and, above all, test and integration facilities) while rarely missing an opportunity to block funding for a similar ESRO facility. Unhappily, this conflict continued after the formation of the Agency and will remain a perennial problem.

Another resolution wrestled with the problem of reconciling the Ariane launcher and Spacelab programs. It was entitled "Launcher and other space transport systems" and arrived at ensuring that both ESA and the Member States would use these European developments in their future programs and would, indeed, plan their missions around the available European launch capacity. Although it won universal support, it was largely an uneasy truce, for the Spacelab could not be considered as a space transport system without the use of the NASA shuttle in which it is designed to fly. With France ferociously promoting the development of the Ariane launcher and Germany enthusiastic—at least in the beginning—for Spacelab, any important agreement in ESA must still strive to provide at least some appearance of equilibration between the support to these two programs and to their successors.

Industrial return could not fail to be a favorite topic in the negotiations leading to the formation of ESA, and there was in fact a separate Sub-Group of delegates charged with a detailed examination of the subject. Their recommendations, mutilated by months of subsequent debate, found their way into an annex of the ESA Convention and did a great deal to rationalize the procedures for the award of industrial contracts. Total satisfaction in this area is elusive, but the groundwork was laid for a transparent system in which the needs of the ESA program could be reasonably evaluated by delegations and measured against their continuing desire to see contracts awarded to their own industry.

To explain the objectives of the new Agency, the whole of Article II of the 1975 Convention is cited: each word and punctuation mark was the subject of vigorous debate, and yet the text still manages to say quite clearly what were the intentions of delegations—at least as far as they were expressed by their appointed Ministers. Article II reads:

> The purpose of the Agency shall be to provide for and to promote, for exclusively peaceful purposes, cooperation among European States in space research and technology and their space applications, with a view to their being used for scientific purposes and for operational space applications systems:
>
> a. by elaborating and implementing a long-term European space policy, by recommending space objectives to the Member States, and by concerting the policies of the Member States with respect to other national and international organisations and institutions;
>
> b. by elaborating and implementing activities and programmes in the space field;
>
> c. by coordinating the European space programme and national programmes, and by integrating the latter progressively and as completely as possible into the European space programme, in particular as regards the development of application satellites;
>
> d. by elaborating and implementing the industrial policy appropriate to its programme and by recommending a coherent industrial policy to the Member States.

During the debates there were many references to giving more authority to the Director General for the conduct of the Agency's business, and as the first token of that new regime, the Secretariat pointedly began to refer to itself as the Executive. This change was difficult to challenge, but life would no doubt have been quieter if one had remained with the title and attitude of the Secretariat. Many Member States have shown themselves to be extremely sensitive to any buildup of executive power in an international organization.

By the end of 1975 ESA had on board its full complement of directors and the new, rather elaborate structure of delegate bodies. The latter is illustrated in Figure 3.1, from which it will be seen that there were no less than thirteen committees.

ESA'S PROGRAM

At this stage it may be helpful to recall briefly the composition of the Agency's program as it emerged from the tunnel of nearly three years' negotiations. In fairness it must be stressed that not all of this period was lost, for ESA had learned from ESRO the value of winning approval for initial studies which, while not binding the Member States to a future commitment to fund the development program, allowed the preliminary work on program definition to be started with industry in parallel with the further discussions with Member States. The approved program consisted of the following:

FIGURE 3.1

ESA'S GOVERNING BODIES

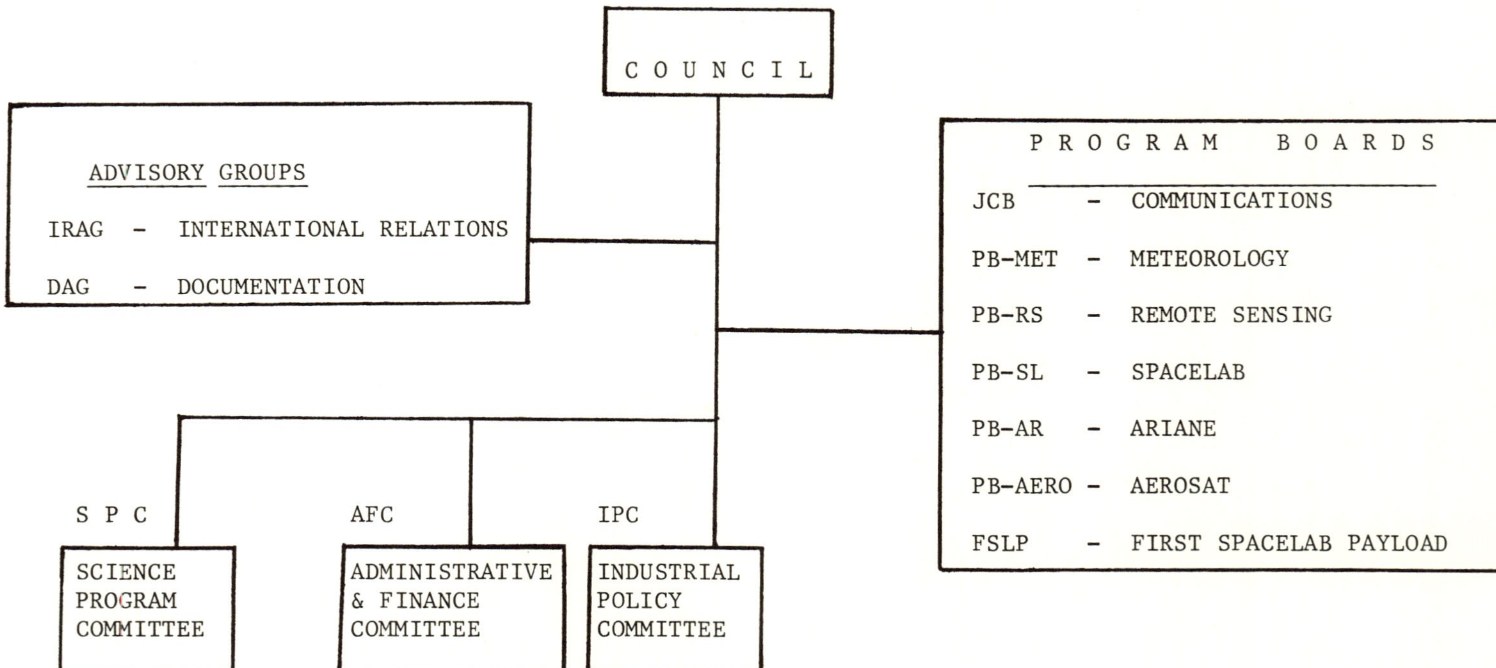

A) Mandatory programs financed by all Member States in proportion to their gross national products:
   - the technology program (the old applied research program);
   - the documentation retrieval service;

B) Optional programs financed by interested Member States at percentages agreed between themselves:
   - Spacelab program including only the development and the first joint ESA/NASA flight;
   - Ariane launcher development program—with funding to include four test firings and the construction of an ESA launch site at the French launching base at Kourou in French Guiana;
   - Telecommunications satellite program (intended first to produce an "orbital test satellite" (OTS) and thereafter a family of telecommunications satellites tailored to meet Europe's internal long-distance communication needs);
   - Maritime satellite program—for telecommunications between ships and shore;
   - Meteorological satellite program—designed to put a satellite in geostationary orbit as Europe's contribution to the World Weather Watch, and designed to demonstrate to the European meteorologists the value of an operational satellite system;
   - Aerosat: an aeronautical communications satellite program intended to be carried out with the USA and Canada.

This added up to a substantial investment and, as can be seen from Figure 3.2, the budget tripled in real terms between 1972 and 1975. In 1975 the Agency spent 336 million accounting units (at that time the equivalent of about $360 million), an amount that was again to be doubled by 1980. This was the period in which Member States all reduced their expenditures on national programs and increased their participation in the European programs. Germany provided the most dramatic example of this: prior to 1975 two-thirds of the space expenditure was national, thereafter the same proportion was allocated to ESA programs.

I realize that the technical content of the various programs has little interest for the reader of this volume; but I should like to devote a little time to some of those programs which throw a revealing light on international cooperation. I hesitate to say that there are lessons to be learned from a study of these programs, but at least they should enable the reader to see various manifestations of Europe's Janus-like approach to European cooperation and integration.

The documentation retrieval service, which I mentioned earlier in connection with the establishment of Frascati (SDS/ESRIN), certainly provides a good example. An early agreement with NASA enabled the service to acquire the NASA principal documentation data base and to obtain regular updating. A not insignificant amount of money was expended in developing

Figure 3.2
DEVELOPMENT OF THE AGENCY'S BUDGETS, 1972-1982
(in millions of units of account)

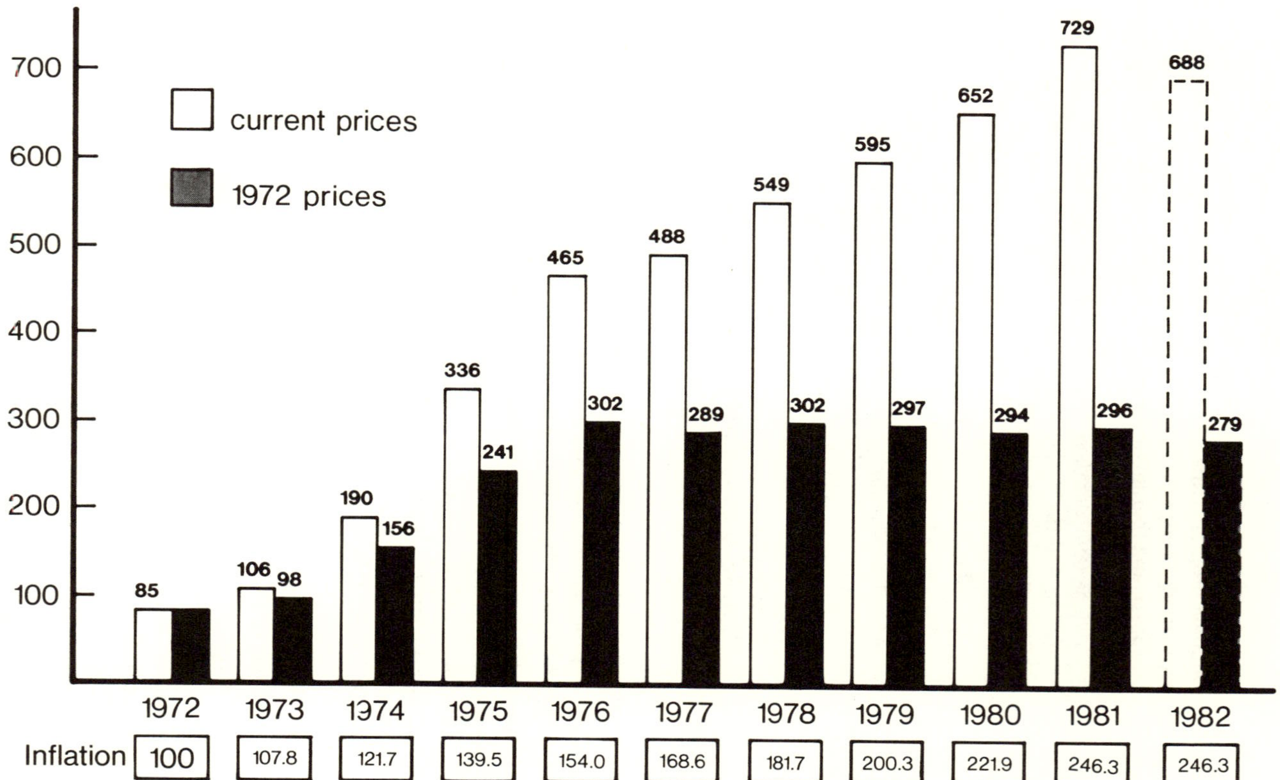

a very advanced system of storage and recovery which enabled this and other data bases to be interrogated from terminals all over Europe. The system was refined and expanded over the years until very few experts would have contested its claim to be the most advanced in Europe. Proof of its capability and of the expertise of its staff was provided when the relevant service of the European Communities sought ESRO's help in establishing the European data network (EURONET). Support from delegations was nonetheless sporadic and largely dominated by the aspirations of those delegates whose own national information retrieval services had plans to enter the market. Their opposition was never sufficient to kill the ESRO/ESA service, and it is at the time of writing still flourishing, but this in spite of the Member States rather than because of wholehearted support. Many of the improvements and innovations were the product of gifted staff working long hours aided by an occasional liberal interpretation of the regulations. Thus, what could have been the keystone of a lucrative European business in an area of rapidly developing interest was relegated to the barely tolerated status, subject at regular intervals to sharp criticisms from delegates who had nothing concrete to criticize except that the operation was more successful than those in Member States or other international organizations.

Applications Satellites

It was obvious to all that once ESA went beyond the relative calm lagoon of the scientific program, the elements would not be so friendly. The progress of the telecommunications program illustrates very well this change of weather. There were to my mind at least two reasons why this was inevitable. In the first place, Europe did not possess an organization capable of speaking authoritatively for its national telecommunications entities, still less one authorized to negotiate on their behalf. (I have earlier referred to the ineffectual efforts of the CETS during the INTELSAT negotiations). There was in fact a Conference Européenne des Postes et Telecommunications (CEPT), but it operated through consensus rather like the CSE. Although CEPT tried to face up to the problem of satellite telecommunications by forming a working group—Comité de Coordination des Telecommunications par Satellites (CCTS)—specially for that purpose, it was not a very effective coordinating body. This made it extremely difficult to have the telecommunications entities specify their needs and, of course, the definition of the satellite program demanded on the formulation of these requirements. It was not until 1979 that the various telecommunication authorities were able to found EUTELSAT, named by analogy with INTELSAT, and to authorize one of their members to negotiate with ESA for the provision of the European Communications Satellite (ECS) system. ESA was, after all, an organization supported by development ministries, and they were justifiably unwilling for telecommunications to commit large amounts from their budgets unless they could have a guarantee that the end users were satisfied and — no less important — were also making a financial effort.

The second factor resided in the potential commercial value of telecommunications satellites. Technical journals all produced articles predicting the coming rash of satellites in many parts of the world, not only for telecommunications, but also for television and data transmission. This immediately led to visions of exports and hence to a greatly enhanced national interest in developing the industrial capacity to compete on the world market. This had in fact been one of the original objectives in forming ESA, but France and Germany became restive at the idea of having to trail the industries of smaller Member States along when the time came to bid for the overseas satellite contracts. The thought of being dropped did not at all appeal to the smaller Member States, who pointed to the significant investment in which they had faithfully participated over the past ten to fifteen years. A satisfactory agreement was signed between ESA and EUTELSAT in 1979, but the seeds of a future clash had been sown; things would never be as calm as in the good old days when ESRO simply had to satisfy the space scientists.

The maritime communications satellite was a variation of the OTS, using the same basic module. Development, however, became involved with the birth of INMARSAT, the international organization created on the INTELSAT pattern, responsible for maritime satellite telecommunications. The Member States of ESA were anxious that their satellites — the so-called MARECS A and B — should be incorporated into a worldwide system. The UK, which had given up its national telecommunications satellite program as part of the general European settlement, was particularly keen to see this happen, but the European front had great difficulty in maintaining unity over the several years of international negotiations. There was, however, a happy ending to this chapter: INMARSAT accepted MARECS A and B, along with other satellites, as part of its first generation system, and MARECS A was launched successfully from Kourou on board the fourth development flight of the Ariane launcher on 19 December 1981.

The ill-fated AEROSAT program is a saga in itself, but in this present context it merits mention because it was largely a European initiative and was intended to bring together the air-traffic-control entities from Europe, the United States, and Canada, and at a later stage those from Japan and Australia. A memorandum of understanding was negotiated between ESA, the US Federal Aviation Agency, and the Canadian Department of Communications; industrial specifications were prepared and contractors chosen. But suddenly there was a US governmental decision not to proceed with the program, and, in spite of the memorandum of understanding, the whole venture collapsed. It was alleged that there had been insufficient consultation with the airlines and with IATA, and these bodies certainly marshalled an impressive lobby against the AEROSAT program. Whatever the real motive, and I believe that there were several, the cancellation gave rise to a lot of ill will in Europe. Luckily, NASA had only been involved at the very beginning of discussions on the program and thus incurred none of the opprobrium. The program continues to maintain a miserable existence, but few people have hopes that it will ever materialize in anything resembling its originally conceived form.

One lesson to be learned from this experience—apart from a certain mistrust of memoranda of understanding—was the increased need to consult and to educate the end user of application satellite systems. This was to be underlined in all the future programs of meteorology and remote sensing, where it was important to put a brake on the aspirations of the satellite engineers and to listen to the needs of those who would be using the end product from the satellites. As has been the case in other parts of the world, ESA had to tread a careful course between the twin rocks of undue pressure on the satellite user and of waiting, cap in hand, until the user knocked on ESA's door requesting a satellite. Nature had to take its course, but it could be judiciously helped and prompted.

Spacelab

The Spacelab program was probably ESA's most difficult undertaking. Not only was it expensive, even as originally estimated, but it was also highly sensitive to changes in the NASA Shuttle in which it was being designed to fly; a large proportion of the Shuttle engineering changes caused significant and expensive changes in the Spacelab. Moreover, this was ESA's first entry into man-rated programs and exposed ESA's staff and European industry to very much more rigorous standards and working methods than ever before experienced. I have mentioned earlier that the program was covered by a memorandum of understanding between NASA and ESA. This provided that ESA would deliver to NASA a complete Spacelab assembly for use in the programs and that ESA would have a half share of space for experiments on the first Spacelab flight. Although these terms were fully known from the outset to all Member States, there was a growing dissatisfaction with them, as the cost of the program rose (and not always, as I have explained, because of any inadequacy in the Spacelab itself). It was often overlooked that the Spacelab/Shuttle cooperation was in fact the result of intergovernmental negotiations leading to a government-to-government agreement, which clearly shows that the provision of Spacelab was Europe's entry ticket into the manned space programs and that it was intended to be a continuing cooperative venture with the United States.

The Spacelab agreement between the participating Member States (all except Sweden) plus Austria, provided a margin of 20 percent for contingencies; in the event, a further 20 percent was required. This caused severe problems with Germany and Italy, the main contributors. Italy was doubly hurt because the areas in which modifications required the additional funds to be spent were not to any great extent in the work being undertaken by Italian industry; the percentage of Italian industrial work compared to its financial participation thus declined. As I have indicated, it was not only the rising cost which caused the disenchantment (an overrun of 40 percent—half of which had been foreseen from the outset—is regrettable but, in the circumstances not—at least in my assessment—dishonorable; most Member States can point to larger overruns on national programs). There was also the growing feeling that ESA had been shortchanged in the deal with the United States. This in turn led to a great reluctance to provide funding for the use of Spacelab by European experimenters (although Germany found money for quite a significant national program) and even less for the improvements to Spacelab essentials later on to maximize its chance of being used as a building block for the future space station.

The flight model of Spacelab was formally handed over to NASA at the beginning of December 1981, and it remains now only to wait for it to be fitted into the Shuttle flight schedule with its payload of several thousand pounds of scientific and technical experiments. The Shuttle in the meantime has proved itself; NASA has ordered from ESA a second Spacelab, this time at NASA's expense; and there are signs that Spacelab is gradually coming back into favor.

New Members

I am conscious that I have stressed the ESRO/ESA crises and expressions of dissatisfaction from Member States, but these were apparently not sufficient to discourage newcomers. Ireland subscribed to the 1975 ESA Convention and became the Agency's eleventh Member State. The quality of their delegates and the constructive attitude they adopted in business meetings were exemplary. The Executive for its part spent a great deal of time learning about Ireland's needs and how best Irish industry could be helped.

Austria, too, expressed desire for a closer relationship with ESA. Participation in the Spacelab program was the first step, and this led in turn to Austria being accepted as an Associate Member in October 1979, with every likelihood of this being upgraded to full membership in due course. Norway, with always an eye on Austria in space matters, followed suit and became an Associate Member in November 1981.

The most surprising new candidate was, however, Canada. Almost since its inception, ESRO had had excellent relations with the Canadian Department of Communications and, aside from the common disappointment of AEROSAT, had cooperated together in the field of satellite telecommunications. There was also a meaningful exchange in the remote sensing area. A

Canadian lady minister informed the meeting of the ESA Council at Ministerial level in February 1977 (the ESA Convention had done away with the need for the CSE and its Committee of Alternates) that Canada wished to become an Associate Member. In spite of the gallant assurances of the Italian president, the procedure was not quite as trouble-free as one could have hoped. The ostensible objection to associate membership was the unfortunate geographical fact that Canada was not part of Europe. The deeper seated reasons were, to my mind, the dangers some Member States saw in accepting a new associate member with a qualified aerospace industry and proven experience in application satellite exploitation.

There followed an embarrassing period of renegotiation, and in December 1978 an agreement was signed giving Canada all the advantages of associate membership, but without that specific title. A certain amount of political pressure was necessary to achieve this agreement because of the need for unanimous approval in Council, but I am convinced that the ESA community will greatly benefit from Canada's refreshingly practical approach to space problems, and her reluctance—thus far—to fuel those long and dispiriting debates which are a specialty of international organization. Canada, too must reckon itself happy with the association—although spelled with a small "a"—because the Canadian representative at the ESA Council meeting in December 1981 announced his country's decision to invest a good deal more money in ESA programs.

External Relations

The sensitivity of Member States was nowhere more evident than in regard to the Executive's excursions into external relations. A certain caution is understandable: there are cases where international organizations take in washing from one another, and where the main aims of the organizations appear to have less priority than their somewhat incestuous relations with other organizations. ESRO and ESA could never justly be accused of that; the main motivation for attempting to extend ESA's external relations came from the evident pleasure which non-Europeans experienced from seeing an active Europe in space. There were opportunities for Europe to benefit from the reputation of its space agency, sometimes intangible but often as a precursor for European industry. Member States were in general, however, very reticent, and I suppose it was a reaction against any desire ESA might have to develop into a supranational authority. Particularly discouraged were attempts to have closer relations with Africa and the Middle East. There is no doubt in my mind that Europe missed several interesting opportunities because of the reluctance to play the ESA card. Non-Europeans with whom ESA officials came into contact were sometimes mystified by the attitude of Member States, and the Executive at times had difficulty in finding an explanation which was acceptable even given habitual diplomatic tolerance. The fact is that most Member States were more interested in improving their own individual relations with developing countries by the provision of training courses and advice in the hope of an immediate commercial advantage for their own industry. That some overseas countries preferred a European approach to assistance and advice, and saw in ESA a guarantee of impartiality, was never really understood by some Member States.

Nevertheless, ESA did have relations with many countries all over the world, and concluded—sometimes with the grudging approval of its Council—agreements with NASA (as already described), the Academy of Sciences of the USSR, the Indian and Japanese Space Research Organizations, and the corresponding authorities in the People's Republic of China. The agreement with the Indian Space Research Organization (ISRO) led to ESA launching an Indian telecommunications satellite (APPLE) on the third development flight of the Ariane launcher. I always had the feeling that ESA had a lot to learn from ISRO: they were not able to saturate technical problems with a hose-pipe of resources; they had relatively little funding available and had to husband their resources most carefully. As a result they often came up with ingenious technical solutions which in Europe—and still less in the United States—would not have been sufficiently elegant to win approval. All ESA staff who worked with ISRO were impressed by the enthusiasm and dedication of their personnel, and there emerged a mutual respect and understanding that certainly had not been anticipated on the European side.

From the outset ESRO had close relations with the Council of Europe, and the ESA Convention specifically provided for this to continue. The Organization received a great deal of support and encouragement from members of parliament from all over Europe, and there developed a very worthwhile cooperation between the two organizations.

Relations with the European Community were kept alive by a handful of staff members from both organizations who could see the value of a cooperation and in particular a demarcation agreement. This was of special importance in remote sensing, where the Community had a real interest and capability, mainly through its center at Ispra, Italy. In spite of one or two high-level meetings, however, I never had the impression that the Commission of the Community was greatly interested by ESA or by space affairs in general. Attempts were made to point out to the Community, even at the highest level, the interest which African nations could have in such programs as METEOSAT which was producing images of the whole of the African continent every twenty-five minutes. The value was recognized by some, but apparently at a level incapable of producing action. Nevertheless, the paths of the organizations continue to cross, and there is always the hope that a time will come when the Community can better exploit what ESA has to offer.

New Programs

The program with which ESA started was so large that it devoured all available funding in most Member States, particularly during the second half of the 1970s when Europe had considerable financial difficulties, and the chances for new programs were thereby very much reduced. The Agency nevertheless proposed new programs in four areas:

– a program of television broadcasting known as L-Sat
– a program of remote sensing
– a utilization and improvement program for Spacelab
– an improvement program for the Ariane launcher

It was clearly imprudent to await the end of the ongoing program before suggesting new ones. The aim was to maintain a steady level of activity within the Agency and also in industry. The ESA Convention contained the mechanism by which it had been hoped to introduce some continuity and to permit realistic medium-term planning by removing the need for unanimity in budgetary votes. However, the ESA Convention came into force only after ratification by all signatories. To cover the intervening period, Member States agreed that they would normally apply the new Convention, unless there was an objection from one or more states. Not only did the normal process of ratification take—as expected—a number of years, but there is reason to suppose that in France the procedure was slowed, if not halted, to provide a useful, if unmentionable, negotiating instrument. The ESA Convention finally came into force on 30 October 1980. Nowhere was this lack of proper framework felt more than in the budgetary area; in the absence of a Convention the Member States agreed that unanimity was required for the three-year level of resources and that in its absence the annual budget of the mandatory program (scientific and general budget) required unanimous approval. The majority of the Member States were prepared to vote both, but others (not the smallest) declined to vote for either until they had gained satisfaction in the area which interested them most. Consequently, for year after year the ESA scientific and general budgets were granted on a monthly basis. The Executive was able to gain sufficient support for an interpretation of the relevant texts, which gave a little flexibility and minimized the damage to the programs, but it was not a pleasant situation. The Council meeting in December 1981 started 1982 again under the "provisional one-twelfth's" regime. The unanimity rule—sacred weapon of national independence against domination by international organizations—continued to impede progress.

Although the atmosphere generated by the continued bickering was not conducive to winning approval for new programs, there was some enthusiasm for the proposed experimental broadcast satellite, principally supported by the UK. France and Gemany were both at best lukewarm, but the remaining Member States agreed to drag out the decision-making process in order to allow time for a change of heart, especially on the part of Germany. I will not strain the reader's patience with a recapitulation of the events, the important and sad thing to report is a victory for the division forces in Europe. The French and Germans decided to proceed with their own program, even thought it was obvious from the start that the choices were between one European satellite program or two, even three, programs by separate groups of countries, for no technologically developed country could afford to opt out of this important activity. All this took an amount of time, but by December 1981, the L-Sat development program was formally approved by its participants, while the French-German program goes its own way—though not, I believe, without the occassional wistful glance at the ESA program.

Remote sensing had for a long time been identified as the next area into which ESA must move. In preparation for this program, a number of studies had been undertaken by ESA, and the Agency had organized a network of ground stations for the retrieval, processing, archiving, and dissemination of images, using as a start those obtained from NASA's Landsat satellites. France had for some time been working on a remote-sensing-satellite program named SPOT, and, in conformity with the same Convention she found for other reasons difficult to ratify, the French delegation offered the program for internationalization through ESA. The offer came, however, at a bad time: money was short and most Member States were still in the process of digesting the large financial commitments which the first batch of ESA programs represented. Hence, France—encouraged financially by a military interest—went ahead with the program outside ESA and subsequently found some interesting bones to offer to Sweden and Belgium.

In this area, however, there was not the same conflict and tension as with the broadcast satellite, and all Member States agreed that an ESA remote sensing program must be undertaken as soon as funds became available. Preliminary studies were commissioned and experts met regularly to define the optimum objectives for Europe's remote sensing program. Perhaps more than in any other area, time was needed to inform and consult end users, and to avoid producing a program too much influenced by satellite designers. It is gratifying to be able to say that the ESA Council in December 1981 decided to go ahead with the first satellite envisaged in this program: one to be devoted mainly to ocean monitoring. The relative success of the European concept in this case probably reflects the fact that neither civil servants nor industry can really prove that there are imminent commercial profits to be made from remote sensing satellites. True, the French SPOT program team are strenuously marketing the potential images from their satellite, but there is not yet the keen demand and commercial competition long demonstrated in satellite telecommunications and now manifesting itself in television broadcasting satellites.

Arianespace

ESA exercised a very minimum of control over the Ariane launcher program; there were never more than twenty staff members occupied on this task, for it had been agreed that the program should be managed by CNES, the French space agency, and under their control by SNIAS as prime contractor. Even this degree of supervision often irked the French, but perhaps not as much as the need to report to, and demand annual funding from, a Program Board consisting of representatives of the participating countries. I have no difficulty in admitting that the development of Ariane was a product of French aerospace talent, nor that the approval of the Ariane program was largely due to French insistence and pressure. Similarly, I would not wish to contest the efficiency with which CNES and SNIAS undertook this difficult and crucial program. I did, however, object—and still do—to the consistent French attempts to represent Ariane as a wholly French program; Ariane would never have been approved without European support, and this support was too significant in size and constant in nature to be forgotten.

The French nonetheless yearned for a free hand with Ariane and even before the first of the four test firings they were proposing the creation of an industrial consortium to take over the production of Ariane—a consortium, needless to say, with more than 50 percent French shareholding. Thus was born Arianespace, a French company with shares held, after two yeas of negotiations, by forty or so European firms and banks, but with the control firmly in French hands. There was initially a good deal of resistance to the notion of giving Arianespace responsibility also for launchings, for many considered that this was incompatible with the character of a commercial enterprise. But as time passed, formulae were devised to satisfy the conscience of one or the other delegation, and the necessary agreements were reached eventually. ESA was left with responsibility up to the successful completion of the development of the Ariane launcher (increasing the size and weight of the satellites it can put into orbit) and for the maintenance and extension of the Ariane launch site in Kourou. Arianespace was charged with the production of Ariane, its marketing, and, of course, the actual launch services.

The fourth development launch was a complete success on 19 December 1981, and there is every reason to believe that the Ariane program will continue to succeed and to attract customers from outside Europe, too. May I be forgiven for wishing that the enterprise could have retained its true European flavor? ESA Member States, and this is more important than personal sentiments, appear to bear no malice for the way in which this recovery operation was conducted by France, for at the end of 1981 they were apparently willing to pay their share of an additional $240 million for the further development of Ariane.

POSTSCRIPT

The ESA Council at the end of 1981 gave abundant indications that the eleven Member States and three associated members had every intention of continuing to cooperate together in space programs and even to extend their cooperation to new areas. This is essential; against this, all the bickering and jockeying for position is unimportant. European cooperation may cause Member States periods of disillusionment and profound irritation, but, whether they realize it or not, progress is made and will continue to be made as long as a minimum of goodwill is present. As I hope the reader will have perceived, in twenty years Europe has come a long way in space, and most of that progress has been made by means of common effort. The European aerospace industry is now in a position to win substantial shares of important world markets, for both satellite systems and launchers. That the prospect of near-term national commercial benefits causes the cooperation to be strained at the seams should not be allowed to detract from the basic fact that the cooperation is a success. This success, moreover, is of importance for the making of Europe as a whole and not solely for aerospace.

Rodger M. Govea 4

THE EUROPEAN RESPONSE TO TERRORISM

THE SCOPE OF THE PROBLEM

Western Europe has experienced more than its share of terrorism. The countries of Western Europe have the dubious distinction of having faced more terrorism than any other region. As Table 4.1 indicates, approximately 38 percent of the terrorist events in the world from 1968 to 1979 took place in Western Europe. Past and present difficulties with the Baader-Meinhof Group, the South Moluccans, the Red Brigades, and a host of transnational acts by such groups as Black September are the most well known in the European experience. Although the casual observer might register surprise at the concentration of terrorist events and campaigns in Europe, there is ample reason for the formation and persistence of such groups. These reasons relate to several attributes of the European countries.

First, the nations of Western Europe contain a significant number of well-educated middle-class citizens. To some, this might seem to weigh against violent campaigns, but in fact it is precisely this type of demography that often yields a terrorist organization. Ted Gurr found that 70 percent of the organizations active between 1961 and 1970 had membership from middle and upper classes; 15 percent had exclusively middle-class participation.[1] Moreover, as Albert Parry points out, the leadership of terrorist organizations is overwhelmingly middle class and well educated.[2] Henry Targ has suggested that the alienation which characterizes postindustrial societies explains this feature of terrorism; [3] whatever the reason, there is ample evidence that terrorism is often present in highly educated middle-class nation-states.

I would like to thank Juliet Lodge, University of Hull, Alexandre Papandreou, Directorate of Legal Affairs, Council of Europe, and the European Community Information Service for their assistance.

TABLE 4.1

DISTRIBUTION OF TERRORIST EVENTS

BY REGION, 1968-1979

Region	Number of Incidents	Percentage of Total Incidents
Western Europe	1267	38.0
Latin America	861	25.8
Middle East/North Africa	531	15.9
North America	381	9.5
Asia	197	5.9
Sub-Saharan Africa	124	3.7
Other	38	1.1
TOTAL	3336	99.9 (rounding)

Source: Adapted from James B. Motley, "International Terrorism: A New Mode of Warfare," International Security Review 6 (Spring 1981), Appendix 1, Table 1, "Geographic Distribution of International Terrorist Incidents, 1968-1979," p. 112.

Second, there is a great deal of residual resentment from the Third World concerning the colonial experience with Europe. For symbolic or real grievances, many transnational groups choose European targets for their actions. The hijacking of European planes was an integral part of Black September and the Popular Front for the Liberation of Palestine (PFLP) strategy because of the connections between Western Europe and Israel, yet these attacks were mostly symbolic in nature, with very minimal tangible gains as goals. By virtue of its past support of Israel, Western Europe was included as part of the international imperialist community, and was thus a symbolic target. A more direct connection may be found between the South Moluccans and Dutch policy toward the East Indies. The South Moluccan desire for self-rule had been thwarted by Dutch policy; the issue was direct and tangible.

A third reason for the persistence of terrorism in Western Europe is the ease with which travel is possible throughout Europe. With national boundaries becoming less significant, it is possible for terrorists to achieve the key attribute of mobility. The travel record of Mehmet Ali Agca, who shot

Pope John Paul II, provides ample evidence of the mobility of individuals and groups through Western Europe, if not a good example of terrorist behavior.

Transnational terrorism is a difficult legal and political problem for nation-states since its very nature defies the strongest traditions of international legal practice. The modal terrorist organization is based on the premise that some internationally recognized government is *not* the legitimate ruler of all or part of its territory. The problem is compounded by the operations of transnational groups who do not confine their activities to one nation-state, region, or even continent. International diplomatic and legal traditions are based on the Westphalian model which defines international politics as a collection of sovereign states; the global scope of terrorist groups was not foreseen in 1648.

It is well known that transnational terrorist groups have been using the vagaries of international law for their own purposes. For example, several nation-states are willing to grant political asylum to entire groups who have violated some international agreement such as The Hague, Tokyo, or Montreal conventions on air piracy. Once asylum is extended, the legal question of the offense becomes meaningless. Compounding the problem is the consistent tendency for nation-states to use insurgent organizations as proxies against another nation-state, another question for which there is no clear legal answer.

The natural response of both governments and scholars to the problem of transnational terrorism has been to seek international cooperation. In 1974 the United Nations began deliberations on the problem of international terrorism in the hope that some consensus might be reached. These deliberations, which caused an acrimonious and wholly unproductive debate, did not even reach agreement on the definition of terrorism. For example, a group of nonaligned nations proposed a definition of international terrorism which included "acts of violence and other repressive acts by colonial, racist, and alien regimes against peoples struggling for their liberation."[4] The nation-states of the West were less than enthusiastic toward that definition, detecting perhaps a barb in their direction. In essence, most attempts at definition were self-serving, and no agreement was reached. In the absence of agreement on the definition of terrorism, the ad hoc committee had little reason to continue.

Other multilateral actions have dealt with the question of aircraft hijacking. However, agreements such as The Hague, Tokyo, and Montreal conventions have been unsuccessful due to either a lack of strong punitive measures or a lack of signatories.[5] The latter is a particularly damaging condition, since countries that have not acceded to the conventions have often given asylum to hijackers. Prominent among this group are Algeria, Libya, and South Yemen.

Despite the failure of global agreements, there was a persistent drive toward achieving international antiterrorist measures in Europe. In 1974

Paul Wilkinson expressed the unsinkable optimism shared by many: "Governments must combat terrorism and win. And to this end the governments of Europe will find strength through unity."[6] Throughout the 1970s, Western European countries attempted to tackle the problem of terrorism through some supranational institutions, most notably the Council of Europe and the European Parliament. These efforts led to a variety of resolutions and the 1977 European Convention on the Suppression of Terrorism.

THE EUROPEAN CONVENTION ON THE SUPPRESSION OF TERRORISM (1977)

The Council of Europe is an international intergovernmental organization (IGO) comprising twenty-one European nation-states. Created in 1949, it was an effort to coordinate various activities and policies of the nation-states of Western Europe, an effort ultimately overtaken by the development of the EC. Nevertheless, the Council remains active as an opinion forum for its member states, and has developed conventions and agreements in such wide-ranging areas as criminal law, public health, and patents.

The Council of Europe was in many ways the logical institution to begin harmonization on antiterrorist policy. First, it had already generated agreements in the somewhat related fields of criminal extradition[7] and human rights.[8] The former is significant given the transnational wanderings of countless terrorist operations and the corresponding problem of political asylum. The latter is significant in light of potential governmental excess in antiterrorist campaigns and the confounding question of political versus criminal offense. Second, the deliberative nature of the Council, and its corresponding inability to initiate binding legislation, made it a "safe" environment in which to negotiate on this sensitive subject.

In 1973 the Consultative Assembly adopted a recommendation on terrorism which condemned both the act and the meager international response to the problem. More substantively, the recommendation called on the Committee of Ministers to establish a common definition of "political" offense. This measure was a direct response to the universal tendency of terrorist groups to justify their actions as redress for unjust political conditions and the corresponding definition of incarcerated comrades as "political prisoners." The ultimate product of the deliberations and resolutions which followed[9] was the Convention on the Supression of Terrorism, drafted in 1976 and signed in 1977.

In essence, the Convention is an extradition treaty, differing from the European Convention on Extradition in that the issue of political offenses is directly addressed. The Convention on the Suppression of Terrorism proscribes the use of the term "political" as a definition for a variety of classical terrorist actions: hijacking, hostage-holding, bombing, and attacks against diplomats. The Convention thus seeks to make extradition mandatory by limiting the use of the term "political offense," which, under previous extradition treaties, constituted an exceptional case in which extradition was not mandatory.[10]

Nevertheless, there are two articles in the Convention that provide loopholes for reluctant nation-states. Article 5 states that extradition may be refused "if the requested State has substantial grounds for believing that the request for extradition . . . has been made for the purpose of prosecuting or punishing a person on account of his race, religion, nationality or political opinion."[11] The distinction between refusing extradition on the grounds that the offense was political and refusing extradition on the grounds that the offender will be punished for political opinion is indeed a technical one; the two statements are probably functional equivalents.

Article 13 adds a second opportunity for countries not to extradite, even though Article 5 probably makes this section unnecessary. Article 13 allows any country to reserve the right to refuse extradition in any offense which it considers to be a political offense. The article more or less warns countries to consider the seriousness of the offense, but puts no other limits on the option to issue such a reservation.[12] Thus, the Convention does little to strengthen already existing extradition treaties.

Curiously, the Council of Europe has attempted to define away the complicating political dimension of terrorist activity. This action is tantamont to combatting terrorism by declaring it illegal. Signatories are thus asked to accept the premise that insurgent terrorist behavior is unacceptable under any circumstances. Not surprisingly, several countries have expressed reservations about the treaty, others have never signed, and still others have not ratified.

The variety of responses to the Convention of Council of Europe members is displayed in Table 4.2. Especially striking is the fact that out of twenty-one nation-states represented, only seven have given unconditional approval of the Convention. The other fourteen show varying degrees of reluctance to approve the document.

The reservations declared by eight of the members deserve some consideration because the reservations are serious. All eight countries—France, Italy, Portugal, Cyprus, Denmark, Iceland, Norway, and Sweden—use Article 13 and reserve the right to refuse extradition in any case involving a political offense (the judgment of which is left to the discretion of the host governments). Portugal also reserves the right to refuse extradition "for offenses punishable by death in the requesting State."[13] The declaration made by France contains a defense of its policy of granting asylum to "anyone persecuted on account of his action for the cause of liberty."[14]

These reservations highlight the dilution of the Convention. The substantive reason for its drafting was the problem of extradition and "political

TABLE 4.2

RESPONSES OF MEMBER STATES TO THE EUROPEAN CONVENTION ON THE SUPPRESSION OF TERRORISM

Countries that have not signed	Countries that have signed, with reservations but have not ratified	Countries that have signed, without reservations, but have not ratified
Ireland	France	Belgium
Malta	Italy	Greece
	Portugal	Netherlands
		Switzerland

Countries that have signed and ratified, with reservations	Countries that have signed and ratified, without reservations
Cyprus	Austria
Denmark	Fed. Rep. of Germany
Iceland	Liechtenstein
Norway	Luxembourg
Sweden	Spain
	Turkey
	United Kingdom

Source: Council of Europe, "Chart Showing Signatures and Ratifications of Council of Europe Conventions and Agreements," March, 1981; Council of Europe, "Declarations and Ratifications to the European Convention on the Suppression of Terrorism," January, 1977 -- 8 Documents.

offenses." By reserving the right to refuse extradition, these countries render the Convention an exercise in symbolic action. Substantively, nothing has changed due to the passing of the Convention; countries that wish to reserve the right not to extradite may do so. Of course, the Convention itself sanctions these reservations, but by issuing reservations, the prospects for a tightening of Western European antiterrorist policy are virtually removed.

The French reservation is also significant in focusing attention on the issue of the justification for terrorism. The seven countries that signed and ratified without reservations—Austria, Germany, Liechtenstein, Luxembourg, Spain, Turkey, and the UK—seem to accept the premise that terrorism is never a political act and is universally unjustified. In contrast, the French seem to assert that there are instances in which terrorism is justified (namely, when the cause of "liberty" is being advanced). The fact that the French have never ratified the Convention demonstrates their displeasure with the posture of the seven unconditional supporters.

While the Convention has been criticized for its numerous loopholes, there is a sense in which this particular European response is in fact an overreaction. The number of cases in which extradition has been contested and the value of a "universal extradition" treaty as a response to terrorism is questionable. For these limited goals, countries are being asked to surrender, not only their ability to make decisions based on political exigencies, but an integral part of their own sovereignty.

A major flaw in the Convention on the Supression of Terrorism is the denial of the term "political offense." The Convention is essentially an attempt to treat terrorism as if it were merely another form of crime. This definition is, in the main, misguided. Terrorists do not spring from the same roots as "common criminals," nor do their motives echo criminal sentiment. The middle-class origin of most terrorist groups, the educational level of the leadership, and the tendency to engage in suicidal acts points to a phenomenon quite different from the behavior of "common criminals." The denial of political motivation, as in Mrs. Thatcher's recent comments regarding the Provisional Irish Republican Army (PIRA) hunger strikes, neither prevents nor discourages continued action. It does, however, provide comfort to those who oppose a particular terrorist group. The denial of a political dimension to terrorism constitutes a symbolic action above all. Certainly, loopholes which remain in the Convention allow a government to refuse extradition due to political circumstances. Thus, the substantive consequences of the Convention are few; the symbolic appeal would appear to be foremost.

EUROPEAN PARLIAMENT ACTION

The European Parliament has deliberated a number of issues relevant to the control of terrorism. These include extradition, control of arms sales, and the expansion of European antiterrorist agreements to the Lomé countries. However, none of these debates has yielded any significant legislation. More typically, Parliament has passed resolutions condemning terrorism as an act or calling for increased cooperation. Where resolutions have been controversial, they have been watered down in the interests of consensus.

A good example of a purely symbolic act by the European Parliament is a motion for resolution on July 6, 1976.[15] This motion called for cooperation among European nations and the United Nations against terrorism and stated that Parliament "welcomes the courageous liberation of the Entebbe hostages."[16] Similarly, after the killing of Aldo Moro, the Parliament went on record condemning the act by the Red Brigades.[17]

The European Parliament has attempted to bring about some harmonization of action, but those attempts have either failed to bring about tangible results or have led to division within Parliament itself. An example of the former is the motion of January 13, 1977, which called on the "governments and parliaments of the Member States of the European Convention on the Suppression of Terrorism."[18] While the Council of Europe no doubt appreciated the effort, there still remained those countries that did not ratify the Convention. An example of the division within Parliament on the issue of terrorism may be found in the Political Affairs Committee Report on acts of terrorism in the Community in late 1977.[19]

On October 12, 1977, Parliament referred two motions on terrorism to the Political Affairs Committee. One motion came from the Socialist Group, the other from a combination of the Christian Democrats, Progressive Democrats, and the Liberal and Democratic Group. The differences between these motions perfectly illustrates the division among Western Europeans on the issue of a response to terrorism.

While both motions condemn terrorism as an act and call upon member governments to harmonize policy, several differences in emphasis appear between the two documents. The centrists' motion is peppered with such terms as "cold-blooded murders," "criminal deeds," "criminal planning." It concludes that "joint efforts are essential in order to provide effective protection for all citizens" and that internal security must be strengthened.[20] The Socialists' motion, in contrast, "encourages governments in their resolve to ensure that restrictions on freedom are kept to a minimum," warns governments that they should "avoid special measures which cause hostility" or suspend such measures as soon as possible, and recommends that governments "eliminate the causes of terrorism."[21]

The difference between the two is clear. While the centrists emphasize the dangers of terrorism itself, the Socialists emphasize the dangers of counterterrorist policy. Moreover, the Socialists seem to believe that governments share some of the blame for terrorist activity. The idea that the causes of terrorism should be eliminated implies that terrorism is a result of social and political conditions; nation-states which experience terrorism may therefore be systematically inducing these actions. It follows from this that terrorism is a symptom of certain systemic problems and that these problems should be addressed by governments. In contrast, the centrist coalition places blame squarely on terrorists and considers terrorism completely unjustifiable. No mention is made of restraints on governmental counter-terror actions.

Actually, this difference of opinion relates directly to the political content of terrorism, raising this issue once again. The centrists believe that terrorism is criminal behavior and that governments must stop it at all costs. The Socialists seem to suggest that terrorism does in fact represent a political force, if not a legitimate form of behavior. Thus, the key issue of terrorism as criminal versus political behavior reappears in this controversy.

The compromise document of November 14, 1977 represents a trade-off of substance for consensus. While incorporating the concerns of both factions in the preamble, the resolution ultimately (1) "condemns unconditionally all acts of terrorism" and (2) calls for multilateral cooperation among member states and the United Nations.[22]

Unfortunately, the issue of an appropriate response to terrorism has not been approached by the European Community. The issue of the preservation of essential democratic rights versus strong counter-terrorist measures is central to the formation of such a policy; in the interest of consensus, Parliament has avoided a crucial issue. The issue of the political content of terrorism, addressed by the Convention on the Suppression of Terrorism and reopened by the various reservations of signatories, was also skirted by the European Parliament.

RESPONSES AMONG THE NATION-STATES

There has been a good deal of cooperation between countries in individual cases of terrorism. The Swedish government cooperated fully with the FRG during the Stockholm embassy attack in April 1975, turning captured Baader-Meinhof Group (BMG) insurgents over to the FRG. The French government engaged in its own search for Hans Schleyer, who was kidnapped in Germany by the BMG and taken to France in 1977. Indeed, in most cases, governments have been willing to assist others which have been victims of terrorist campaigns.

Nevertheless, there remains the problem of political asylum. France is the best example of a country that has reservations concerning an EC counter-terrorist policy. The long tradition of France as a haven for political outcasts accounts for these reservations and poses an age-old question for the Community: the question of sovereignty versus multilateralism.

The most committed antiterrorists endorse a policy of universal condemnation of terrorism. Pursuant to this premise, all nations should cooperate completely with any government in the throes of a terrorist campaign. Countries that extend political asylum are "thorns in the side" of the battle against terrorism. In short, the individual desires of each country are less important than the overall goal of attacking terrorism.

Others would see the situation differently. The idea of asylum is an old tradition; in France it made it possible for thousands to escape the repression of dictatorships around the world. To give up this tradition would be counter to the notion of human rights. Furthermore, the option to grant asylum is inextricably linked to the notion of sovereignty; a country giving up this option is voluntarily relinquishing its own sovereignty.

It should not be concluded that the French are unalterably opposed to the idea of extradition. The same government that refused to hand over four Black Panthers accused in the United States of hijacking also sent four Basque separatists to Spain after the reforms of a few years ago. The same government that refused to hand over Abu Daoud, who was involved in the 1972 Munich incident, to German and Israeli officials extradited BMG lawyer Klaus Croissant to the German government. The point here is that the French, ever sensitive to political conditions, prefer to make their own judgments on extradition.

Despite differences in opinion on the issue of extradition, EC countries have informally accepted some basic principles concerning terrorism. First, there is widespread acceptance of the advisability of maintaining liberal-democratic principles even in the midst of a terrorist campaign. The Community looks with disfavor on those countries whose counter-terror "emergency measures" lead to excesses. However, specific questions related to special measures have not been resolved. An example of this problem is the case of *Ireland vs. United Kingdom.*[23] This case was brought to the European Court of Human Rights in Strasbourg under procedures contained in the Council of Europe's European Convention on Human Rights. The Strasbourg Court was called upon to evaluate five alleged antiterrorist actions by the British government. The five techniques—wall standing, hooding, sleep deprivation, nutritional deprivation, and abuse of noise—were considered torture by the Republic of Ireland which sought redress on behalf of the abused prisoners. The Court found that the techniques were not "torture" but rather only "inhuman" and as such did violate the European Convention on Human Rights. Yet, even though the UK government freely admitted to these practices (by the time the judgment had been reached, the UK had ceased the techniques), the decision went only as far as admonishing the UK for past practices.[24] Clearly, Western Europe did not wish to encroach upon the sovereignty of the UK government, preferring instead to issue a meek reprimand.

Second, there is an acceptance that, while political motivations do exist in terrorist campaigns, a terrorist insurgency is generally unjustified. However, the more understandable the grievances of an insurgent group, the more likely it is that some countries will tolerate the presence of terrorist "refugees." Thus, Basque insurgents in France were protected from France's extradition attempts, but were returned to Spain when democracy was established because they could no longer claim an unjust political order in that country. Similarly, the BMG, whose motives are still in question (there is yet a debate as to whether the group has an identifiable ideology), have no sympathetic audience in Europe. Third, as Juliet Lodge points out, there is the basic acceptance of the principle of "extradite or try".[25] Even though extradition has at times been an uneasy process, no nation-state in Western Europe wishes for terrorists to go unpunished.

Unilaterally, the nations of the EC have pursued different antiterrorist policies. The UK has been thoroughly intransigent in dealing with the Provisional IRA. The Netherlands, in contrast, has chosen to negotiate with terrorists in different circumstances. A completely different approach is the FRG's mixture of counter-terror (the highly trained GSG-9, which conducted the dramatic Mogadishu rescue), negotiation, and intransigence. The French, having had little resistance to its own government, have adopted a relatively tolerant attitude; Paris is known as a haven for fugitive terrorists.[26]

Of course, these differences are not so much a product of ideology or attitude as they are responses to the situations that have arisen. The Dutch were able to conduct some negotiations with the South Moluccans because the latter were willing to accept such overtures. In contrast, the FRG had little choice in dealing with the Baader-Meinhof Group, for negotiation was virtually impossible. Thus, the peculiarities of each campaign has significantly framed the response.

The importance of these differences in policy is that they represent an obstacle to the harmonization of anti-terrorist policy. The diversity of unilateral approaches demonstrates a lack of consensus on the nature of a uniform Western European response.

SUMMARY AND CONCLUSIONS

Overall, it is clear that there has been little progress in the way of a unified European response to terrorism. On the isolated issue of extradition, there has been occasional friction between countries. The European Convention on the Suppression of Terrorism has not been ratified by all signatories, and countries which have not even ratified have expressed reservations in the event that they accede to the Convention. The European Parliament has taken few actions and has shown an inability to generate concrete guidelines for a concrete antiterrorist policy.

It should be obvious that there has been no appreciable abatement of terrorism in Western Europe. As Table 4.3 indicates, well over 100 terrorist events take place yearly. The Red Army Faction is apparently experiencing a third or fourth incarnation with recent attacks on US military installations and personnel. Italy and the UK still have major problems with terrorism. Thus, whatever consensus has been achieved among EC countries has had absolutely no effect on the vitality of the terrorist enterprise. Certainly, the Convention's assertion that terrorism is not a political offense has done little to deter any activities.

TABLE 4.3

TERRORIST EVENTS IN WESTERN EUROPE

1968-1979

YEAR	NUMBER OF EVENTS
1968	16
1969	31
1970	58
1971	38
1972	112
1973	141
1974	151
1975	109
1976	179
1977	129
1978	166
1979	137
TOTAL	1267

Source: Adapted from James B. Motley, "International Terrorism: A New Mode of Warfare," International Security Review 6 (Spring 1981), Appendix 1, Table 1, "Geographic Distribution of International Terrorist Incidents, 1968-1979," p. 112.

Still, the above criticisms are perhaps a bit harsh. Western Europeans have deliberated the question more successfully than did the UN, where discussions became fruitless as soon as the definition of terrorism was discussed. Given that no multilateral institution has successfully framed an antiterrorist policy, it is unfair to score Western Europe for its failures.

In fact, Western Europeans have achieved some positive results in framing a response to terrorism. Some consensus has formed on a few issues, and despite disagreement on the issue of fugitive terrorists, there is agreement in principle that they should be extradited or tried. Bilateral cooperation in various instances is also a positive development.

Perhaps the most encouraging development is the idea of extending some of this cooperation to the Lomé countries. Part of the problem in Western Europe's approach to terrorism is that terrorism itself is a global phenomenon. The greater the breadth of agreement internationally, the more effective agreements will be. If the Lomé countries can be encouraged to cooperate on the issue of terrorism, a large step toward international consensus will be taken.

The prospects for a concerted Western European response to terrorism are not particularly bright. Terrorism is an explosive issue. Its volatility derives in part from its challenge to national security and the legitimacy of the nation-state itself.[27] Some suggestions by members of the European Parliament for an international body of jurisdiction and enforcement[28] within the EC, while attractive, require a selfless cession of sovereignty by a nation state. When terrorism is directed against a single government, that government will necessarily insist on directing counter-measures because it has been directly challenged. It is inconceivable that governments faced with a threat to internal security will allow another political body to decide its fate. Chances for such a supranational authority are therefore remote. Similarly, the prospects for multilateral cooperation are constrained by these factors.

The sensitivity of the issue of terrorism is a further obstacle to increased cooperation. There is a natural tendency for countries to avoid dealing with terrorism outside their borders, partly because of a reluctance to encroach on the domestic politics of another country, but more so out of a desire to evade the difficult political problems caused by a sustained terrorist campaign. Western European countries outside of Britain are relieved that they do not have a Northern Ireland. It is understandable that they do not adopt the conflict as their own; by similar logic, other terrorist campaigns are avoided whenever possible.

A similar difficulty arises in two-party disputes concerning terrorism. Friction between Italy and France during the Moro affair, for example, was not alleviated by Community action because it was seen essentially as a Franco-Italian dispute.[29] If such disputes are consistently avoided by Community members, multilateral progress becomes all the more difficult.

Aside from the basic issues of sovereignty, legitimacy, and national security, there are some serious differences among EC countries that weigh against future collaboration in antiterrorist policy. First, the countries of the EC have had different experiences with terrorism. The UK and FRG attach more salience to the issue than the French, who have been relatively unscathed. Second, there is a basic disagreement on proper antiterrorist policy among the various EC governments. The measures taken by the UK in Northern Ireland bear little resemblance to the policies of other member states. The differences among the various policies are marked, and the reconciliation of these approaches may be difficult. Third, the problem of countering terrorist groups raises ideological and human-rights-related issues. To leftists, the idea of "emergency measures" to combat terrorism raises the specter of fascist regimes, who justified their excesses in an uncomfortably similar fashion. The debates in the European Parliament demonstrate effectively differences between rightists and centrists, who emphasize effectiveness against insurgency, and leftists, who emphasize the sanctity of democratic institutions and traditions.

The problem of accommodating both views may well be insoluble. No one has yet invented a counter-terrorism formula that combines maximum effectiveness with the preservation of human rights. Countries such as Uruguay suffered from the suspension of a previously stable democracy by a military government that promised and delivered the return of order. In the case of Europe, it might make it easier for authorities to track down domestic terrorists if Western Europe reverts to a time when lengthy border checks slowed international travel. Indeed, such careful checks would have made it more difficult for Mehmet Ali Agca to travel throughout Europe prior to his shooting Pope John Paul II. Still, there is no assurance that the shooting would have been prevented; what is clear is that it would take a longer time to travel through Western Europe if the EC were to reinstate obstacles to international travel. Ironically, such a response to this problem would be cooperation among Western European governments to dismantle one of the most successful EC efforts to date.

Ultimately, one is forced to ask if European efforts have been ill-advised from the start. Beyond the complications of developing a unified anti-terrorist policy, there is the question of the very utility of harmonizing the European response. There have been no terrorist campaigns in Western Europe in which other EC countries have provided terrorists with support and sanctuary, nor have there been any major campaigns threatening the well-being of more than one nation-state, save the ethereal "world revolution" attempted by the Red Army Faction. The actions of terrorist groups have not been aimed at the Community as a whole; the destruction of the Community is irrelevant to these insurgents.

Moreover, the institutions of the EC have no more credibility than nation-states to the terrorist group. In the case of subnational ethnic terrorism, the EC has perhaps less credibility, since its attempts at harmonization are diametrically opposed to the nation-state dissolution favored by the insurgents. To ideologically radical terrorist organizations, the decidedly nonrevolutionary EC must appear to be an apologist for the status quo.[30] In neither case is there any evidence that a multilateral antiterrorist policy will have either credibility or deterrence in the minds of the terrorist themselves.

Certainly, the scope of the problem of terrorism severely limits the efficacy of a Western European response. It has been noted that the EC does not operate in a self-contained environment, contrary to the approach many Western scholars found appealing in the 1960s. The effectiveness of EC policies is often limited by external considerations: economic policy may move toward harmonization, but with an unstable global economy, the measures have a limited impact. Nowhere is this condition as pronounced as in the case of terrorism. If the international milieu is sufficiently conducive to transnational terrorism, will the existence of a small unified pocket of resistance affect terrorism at all? As long as South Yemen and Libya remain sympathetic to a variety of terrorist organizations, there will be haven for those who conduct campaigns against Western governments. The fact that these havens are not located in Europe scarcely matters in an age of air travel.

There is also the question of a single set of standards in responding to terrorism. Terrorism is not a single, easily identifiable phenomenon, but a host of different types of behavior which have violence and intimidation in common. It is one thing to negotiate a customs union, since commerce is in the main predictable and nation-states have understandable and identifiable positions in the discussions. It is quite another to confront a phenomenon characterized by peculiar and sporadic events. Our understanding of terrorism is revised virtually every time a new campaign is launched, and old responses are rendered obsolete. Furthermore, the peculiarities of terrorist groups prevent generalizations, which are necessary for the promulgation of supranational policy. The British have in mind the PIRA, the Dutch the South Moluccans, the Italians the Brigati Rosa; none have identifiable similarities.

In the absence of reliable generalizations and theory, there is little on which to base a policy for the EC. Worse yet, if there isn't even basic agreement on what the phenomenon entails, it seems futile to hope for a solution to even the simplest issues related to terrorism. This particular problem confounds individual nation-states; there is no reason to believe that the EC should fare better.

A final comment on the phenomenon of terrorism concerns the symbolic appeal of European Parliament resolutions and the Convention. Thornton suggests that terrorism is primarily symbolic behavior,[31] and Bell agrees that the total destruction caused by terrorism is really quite small.[32] The symbolic content of terrorism, rather than its actual physical effects, represents the real impact of terrorism. Curiously, it is appropriate that the EC response has been primarily symbolic gestures assuring nation-state cooperation in Europe. Undoubtedly, the biggest effect of the European response to terrorism is to have provided reassurance to those citizens who are aware of Community activities. Since true security against terrorism is impossible, perhaps the nations of Western Europe, in posturing against terrorism, have done virtually all that can be done.

NOTES

1. Ted Robert Gurr, "Some Characteristics of Political Terrorism in the 1960s," in *The Politics of Terrorism*, edited by Michael Stohl (New York: Marcel Dekker, 1979), pp. 23-49.

2. Albert Parry, *Terrorism: From Robespierre to Arafat* (New York: Vanguard Press, 1976), p. 12.

3. Henry R. Targ, "Societal Structure and Revolutionary Terrorism: A Preliminary Investigation," in *The Politics of Terrorism*, edited by Michael Stohl (New York: Marcel Dekker, 1979), pp. 119-143.

4. United Nations, General Assembly, *Report of the Ad Hoc Committee on International Terrorism*, General Assembly Official Records, 28th Session, Supplement No. 28 (A 19028), 1973, p. 21.

5. J. Bower Bell, *Transnational Terror* (Washington: AEI-Hoover, 1975), p. 81.

6. Paul Wilkinson, *Political Terrorism* (London: The Macmillan Press, 1974), p. 151.

7. These include the European Convention on Extradition (1957), Additional Protocol to the European Convention on Extradition (1975), and the Second Additional Protocol to the European Convention on Extradition (1978).

8. The Convention for the Protocol of Human Rights and Fundamental Freedoms (1950) and Five Additional Protocols.

9. An excellent summary of these actions appears in Juliet Lodge, "The European Community and Terrorism: Establishing the Principle of 'Extradite or Try,'" in *Terrorism: A Challenge to the State*, edited by Juliet Lodge (New York: St. Martin's, 1981), pp. 164-194.

10. Ibid., p. 170.

11. *Explanatory Report on the European Convention on the Suppression of Terrorism* (Strasbourg: Council of Europe, 1977), p. 23.

12. Ibid., p. 23.

13. Council of Europe, *Declarations and Reservations—Portugal* (translated), 27 January 1977.

14. Council of Europe, *Declarations and Reservations—France* (translated) 27 January 1977.

15. European Parliament (EP) Working Documents 222/76.

16. Ibid., p. 1.

17. EP Working Documents 50/78.

18. EP Working Documents 513/76.

19. EP Working Documents 372/77.

20. Ibid., Annex II, p. 9.

21. Ibid., Annex I, pp. 7-8.

22. EP Working Documents 372/77, pp. 5-6.

23. See Leon Hurwitz, *The State as Defendant* (Westport, Conn.: Greenwood Press, 1981), pp. 150-155.

24. Ibid., p. 152.

25. Lodge, "The European Community and Terrorism."

26. See Philip C. Cerny, "France: Non-Terrorism and the Politics of Repressive

Tolerance" in *Terrorism: A Challenge to the State,* edited by Juliet Lodge (New York: St. Martin's, 1981) esp. p. 105.

27. Rodger M. Govea, "Terrorism and American Foreign Policy," paper presented at the Annual Meeting of the International Studies Association, Washington, D.C., 1978, p. 3.

28. Lodge, "The European Community and Terrorism," pp. 189-190.

29. At issue was the extradition of Franco Piperno (an alleged organizer of the Red Brigades). See EP Working Documents 1-435/79.

30. Brian Jenkins, *International Terrorism: A New Mode of Conflict* (Los Angeles: Crescent Publications, 1975), p. 10.

31. Thomas P. Thornton, "Terror as a Weapon of Political Agitation," in *International War,* edited by Harry Eckstein (New York: Free Press, 1964), pp. 71-99.

32. Bell, *Transnational Terror,* p. 77.

David M. Wood 5

FUTURE TECHNOCRATS? RECRUITS TO THE HIGHER CIVIL SERVICE OF THE EUROPEAN COMMUNITY

The Commission of the European Community is a bureaucracy that is located at the conjunction of political and administrative functions. As the Executive of a transnational organization it is charged with the responsibility of taking policymaking initiatives and seeking to reconcile the conflicting interests of member states, as well as implementing policies made by its political superiors, the Council of Ministers. The staff of the Commission is an international civil service whose members must wed their perspectives as nationals of their native countries to their commitments to the international or European mission with which the Commission is entrusted. A considerable amount of the work of the Commission is of a technical, specialized nature, reflecting the largely economic policy/administration role of the organization. Thus, in addition to political sensitivity and administrative skill, the job description for the European civil servant often includes technical competence in professional/academic disciplines whose skills are in demand for employment at the national as well as the international level, in the private sector as well as the public. This study examines the following question: what sorts of professional specialties has the Commission sought in recruiting European civil servants?

Different objectives have oriented Commission personnel policy at different times since the creation of the High Authority of the European Coal and Steel Community in 1952.[1] In the early years, the staff of the Executive was characterized by a high European *esprit de corps,* owing in part at least to the fact that many of the early *fonctionnaires* of the Coal and Steel Community, Euratom, and the Common Market were individuals who had played a role in the European movement of the 1940s and 1950s and in the negotiations of the treaties establishing the Communities. They were often European federalists, or they shared a common functionalist commitment with Jean Monnet and Walter Hallstein.[2] In short, these were civil servants with a high level of organizational loyalty.

With the onset of the de Gaulle-generated crisis of the Community in the 1960s, recruits to the European civil service came increasingly from the national bureaucracies of the member states. This development was severely criticized, partly because it detracted from the European character of the Commission staff, and partly because it violated good personnel administration principles by bringing people in laterally from outside at high levels, thus curtailing promotion prospects for indigenous staff.[3] There is evidence to suggest that the Commission may have had difficulty socializing those new recruits from member governments who viewed employment with the Commission to be a temporary part of the overall career pattern within their various national contexts.[4] Pressure mounted during the 1960s from staff representatives to develop sounder personnel policies and bring this lateral recruitment to an end.[5]

The Commission responded to this demand by various steps, one of the most noteworthy of which was the establishment of a system of competitive examinations for entry into the European civil service at the junior grades, which began in 1968. Virtually all recruitment to the junior grades of the A-Category[6] is now by competitive examination. According to Hans Michelmann, promotion from the lower grades "is now the rule" for all but the top policy grades.[7] The exception is an important one, of course. Lateral recruitment may still be an important mode of entrance for precisely those civil servants who will be making the most important decisions; entry by examination may still give an individual an opportunity to rise only to the middle grades of the A-Category. The data examined in the present study do not enable a judgment as to whether the Commission's intention of providing upward mobility to the highest levels has yet borne fruit. If it has begun to do so, or if we can expect this development in the near future, then a study of the recruitment patterns to the junior grades has distinct policy implications. For example, while one might applaud the advent of greater professionalism in the recruitment process, David Coombes has expressed the fear that the emphasis upon greater bureaucratic standardization is leading toward bureaucratic stagnation and away from an activist role for the Commission.[8] Others have argued almost the opposite, that Commission personnel policy may be producing a new postindustrial breed of *technocrats*, whose narrow-minded activism might actually lessen the Commission's ability to steer a safe course through highly troubled political waters.[9]

The implications of the proposition that the Commission staff is becoming increasingly technocratic in composition are far-reaching. According to Robert Putnam, the literature on technocracy attributes a distinct set of orientations to what we might call a technocratic ideology: (1) conviction that techniques must replace politics; (2) skepticism and even hostility toward politics and political institutions; (3) lack of sympathy for the openness and equality of political democracy; (4) the belief that social and political conflict is misguided; (5) preference for practical over ideological or moralistic criteria; and (6) commitment to material progress over social justice.[10] Extrapolating from Putnam and other definitions in the literature, one might expect technocratic civil servants: (1) to prefer policies promoting material progress rather than other values such as social justice or environmental protection;[11] (2) to be incrementalist rather than either fashioning policy to serve utopian ends or slavishly adhering to bureaucratic routines; (3) to make policy that is insensitive to those group demands or anticipated political consequences that the civil servant does not recognize as legitimate and; (4) to show a preference for centralized control over the implementation of policy.[12]

The foregoing suggests the potential significance of a study of technocracy among European civil servants. A thorough study would examine the policy orientations of the A-Category civil servants, but this undertaking is beyond the reach of the present study. This essay attempts to test whether one of the features that would logically accompany technocratization is occurring in the A-Category: whether or not recruitment to the junior grades of the A-Category is producing a preponderance of civil servants at those levels whose academic and professional backgrounds are, in an objective sense, technocratic. Certain professions are more frequently associated with technocracy in the literature. We can regard them as indirect evidence of the phenomenon, while recognizing that technocracy in the fullest sense is a subjective and behavioral phenomenon, a set of orientations that certain members of the reputedly technocratic professions will share while some will not, and a set of behaviors that reflect these orientations. The burden of the present study is not to show that members of certain professions share certain attitudes and behaviors. If the study finds that recruits with "technocratic" academic and professional backgrounds are predominant among entrants to the European higher civil service, it will contribute ever so slightly to the plausibility of the technocracy thesis. If a contrary finding emerges, the thesis will have been slightly dented, but scarcely discredited.

In asking what professions would be most likely to socialize their recruits to hold technocratic orientations (or, alternatively, to attract recruits who already hold them), the following criteria have been identified:

(1) *Applicability of the profession to "postindustrial" needs.* Technocratic professions would be newer professions, or older professions which have adapted themselves to advanced industrial conditions. For example, economists are increasingly in demand as the economy becomes more complex and the role of the state in the economy more crucial. Chemical engineers find themselves called upon for assistance in finding ways to combat pollution. Political scientists seek to adapt to the new conditions by discovering their vocation as public policy specialists.

(2) *Tendency toward quantification and computer applications.* Professions with this characteristic may socialize new members to prefer to deal with those prob-

lems that can be measured and to ignore the broader qualitative questions, dismissing them as political or utopian. One sign is that academic disciplines such as history and modern languages are joining the trend toward computerization, following the path taken by the softer social sciences. But the model all are following is found in the hard basic and applied sciences, as well as in economics.

(3) *Problem-solving, applied nature, as opposed to pure speculation.* Technocratic professions would be those that pride themselves on their reputation for getting things done. Given a problem, they will come up with a solution, perhaps in ignorance of the process by which the problem was identified in the first place. Engineers would seem to be more technocratic than natural scientists by this criterion; certain kinds of economists more than others.

(4) *Tendency to focus more on things than on persons, on systems more than on individual behavior.* The things-over-persons tendency is, of course, truer of the hard sciences than of the social sciences, the legal profession, or the humanities. In the latter fields, economists and certain kinds of sociologists and political scientists tend more to be systems thinkers. The systems orientation seems most likely to lead to a preference for centralized modes of decision making.

By these criteria, the engineer is judged in his various guises as the technocrat par excellence, followed by the economist. The natural scientist and the mathematician fall short only to the extent that concrete problem solving is not their immediate focus. Certain types of political scientists, sociologists, and psychologists could probably be labeled technocratic by some of these criteria, but their disciplines as a whole should not be so labeled; nor should law and the humanities; neither should training in "European studies," an option that nearly 15 percent of the recruits to the A-Category have taken. This involves postgraduate study at an institute or center for European studies, such as the Collège d'Europe at Bruges or the Centre Universitaire des Etudes Communautaires Européennes at the University of Paris. Few of the students who attend these schools have degrees in technocratic disciplines. While some work in economics is featured in the programs, the orientation is usually more of a legalistic or humanistic nature.

The above interpretations should be taken with caution for a number of reasons. For one thing, economics training in continental Europe typically does not institutionally separate theoretical, or what Americans regard as academic, economics from applied economics, or what are business school disciplines in the United States.[13] Another reason for caution is the possibility that different educational traditions for the training of civil servants in different European countries may mean that different mixes of professional types are being recruited by the Commission from different countries, resulting in an overall staff of a mixed, and difficult to interpret, character.

In most Western European countries, a university student preparing for a government career will most likely be pursuing a law degree. Among the larger countries, Germany and Italy have long been noted for the heavy preponderance of lawyers in the highest ranks of the bureaucracy.[14] In West

Germany, most ministries at both the federal and state levels are staffed at the top generalist ranks by civil servants with law training. Specialists are found in similar positions in certain ministries such as the economists in the Ministry of Economic Affairs, but more often in special autonomous agencies with mainly administrative rather than policymaking functions.[15] One might expect that German and Italian recruits to the Commission will be predominantly lawyers, as will those from the smaller member countries. A counter-expectation would be that a *reverse* process is occurring in which students who are trained in disciplines not favored by their home bureaucracies seek and find employment in the European Community more by default, because the best graduates of the law faculties are staying at home. It should be noted, however, that those with training in economics and the more technical disciplines are more likely than lawyers to be favored for employment in the private sector in the same countries.

By contrast, in Britain lawyers in the public service tend to be regarded as specialists, along with economists, natural scientists, and engineers holding advanced degrees, and are thus found more in advisory roles, subordinate to the social scientists and humanists at the very top of the ministerial hierarchies.[16] If this pattern prevails among the British recruits to the European civil service, we would anticipate an offsetting of the expected continental emphasis on the legal profession. However, because the British pattern is so different from what prevails elsewhere in the EC, we might expect an influx of British lawyers and other "specialists" who are frustrated by the generalist biases of the home recruitment process. Another peculiarity of the British administrative recruitment pattern is that students of whatever academic subject are not encouraged to go beyond an undergraduate degree, whereas aspirants for the national higher civil services on the continent are likely to have taken advanced work; in West Germany, for example, the lawyers will take a second state law examination after advanced work in a university and a period of apprenticeship in a federal or state ministry.[17]

The "technocratic" character of the French higher civil service is widely reputed, with the strong advantage given in the recruitment process to engineers graduating from the Ecole Polytechnique and economists-public administrators emerging from the Ecole Nationale d'Administration (ENA).[18] It should be noted, however, that the latter of these institutions itself recruits from graduates of a variety of faculties. A French aspirant with advanced work in economics is, in fact, as likely to have a first degree in law or political science as a degree in economics. But the monopoly by the law faculties of the formation of future civil servants, broken for good by the creation of ENA after World War II, was never so great as in other continental European countries, given the long-standing advantageous position of former *polytechniciens* in some of the central ministries and in the state-owned industries. If a French pattern is found among recruits to the European civil service, it would take the form of recruits with a relatively wide variety of first degrees (though not as wide as the British pattern), frequently having advanced degrees or certificates in economics and engineering. However, given the favored positions of French students emerging from the *hautes écoles* and the exceptional prestige of the *grands corps* of the French civil service, it might be expected that whatever the undergraduate degree displayed, graduates of these prestigious schools would not be readily available at the beginning of their careers to the European Commission.

OVERALL PATTERNS OF RECRUITMENT

The findings reported here are from data collected at the headquarters of the Commission of the European Community in Brussels in 1975 and again in 1979.[19] The data examined consist of information contained in the applications for employment of 997 candidates who passed the written examination for the junior ranks of the A-Category of European civil servants. The 997 cases consist of nearly the entire set of individuals who passed the various specialized examinations during these years.[20] Information gathered concerns the higher educational experiences of the candidates, their employment experiences subsequent to graduation, and the foreign languages they are able to speak competently. The examinations were held as and when vacancies were anticipated and one or more were held during each year between 1972 and 1978, excepting 1976. Examinations were specialized, concentrating on fields such as law, economics, social sciences, public administration, computer science, nuclear energy, and agriculture. In the next section the cases will be divided into three subsets: 1972-73 (291 cases), 1974-75 (366 cases), and 1977-78 (340 cases). The first of these periods was noteworthy for the expansion of the Community to include Britain, Denmark, and Ireland as members. This required a recruitment bias in favor of candidates from these countries. In fact, only nationals of Britain, Denmark, and Ireland were eligible for the 1973 competition. After 1974, which might be regarded as the only really "normal" year, budgetary stringencies required that only a very restricted competition be held in 1975, no competition in 1976, and competitions in 1977 and 1978 which produced approximately the same number of *laureats* (persons passing the examinations) as in 1974 alone.

Once a candidate passes the examination, he or she is not automatically assured of a position with the Commission. As must any governmental personnel administration, DG IX, the unit within the Commission responsible for recruitment as well as for administering other aspects of personnel policy, must be sure that it has available enough candidates to fill the potential demand from various subunits of the organization. Thus, it consciously positions and which had not. For the entire set of 997 candidates, 537, or 53.9 percent, had been hired by the Commission. One of the criteria to be used in assessing the varying emphases which the Commission places upon different categories of candidates will be this percentage, or what is termed the "success score."

Table 5.1 breaks the 537 successful cases down by academic discipline, first by subjects of concentration pursued for the first degree, and second by those pursued in postgraduate work. The percentages in each column total more than 100, since candidates often listed more than one discipline at both levels. Economics and law are easily the predominant subjects represented in both columns, followed by political science, engineering (coupled with the natural sciences in the second column), and mathematical sciences, appearing in different orders in the two columns. European studies is ranked third in the postgraduate column. These higher ranking disciplines include three that are labeled "technocratic" and three that are not. It is noteworthy that economics leads both lists. But a counterfinding is that political science improves its position as we move to the higher level of education, especially if we combine it with the allied fields of public administration and international relations which place sixth and seventh on the advanced list. Moreover, political science is often an important component of European studies. One might speculate that advanced work is more necessary for those in nontechnocratic disciplines to improve their employment opportunities than it is for those in economics, engineering, mathematics, or statistics. But law does not similarly improve its position from the first list to the second. It is also worth observing, lest we try to overinterpret the table in a technocratic direction, the very low positions of agriculture on the first list and computer science on the second.

The rankings change substantially as we turn with Table 5.2 to the success scores[21] of the various disciplines; and moreover the rankings differ noticeably between the two columns in the table. Looking at first-degree disciplines first, the divergence in position of economics and law, the two highest frequency disciplines, is perhaps the most significant finding. Economics retains its leading positions, while law is found down in the ninth position, the 51.9 success score being below the overall average (53.9). In addition to economics, only the social sciences and history-letters[22] are above that average, giving the success scores rankings for the first degree a rather British flavor. This should not be so surprising, when it is considered that British civil servants are not expected to have gone beyond the first degree and that British candidates were favored over candidates from the original six countries during the early years of the period studied.

Law moves back up the table when we look at postgraduate disciplines. Six disciplines rank above the overall average, four of which (European studies, law, international relations, and secondary education) are decided-

TABLE 5.1

PERCENTAGE OF TOTAL CANDIDATES HIRED, BY ACADEMIC DISCIPLINE

(1972-1978)

First Degree Disciplines	Percentage	Post-Graduate Disciplines	Percentage
Economics	35.8	Economics	25.5
Law	32.8	Law	20.1
Mathematical sciences	11.0	European Studies	13.8
Engineering	10.6	Political Science	5.4
Political Science	8.9	Mathematical sciences	5.2
History-letters	6.0	Natural sciences-engineering	4.6
Languages	5.2	Public Administration	2.6
Natural sciences	5.0	International relations	2.4
Social sciences	4.5	Computer science	2.0
Agriculture	2.2	Secondary education	1.7
Public administration	1.1	History-letters	1.7
		Languages	1.5
		Social sciences	1.3
		No post-graduate study	35.8

oversubscribes by adjusting the threshold of acceptability in the examination to the expected demand for personnel, plus whatever additional number is needed to provide the necessary cushion. This means there is an additional hurdle that the candidate must successfully overcome. He or she must find a sponsor, in the sense that some unit of the Commission makes a special request that the candidate be assigned to it. On the one hand, the personnel administration must try to accommodate the specific needs of units of the Commission. On the other hand, from the generalized perspective of DG IX, it is necessary to be sure that the most highly qualified candidates find positions. As an additional consideration, there is the requirement, common to international organizations, that a balance be struck between nationals of the member nations, roughly proportional to population differences between them. Findings related to this last matter will be discussed in a later section.

Given these competing criteria, which professional categories seem to have had advantages in this process over others? Fortunately, data included information as to which candidates had, as of the end of May 1979, found

TABLE 5.2

SUCCESS SCORES BY ACADEMIC DISCIPLINE (1972-1978)

First Degree	Success Score	Post-graduate	Success Score
Economics	63.2	European studies	63.2
Social sciences	57.8	Mathematical sciences	62.2
History-letters	56.1	International relations	61.9
Engineering	53.8	Economics	61.7
Languages	53.8	Law	58.7
Political science	53.3	Secondary education	56.3
Mathematical sciences	53.2	Political science	54.7
Agriculture	52.2	No post-graduate study	49.0
Law	51.9	Languages	47.1
Public administration	46.2	Natural sciences	46.3
Natural sciences	40.9	Public administration	43.8
		History-letters	37.5
		Computer science	36.7
		Social sciences	29.2

ly nontechnocratic. The latter two of these are very low-frequency disciplines, however, which makes the high rankings of mathematical sciences and economics appear of some significance. It would be tempting to suggest that this listing has a distinctly French flavor, but the natural sciences and engineering have a relatively low position. Perhaps it is more appropriate to speculate that this ranking represents a mixture of continental patterns, in all of which advanced work is more the norm for civil service recruits than it is across the Channel. The low rankings of subjects more likely to be favored in Britain strengthens this possibility; modern languages, history-letters, and social sciences are all well below the overall average.

VARIATIONS IN RECRUITMENT PATTERNS OVER TIME

To the extent that overall patterns are discernible in the above analysis, the question is readily posed: are these patterns reflective of longer-term trends? Are the recruits to the European civil service more technocratic than their predecessors? Lacking data for the 1960s, the question cannot be answered directly; however, it is possible to compare the early 1970s with the latter part of the decade to see if any trends emerge. Changes in percentages of those hired according to academic discipline are displayed in Table 5.3, with comparisons between the years 1972-73 and 1977-78. A rather clear pattern appears for first-degree disciplines, but the same can not be said of the postgraduate disciplines. Three first-degree disciplines show a gain during the decade, all falling in the technocratic category: engineering, mathematical sciences, and natural sciences. Economics, however, registers a percentage loss during the period, while law holds its position. Thus, the "technocratization" is a selective one.

When one turns to the postgraduate disciplines, the most striking trend is the gain registered by law. Economics loses ground here as well, while mathematical sciences, natural sciences, and engineering remain constant. Computer science exhibits a noteworthy gain. At the postgraduate level it is difficult to see consistent trends. Most disciplines show very small percentage changes. What does seem clear is that the Commission continues to look for a variety of talents in its recruits. It remains to be seen whether this variety is explicable by the fact that several distinct *national profiles* prevail.

NATIONAL PROFILES

Earlier it was noted that a consideration the personnel administration of an international organization must take in hiring is the necessity to strike a balance between nationals of the member countries, presumably on the basis of respective population sizes. The literature indicates that the Commission of the European Community is no exception.[23] However, the 1973 expansion of the Community meant a bias in the early part of the period examined in favor of recruits from Britain, Denmark, and Ireland. Table 5.4 shows that the latter was the case. Candidates from the three new countries all registered success scores of 60 or above, the Irish score of 65.0 being the highest. That a national balance was struck is not so certain, however. While most of the success scores are in the vicinity of 60, those for the Germans, the Italians, and the Flemish Belgians (who are considered separately from the French-speaking Belgians) are substantially lower. When we look at the *percentages* in the first column, anomalies arise. We would expect the French, German, and Italian percentages to be below the British, but roughly equal to one another. In fact the French percentage (23.1) is equal to the British and substantially above the German (15.4) and still more substantially above the Italian (8.8). These differences are due in part to the differences in success score, but also to the fact that there are differences,

TABLE 5.3

VARIATIONS IN PERCENTAGES OF TOTAL CANDIDATES HIRED, BY ACADEMIC DISCIPLINE (THREE TIME PERIODS)

First Degree	1972-73	Percentage Hired 1974-75	1977-78	Change (1972-73 to 1977-78)
Economics	44.4	26.7	37.9	-6.5
Law	32.6	33.3	32.1	-0.5
Mathematical sciences	8.6	10.5	15.0	+6.4
Engineering	4.8	12.9	15.0	+10.2
Political science	11.8	9.5	4.3	-7.5
History-letters	8.1	5.7	3.6	-4.5
Languages	5.9	4.3	5.7	-0.2
Natural sciences	1.6	6.7	9.4	+7.8
Social sciences	8.6	2.4	3.6	-4.5
Agriculture	4.8	1.0	0.7	-4.1
Public Administration	1.6	1.0	0.7	-0.9
Post-graduate				
Economics	30.5	20.4	26.4	-4.1
Law	15.5	21.3	24.3	+8.8
European studies	11.8	15.2	14.3	+2.5
Political science	3.2	8.1	4.3	+1.1
Mathematical sciences	5.9	4.7	5.0	-0.9
Natural sciences-engineering	5.9	2.8	5.7	-0.2
Public administration	2.7	2.4	2.9	+0.2
International relations	2.1	3.3	1.4	-0.7
Computer science	0.0	2.4	4.3	+4.3
Secondary education	3.2	0.9	0.7	-2.5
History-letters	0.5	2.4	2.1	+1.6
Languages	0.0	2.4	2.1	+2.1
Social sciences	2.1	0.9	0.7	-1.4
No post-graduate study	32.3	38.9	32.1	-0.2

TABLE 5.4

RECRUITMENT OF MEMBER-COUNTRY NATIONALS (1972-1978)

Nationality	Percentage Hired	Success Score
Belgian (Flemish)	3.0	39.0
Belgian (French)	7.5	60.6
British	23.1	60.0
Danish	8.3	60.3
Dutch	4.3	57.5
French	23.1	61.8
German	15.4	49.1
Irish	4.9	65.0
Italian	8.8	32.0
Luxemburger	1.5	57.1

although not as great, between these national subsets in the number of candidates who passed the examinations in the first place. British and French candidates both constitute 20 percent of the entire set of laureates, while Germans constitute 17 percent and Italians 15 percent. It is possible that fewer Germans and Italians attempted the examination in the first place, but, whatever the case, the Commission found the French candidates who passed the examination more employable than their German or Italian counterparts.

Among the smaller countries, the most interesting findings are the relatively small percentage of Dutch candidates hired and the strikingly lower percentage and success score of Flemish Belgians than of French-speaking Belgians. In the first case there was an even smaller percentage of Dutch candidates in the total set (4.0) than in the subset of those hired (4.3), and the Dutch success score (57.5) is above the overall average. It seems unlikely that there is a bias in the recruitment process against the Dutch; rather, proportionately fewer Dutch candidates presented themselves in the first place. The same is less likely to be true of the Flemish Belgians. Here one can speculate that the general cultural bias within Belgium in favor of francophones is operating in the EC recruitment process itself. But without data on the number of Flemish Belgians who took the examinations in the first place, it cannot be said with certainty that there is not the same phenomenon taking place among them as appears to be taking place among othe Dutch.[24]

First-Degree Disciplines

In examining the patterns of academic disciplines most favored for each country, emphasis is given to the four major Community members, Britain, France, West Germany, and Italy, noting unusual patterns for smaller countries as well. Tables 5.5 and 5.6 show the breakdown by first-degree discipline for each nationality, depicting percentages of candidates hired and success scores. Of the four major national subsets, the British present the most distinctive pattern. Reading across the British row in Table 5.5 we see the expected low percentage of British candidates with undergraduate law degrees, compared with high percentages of those with economics, political science, mathematical sciences, languages, natural sciences, and social sciences. Reading down the columns, the British rank higher in all of these core academic disciplines than they do in engineering and law, where they rank lowest and second lowest, respectively. In fact, in Britain neither engineering nor law is typically taught at the undergraduate level in the university. The relative percentages of engineering and mathematical sciences exemplify the British pattern well. The latter is an academic subject par excellence; the former is not the sort of subject one would take if one were preparing for the higher civil service in Britain. This comparison holds with respect to the success scores displayed in Table 5.6. The British have the lowest success score in the engineering column and the highest in the mathematical science column. In this table the British with legal studies fare somewhat better than the British average (62.2 versus 60.0), but the success score for British economists (72.0) is the highest in the column.

The French pattern seems in most respects to be the opposite of the British, but it is not such a close fit to expectations. The comparison between law and economics clearly favors law in this case. Only 25.4 percent of the French candidates had undergraduate work in economics, a percentage that is lower than any but the francophonic Belgians and Luxemburgers. Not only are former law students the highest percentage of the French candidates (41.0), but their success score (68.5) is second highest in the law column. The French success score in the economics column (50.8) is the third lowest. These findings suggest the possibility that the best French economics students are not attracted to the Community, having more attractive opportunities at home, while the Community holds out more advantages to the job seeker with a background in legal studies. This possibility will be explored further when we get to postgraduate disciplines. It is further supported at this point by the very high success scores of French candidates with backgrounds in political science, languages, and the social sciences, fields of probably less employment potential in France. The plight of French candidates with engineering, mathematical, and natural science backgrounds is at about the average for these disciplines in terms of the per-

TABLE 5.5

PERCENTAGES OF TOTAL CANDIDATES HIRED, BY NATIONALITY, BY FIRST DEGREE DISCIPLINE (1972-1978)

Nationality	Law	Economics	Political Science	Engineering	Math Sciences	Languages	Natural Sciences	Social Sciences
Belgian (Flemish)	12.5	31.3	6.3	43.8	6.3	6.3	0.0	6.3
Belgian (French)	30.0	20.0	5.0	30.0	10.0	5.0	10.0	2.5
British	18.7	43.9	13.0	2.4	18.7	11.4	7.3	8.1
Danish	34.1	43.2	0.0	4.5	6.8	4.5	2.3	2.3
Dutch	52.2	43.5	0.0	8.7	0.0	0.0	4.3	0.0
French	41.0	25.4	13.1	11.5	9.0	4.1	4.9	3.3
German	39.0	42.7	1.2	6.1	6.1	1.2	3.7	3.7
Irish	19.2	50.0	26.9	3.8	15.4	7.7	3.8	11.5
Italian	34.0	31.9	8.5	19.1	12.8	0.0	4.3	4.3
Luxemburger	50.0	12.5	0.0	25.0	12.5	0.0	0.0	0.0

TABLE 5.6

SUCCESS SCORES OF NATIONALITIES BY FIRST DEGREE DISCIPLINE (1972-1978)

Nationality	Law	Economics	Political Science	Engineering	Math Sciences	Languages	Natural Sciences	Social Sciences
Belgian (Flemish)	15.4	50.0	33.3	58.3	33.3	50.0	--	50.0
Belgian (French)	63.2	66.7	66.7	54.5	57.1	100.0	57.1	50.0
British	62.2	72.0	64.0	42.9	71.9	43.8	56.3	47.6
Danish	65.2	65.5	--	50.0	37.5	66.7	33.3	50.0
Dutch	66.7	66.7	--	100.0	--	--	33.3	--
French	68.5	50.8	80.0	56.0	50.0	83.3	50.0	80.0
German	46.4	63.6	100.0	38.5	29.4	50.0	27.3	75.0
Irish	83.3	65.0	77.8	50.0	66.7	66.7	50.0	75.0
Italian	23.2	62.5	18.2	52.9	54.5	--	28.6	100.0
Luxemburger	57.1	50.0	--	100.0	50.0	--	--	--

centages in Table 5.5 and somewhat below the French average in terms of the success scores in Table 5.6. Clearly the French profile for first-degree disciplines does not live up to the French technocratic reputation.

What is striking about the Germans in Table 5.5 is the heavy concentration in the law and economics columns. A relatively high number of successful Germans took law at the first-degree level, but the number is exceeded by those who took economics, a discipline that is less well established for employment in the higher civil service in Bonn. The success score for Germans in the law column (46.4) is the third lowest in the column, while that in the economics column (63.6) far exceeds the German average (49.1). As with the French, the "reverse interpretation" is tempting. This would argue that, with less attractive opportunities at the national level, German economists of high quality are more apt to seek employment in the European Community than are lawyers better favored by the national market. Again, we must look at the postgraduate disciplines to see if there is corroborating evidence.

What strikes one most about the Italian candidates is the low level of their success scores generally, and particularly the unexpectedly poor performance of those with law degrees. Italian lawyers dominate the national bureaucracy, but they are rivaled by the economists among successful Italian candidates for employment with the Commission. This is true not only in terms of percentages, but especially in the disparity between the 23.2 success score for lawyers and the 62.5 success score for economists. The latter is truly remarkable, given that the overall Italian success score is 22 points below the 53.9 success score for the entire set of 997 candidates, while the Italians with first-degree work in economics are less than one point below the success score for all candidates in that category (62.5 versus 63.2). The findings for success scores of Italians in the engineering and mathematical sciences columns are very similar to those for economics. Again, a reverse interpretation seems difficult to escape. The better Italian law graduates are not seeking employment in Brussels; the better economics, engineering, and mathematical science graduates are. Of the four larger countries' candidates, those from Italy display the most technocratic profile.

A look at the smaller countries shows that the Italians are matched in this respect by the Flemish Belgians, and quite possibly for the same reasons. In the engineering column of Table 5.5, we see that the two categories of Belgians lead the field. Going across the two Belgian rows, we discover that by far the largest category of Flemish Belgians are engineers, while French-speaking Belgians with engineering degrees equal those with law degrees as the largest category. The seeming technocratic character of the francophones does not hold up as well when we turn to Table 5.6 to examine success scores; but the Flemish outdo the Italians with higher success scores for engineers (but not for economists or mathematicians) and lower scores for lawyers (but not for political scientists). If the Italian and Flemish Belgian patterns applied generally, the conclusion would be that the Commission exhibited a technocratic bias in its recruitment policies. But the Dutch pattern is there to remind us that legal studies are not everywhere a liability. The Dutch resemble the Germans in the strong concentration in the law and economics columns, but the ratio is reversed. The Dutch percentage (52.5) is the highest in the law column of Table 5.5, and the Dutch success score for law (66.7) is third highest in the corresponding Table 5.6 column.

Postgraduate Disciplines

As expected, a high percentage of French candidates (86.2) went on to postgraduate work (see Table 5.7), while the percentage of Italians who did so is quite low (36.2). At 63.9, the percentage of British candidates with advanced work is unexpectedly high, but Table 5.8 reveals that the British who went beyond the first degree had success scores that were below the British average. The same is true of Italians with advanced work. Advanced study did, however, appear to give an advantage to Germans taking it over other Germans, while for the French it made no appreciable difference. When we look at the academic disciplines arrayed in Tables 5.7 and 5.8, we see some familiar patterns and some that are new.

The British profile in Table 5.7 is not as distinct from the other national profiles as was true of Table 5.5. The distance in *percentages* between economics and law is not as great, and law is now clearly the second most frequent discipline. This is due to a very high success score for British candidates with advanced work in the legal discipline (72.7). Economics, on the other hand, has a lower score (63.2) at this level than at the first-degree level (72.0). This accords with the fact that, as with more strictly academic subjects in Britain generally, the first degree in economics suffices for entry to the higher civil service. Advanced work is more appropriate for an academic career and may even overqualify one for the public service. In law, on the other hand, advanced work involves the distinction between the barrister and the solicitor. Because of the "trade school" stigma attached to the training of solicitors, they may be at a distinct disadvantage in competing with their counterparts in Europe. Quite the opposite should be the case of the prestigious barrister.

The relative standings of academic disciplines in affecting the recruitment chances of French candidates do not change much as we move from the first degree to the postgraduate level. Law continues to lead economics in both tables, but the distance between them is not as great. Advanced work in both disciplines brings with it higher success scores than does first-degree work. Still, the finding remains that French lawyers do better in gaining

TABLE 5.7

PERCENTAGES OF TOTAL CANDIDATES HIRED, BY NATIONALITY, BY POST-GRADUATE DISCIPLINE (1972-1978)

Nationality	Any P.-G. Study	Law	Economics	Political Science	Mathematical Science	Natural Science-Engineering	European Studies
Belgian (Flemish)	56.3	6.3	31.3	0.0	6.3	0.0	6.3
Belgian (French)	65.0	15.0	27.5	2.5	10.0	7.5	12.5
British	63.9	13.0	29.3	4.1	7.3	2.4	12.2
Danish	47.7	11.4	20.5	2.3	0.0	4.5	13.6
Dutch	52.2	17.4	21.7	0.0	0.0	4.3	13.0
French	86.2	36.6	30.9	10.6	5.7	4.9	15.4
German	62.2	25.6	23.2	2.4	1.2	6.1	9.8
Irish	73.1	19.2	34.6	3.8	19.2	3.8	19.2
Italian	36.2	2.1	6.4	12.8	0.0	4.3	19.1
Luxemburger	75.0	37.5	0.0	12.5	12.5	12.5	0.0

TABLE 5.8

SUCCESS SCORES OF NATIONALITIES BY POST-GRADUATE DISCIPLINE (1972-1978)

Nationality	Any P.-G. Study	Law	Economics	Political Science	Mathematical Science	Natural Science-Engineering	European Studies
Belgian (Flemish)	39.1	12.5	62.5	--	50.0	--	14.3
Belgian (French)	61.9	66.7	73.3	100.0	80.0	60.0	55.6
British	57.4	72.7	63.2	50.0	64.3	60.0	75.0
Danish	75.0	71.4	75.0	50.0	--	66.7	85.7
Dutch	57.1	57.1	83.3	--	--	33.3	50.0
French	62.7	77.6	58.5	59.1	53.8	50.0	70.4
German	55.4	50.0	67.9	100.0	50.0	45.5	61.5
Irish	65.5	62.5	64.3	100.0	71.4	50.0	83.3
Italian	27.9	5.3	20.0	46.2	--	33.3	50.0
Luxemburger	66.7	100.0	--	--	100.0	100.0	66.7

employment with the Community than do economists. Given that advanced work is the norm among French aspirants for public service, the interpretation given above for the British does not apply here. Essentially, the "reverse interpretation" broached for French first-degree holders still seems worth entertaining. Much the same can be said of Germans with advanced study. The predominance of law and economics prevails at this level as at the first-degree level, and while both disciplines show higher success scores than they did at the first-degree level, that for economics is higher than that for law. Thus, the "reverse interpretation" still appears a possibility for the Germans as well as for the French.

Of the major countries, Italy shows the greatest difference in pattern between the two levels of higher education. At the postgraduate level, advanced European studies and political science assume first and second position, with 19.1 percent and 12.8 percent of the successful Italian candidates. Only 2.1 percent of the successful Italian candidates took advanced work in law; only 6.4 percent went beyond the first degree in economics. This reflects success scores that are extraordinarily low for both disciplines: 20.0 for economics and 5.3 for law! On the other hand, advanced European study and postgraduate political science yielded 50.0 and 46.2 success scores, both considerably above the Italian average. Almost all of the students taking advanced European studies studied in institutions outside Italy, incidentally. The finding regarding postgraduate study in political science is unique. In general, given the relatively small percentage of Italians taking advanced work, it seems best to place the burden of interpretation for the Italian subset on the data concerning the first-degree discipline.

The Belgians are no longer found in the engineering column when it comes to postgraduate work. But they do show relatively high frequencies and success scores in economics and the mathematical sciences: the technocratic interpretation still prevails. At this advanced level, the ratio of Dutch lawyers to Dutch economists is reversed, with Dutch economists showing an exceedingly high success score (83.3). What this suggests is not the "reverse interpretation" offered for Flemish Belgians earlier, since we should not doubt that Belgian and Dutch economists are in demand at home. Rather, it seems that in these two smaller countries candidates with very marketable professional credentials who nevertheless seek employment with the European Commission are attractive to the Commission, not only for their credentials, but also because their willingness to forgo attractive oportunities at home bespeaks a strong attraction to European employment.

A related point can be made regarding advanced European studies. Of the larger countries' candidates, only the Germans do not seem to have taken much advantage of this opportunity to improve their employment potential. Success scores show that the upgrading effect was working for candidates in all four major countries and for the Danes and Irish as well. In all these countries success scores for candidates with advanced European studies were higher than the national average for candidates with postgraduate work (see first column, Table 5.7). However, the reverse was the case for both categories of Belgians and for the Dutch. This suggests the possibility that the Commission saw European studies as an indication of the *European* credentials of the candidate, whatever his professional credentials may or may not have been. Given the very solid commitment to Europe of the Belgians and Dutch as a people, such an attestation may not have been additive. But it may have strengthened the credentials of nationals of the larger countries, where loyalty to Europe conflicts with national pride, and of candidates from the smaller countries most recently admitted to membership.

CONCLUSION

The findings of this study are mixed. There are three distinct findings that would support the technocratic pattern if they were not accompanied by counterfindings. The least ambiguous is that economics is the academic discipline found most frequently among successful candidates, whether the economics be at the first-degree or the postgraduate level; and that economics exhibits the highest success score among first-degree disciplines and fourth highest at the postgraduate level. The second is that engineering and mathematical sciences join economics among the five most frequent disciplines at both the first-degree and postgraduate levels. Mathematical sciences are also in first position in success scores at the postgraduate level. However, the overall record of natural sciences is undistinguished, and the success scores of engineering and mathematical sciences are inconsistent. The third is that at the first-degree level, the percentages of successful candidates who have studied engineering, mathematical sciences, and natural sciences increased from 1972-73 and 1977-78. However, the same did not occur at the postgraduate level, and economics registered decreases at both levels during the same period.

The first and third findings are probably the most important. It is probable that the position of economics has been strong from the very beginning of recruitment to the higher European civil service. If success scores in the pure and applied hard sciences have not been impressive, it may well be because the Commission has had difficulty competing with national-level employment opportunities for the best people in these fields. The third finding, that an increasing percentage of those the Commission hires are from the hard sciences, is a sign that this may be changing.

The findings drawn from national profiles make it impossible to affirm the technocratic hypothesis because different professional mixes appear for different countries, each with its own explanation. Of the major countries' candidates, only the Italians assumed a noticeably technocratic appearance. The British exhibited an unusually wide array of first-degree disciplines with notable lack of emphasis on law or engineering, a pattern similar to what is found among recruits to the British higher civil service. The "reverse" phenomenon noted for other countries did not appear for Britain. But the "French" pattern seemed more appropriate to the Belgians and even the Italians, while the "German" pattern seemed truest of the French. As for the Germans, the expected emphasis on law was partly replaced by an emphasis on economics. It is possible that the British adhered to their expected national pattern because of the freshness of enthusiasm for membership in the Community and the momentarily wide-open opportunities that seemed to be available for British nationals. Conversely, nationals of the original members could see opportunities temporarily diminishing, which may have detracted from the incentive for highly qualified candidates to come forth, especially when better employment opportunities appeared at home.

However, there are reasons why the "reverse interpretation" is too bleak and, indeed, cynical. First, it rests upon the assumption that candidates with academic backgrounds that are not favored in national administrative recruitment processes have no other options at home. French lawyers and German and Italian economists *are* recruited into the public sector, although not to the most prestigious jobs in the case of French lawyers and more often in autonomous agencies or nationalized industries in the case of German and Italian economists. Moreover, given that many German and Italian economists have "applied" rather than "basic" training, their services are in demand in the private sector as well. Thus, it would seem to be stretching things to suggest that very many of them seek employment in the European Community by default. Second, those professional categories which are favored in the home civil service (French economists and engineers, German and Italian lawyers) do supply a nonnegligible proportion of the recruits to the European civil service. While these are in a minority, they are persons who would presumably not have difficulty finding professionally rewarding employment in their home countries, but who have opted for the Community instead, exhibiting a motivation that must be more than expediential. In examining the dossiers of candidates from all nine countries and in virtually every profession, the high quality of recruit who is being attracted is obvious. This relates to the third reason to conclude on an upbeat note: the behavior of the Commission itself in the recruitment process.

As noted above, the Commission has made a substantial effort to upgrade the professional quality of its personnel practices, including the recruitment process. Recruitment is handled in a highly professional fashion, with every effort made to ensure that new entrants will be of superior quality. One indication of this is that the Commission has not adhered slavishly to national quotas, but has in fact discriminated in favor of some nationalities over others (using "discrimination" in a technical sense and not implying willful intent). Another indication is that recruitment has not been one-sidedly technocratic or, for that matter, one-sidedly juridical. Efforts seem to have been made to adjust to differences in the mixes of talent most readily available from different countries, as is most notable in the British case. Still another indicator, not reported here, is the preference for candidates with superior language skills, other factors being equal.[25] And finally, the data have shown that the Commission tends to reward European experience when it finds it, suggesting that the intention to instill an institutional loyalty in its employees has not seriously diminished.[26]

NOTES

1. David Coombes, "The Education and Training of International Officials: Special Problems of Educating and Training Officials of the European Communities," paper presented for the Semaine de Bruges Colloquium on the Basic and Advanced Training of International and European Civil Servants, May 1975. (Copyright ©, College d'Europe, Bruges, Belgium.)

2. For the distinction between federalism and functionalism, see Charles Pentland, *International Theory and European Integration* (London: Faber, 1973).

3. See the discussion by R. L. Peterson, "Personnel Decisions and the Independence of the Commission of the European Communities," *Journal of Common Market Studies* 10 (December 1971): 117-37.

4. Studies by Smith and Pendergast showed that experience with the Community made national civil servants more realistic about, but not necessarily more positive toward, European integration. Keith A. Smith, "The European Economic Community and National Civil Servants of the Member States—A Comment," *International Organization* 27 (Autumn 1973): 563-68; William R. Pendergast, "Roles and Attitudes of French and Italian Delegates to the European Community," *International Organization* 30 (Autumn 1976): 669-77.

5. David Coombes, *Politics and Bureaucracy in the European Community* (London: George Allen and Unwin, Ltd., 1970), p. 145.

6. A-Category civil servants are those in the top ranks of the permanent civil service, a distinction similar to that of the former Administrative Class of the British Civil Service.

7. Hans J. Michelmann, *Organisational Effectiveness in a Multinational Bureaucracy* (New York: Praeger Publishers, 1978), pp. 23-24.

8. Coombes, *Politics and Bureaucracy*, ch. 11. Cf. Brian Hocking, "International Administration and the Commission of the EEC," *Public Administration* (Australia) 33 (December 1974): 318-31.

9. Lawrence Scheinman, "Economic Regionalism and International Administration: The European Communities Experience," in Robert S. Jordan, ed., *Interna-*

tional Administration: Its Evolution and Contemporary Applications (New York: Oxford University Press, 1971), pp. 204-5, 208-9, 225-26.

10. Robert D. Putnam, "Elite Transformation in Advanced Industrial Societies: An Empirical Assessment of the Theory of Technocracy," *Comparative Political Studies* 10 (October 1977): 385-88.

11. See Leon N. Lindberg, "Energy Policy and the Politics of Economic Development," *Comparative Political Studies* 10 (October 1977): 355-82.

12. For evidence of the centralizing tendency of technocracy, see Jeffrey D. Straussman, *The Limits of Technocratic Politics* (New Brunswick, N.J.: Transaction Books, 1978), chaps. 3 and 4.

13. Putnam, "Elite Transformation," p. 390.

14. Dietrich Rueschmeyer, *Lawyers and Their Society: A Comparative Study of the Legal Professions in Germany and the United States* (Cambridge, Mass.: Harvard University Press, 1973), pp. 32-43, 75-78; Stefano Passigli, "The Ordinary and Special Bureaucracies in Italy," in Mattei Dogan, ed., *The Mandarins of Western Europe: The Political Role of Civil Servants* (New York: John Wiley & Sons, 1975), pp. 231-32.

15. Nevil Johnson, "Western Germany," in F. F. Ridley, ed., *Specialists and Generalists* (New York: Barnes & Noble, 1968), pp. 145-46.

16. For the traditional British pattern, see John A. Armstrong, *The European Administrative Elite* (Princeton: Princeton University Press, 1973), pp. 149-61. The reforms stimulated by the Fulton Report (1968) were designed in part to break down the distinction between generalists and specialists. Evidence as to its effect on recruitment patterns remains inconclusive. For fragmentary indications, see G. K. Fry, "Some Developments in the British Home Civil Service since 1969," *Public Administration* (Australia) 31 (September 1972): 202-17; and L. J. Sharpe, "Whitehall—Structures and People," in Dennis Kavenagh and Richard Rose, eds., *New Trends in British Politics: Issues for Research* (Beverly Hills: Sage Publications, Inc., 1977), pp. 67-71.

17. Johnson, "Western Germany," p. 142.

18. For differing views on how technocratic the higher French civil servants are, compare F. F. Ridley, "French Technocracy and Comparative Government," *Political Studies* 14 (1966): 34-52; and Ezra N. Suleiman, "The Myth of Technical Expertise: Selection, Organization and Leadership," *Comparative Politics* 10 (October 1977): 137-58.

19. I wish to acknowledge the cooperation of officials and staff of DG IX of the Commission in providing access to the data analyzed here. Funds to conduct the research were provided by the University of the Saarland in 1975 and the Research Council of the University of Missouri-Columbia in 1979.

20. There are seventeen cases not included in this study. They are candidates who passed the examination, were offered employment by the Commission, but refused it.

21. The reader is reminded that "success score" refers to numbers of candidates hired *as a percentage* of the total number of candidates in a given category.

22. The category "social sciences" does not include economics or political science. Most candidates in this category have taken work in sociology or psychology. The category "history-letters" encompasses the academic disciplines of history, literature, philosophy, and classical studies.

23. Coombes, *Politics and Bureaucracy*, pp. 128-30; Hans J. Michelmann, "Multinational Staffing and Organizational Functioning in the Commission of the European Communities," *International Organization* 32 (Spring 1978): 447-96.

24. Michelmann finds the same disparity between Belgians and Dutch in the A-Category staff as of mid-1974. He does not discover the same disparity as among French, Germans, and Italians. Most of the civil servants in his study would have been recruited before 1972. Michelmann, "Multinational Staffing," p. 479.

25. Success scores rise substantially with an increasing number of languages spoken by the candidates. See David M. Wood, "Eurocrats or Technocrats: The Educational and Professional Backgrounds of Recruits to the European Civil Service," paper presented to the 1980 meeting of the Midwest Conference of Political Scientists, Chicago, April 1980, p. 25.

26. Success scores for candidates with prior employment with the European organizations are substantially higher than success scores for other previous occupational experiences. Ibid., p. 22.

John Goormaghtigh 6

SCIENTIFIC COOPERATION: THE EUROPEAN SCIENCE FOUNDATION

Efforts to harmonize the science policies, to promote cooperation among scholars, scientists, and technicians, and to structure the research community in Western Europe after the Second World War were not given priority by the founders of the European movement or by the political leaders of the time. One can read through speeches and documents of that period without finding reference to the need for harmonizing science policies, pooling resources, or undertaking joint projects as steps toward the construction of Europe. Even functionalists such as Jean Monnet who pressed for integration of vital industrial sectors, which led, for instance, to the creation of the European Coal and Steel Community (ECSC), did not envisage similar steps in science and technology. The European Atomic Energy Community (Euratom) was more concerned—at least in its early stages—with the applications of nuclear energy than with fundamental research, and even so, it is far from being an unqualified success. Emphasis was placed quite clearly on the various aspects of economic, social, and—to some extent—political integration; the nature of the institutions which were set up by the successive treaties or conventions naturally reflect this state of affairs. Nongovernmental European organizations created by private initiatives roughly follow the same trend.

No formal intergovernmental European agency has today as its main objective to harmonize science policies of member states or to promote scientific cooperation in general. Nor is there a regional equivalent of UNESCO. Key regional organizations with broad fields of competence, such as the Organization for Economic Cooperation and Development

---

This essay is unable to take into consideration any events subsequent to December 1981.

(OECD), the European Community (EC), and the Council of Europe, have, however, become progressively involved in one way or another in scientific matters. Also, at the general policy level, as well as on specific issues of cooperation in science and technology, unofficial consultations regularly take place between responsible national civil servants from the larger European countries.

A growing number of bilateral or limited multilateral agreements, of exchange programs and fellowship schemes, of nongovernmental organizations and professional associations, of congresses and meetings all contribute to consolidating a European science subsystem. Two observations should be made at this point: (1) the trend toward integration is not regular —the fluctuating number of fellows moving from one country to another could be taken as one indicator among many; and (2) in some disciplines, there is more intra-European cooperation than in others—the most favorable areas are the natural sciences, geosciences, mathematics, and engineering; the least favored are the humanities and social sciences.[1]

The organizations and laboratories which have been established to promote cooperation and to pool European resources in specific fields, mainly in the so-called big sciences (those requiring very expensive equipment, such as high energy physics, space science, and astronomy) have, on the whole, been scientifically productive and have contributed to the creation of genuinely European research communities. They have been, and remain, important meeting places for specialists from many fields, but by the very nature of their subject matter, they are open to collaboration with scientists from all countries. They could not operate efficiently if they were restricted to Europe; although part of the European system, they are also part of the universal science system.

SOME EUROPEAN ORGANIZATIONS

The Organization for Economic Cooperation and Development

In October 1963, the Organization for Economic Cooperation and Development convened the first Ministerial Meeting on Science. The background paper for the Conference, prepared by an eminent group of scientists and economists, entitled "Science and the Policies of Governments," marked a significant step toward recognition of the importance of strengthening national science policies and of harmonizing these policies among Member States. It also stressed the relations between science and economic growth. Article 2(b) of the OECD Convention, to which the governments of nineteen European countries as well as the United States and Japan are party, stipulates that "Members agree that they will, both individually and jointly . . . in the scientific and technological field, promote the development of their resources, encourage research and promote vocational training." On this text is based the ongoing involvement of the Organization in science policy and the promotion of research at the international level. These questions are considered at OECD essentially in relation to the economic and social situation in the noncommunist industrial countries but they are no longer given the attention they received in the early 1960s.

The Council of Europe

The Council of Europe, with a strictly Western European membership, has a very broad mandate. It has taken a number of initiatives in education and cultural affairs, but its activities in science and research as such have been more limited. The Secretariat comprises a division for Higher Education and Research, and in January 1978 the Committee of Ministers set up the Standing Conference on University Problems (CCPU) composed of senior government officials and academics. Although the stated objectives of the Conference are to promote cooperation in both higher education and research, so far its principal focus has been on university teaching, cooperation among universities, and on facilitating the mobility of students. This latter function is of course important in the present context, as it could contribute toward bringing about a European scientific community, which is still far from being a reality today. Mobility of students, researchers, and senior scientists within the region is not what it should be to optimize resources. On the one hand, many obstacles remain in the way of the movement between universities, institutes, and laboratories in the various countries; on the other hand, the United States still constitutes a very strong pole of attraction in many fields of science and advanced technology.[2] The Science Fellowships, Advanced Study Institutes, and Research grants which are sponsored by the NATO Science Committee encourage this transatlantic mobility.

In early June 1980, the Council of Europe organized its Fifth Parliamentary and Scientific Conference in Helsinki, on "Democracy and Technology: Impact of Technological Development on Society and European Civilization." The Conference expressed the opinion that Europe should provide itself with a strategy for long-term technological development. Participants recommended setting up a Consultative Committee to establish priorities; the creation of a European research fund to promote a network of high-level scientific teams; they also called for "a more meaningful dialogue" between politicians and the European Science Foundation. *The Times Higher Education Supplement* detected "a new-found desire to pool the efforts of the Council of Europe, the EEC, and the OECD, the overwhelming support for a comprehensive approach to research problems, and the key role accorded to the European Science Foundation."[3]

The European Community

By far the most ambitious cooperative science program is the one which has been developed by the European Community. Although individual projects had been initiated by the ECSC and Euratom, it was not until the Council of Ministers' Resolution of 14 January 1974 that the outline of a general program in science and technology was formulated. Its definition was extremely broad since, "with the exception of matters military or industrially classified as secret, no sphere of action in the field of science and technology should be excluded from the Community research policy."

The Community can finance its own research as it does, for example, in the context of the "Joint Research Center" (JRC) which was created in 1957 under the Treaty on the Establishment of the European Atomic Energy Community. JRC runs four research institutes: Ispra in Italy, Karlsruhe in the Federal Republic of Germany, Petten in the Netherlands, and Geel in Belgium. The experience of JRC clearly illustrates some of the major pitfalls of international scientific cooperation. The main initial objective of the Center was to place Europe on the map among the major industrial powers in the area of the peaceful uses for atomic energy, so JRC focused its research on the development of new commercial types of reactors and on the fuel cycle. One of its first projects was the design of a heavy-water reactor (ORGEL). However, this joint action, decided upon and funded by all members of the Community, did not prevent the largest among them from developing their own highly sophisticated and perfectly competitive nuclear industries. These events were, of course, very discouraging for the smaller countries who had hoped to find in JRC a safeguard against the technological and economic superiority of their larger partners. There was nothing left for JRC but to turn its attention to other matters. After a crisis which nearly terminated its existence and following the consequent loss of scientific prestige, the Center worked out a new program, starting in 1973, which concentrated on such questions as solar energy, protection of the environment, and nuclear safety. To give an idea of their scale, the research establishments, which are fully financed by the Community, employ, in 1981, about 2,260 scientists.

In addition, the Community concludes research contracts with national teams, institutes, or laboratories which have as their main objective the fostering of collaboration between the best experts from Member Countries on a given topic. These so-called indirect action programs are only partly funded by the Community, the rest of the money coming from national sources. A third mode of action of the Community is limited to coordination and to bringing scientists working on the same problems together.

The Community has in fact, since 1974, set itself the goal not only to promote collaboration and assist research in certain areas, but to conceive and implement its own policy in four major areas of applied science: (1) security and supply of resources (energy, food, raw materials); (2) promotion of internationally competitive industry; (3) improvement of living and working conditions; and (4) protection of the environment. In recent years the largest proportion of the Community's research funds were spent on energy (nearly 70 percent in 1978): conventional, nuclear, alternative sources, and energy conservation. In addition to the work on solar energy conducted in the framework of JRC, the Commission has, for instance, concluded 135 research contracts on different aspects of geothermal sources of energy. And, at present, nearly all research on nuclear fusion in member states is being coordinated by the Community and jointly financed. JET (Joint European Torus) is being constructed in Culham, England, to develop a controlled fusion reactor for the future.

As in all other areas of Community action, the decisions of the Council in the field of science are prepared by the Commission. The Scientific and Technical Research Committee (CREST), composed of senior government officials from each of the ten member countries and members of the Commission staff, as well as the European Research and Development Committee (CERD), composed of specialists serving in their personal capacity, act as advisory bodies. CREST also follows scientific developments in the various countries and plays a coordinating role. To prepare for long-term developments and to define priorities for a future research policy, a program known as FAST (Forecasting and Assessment in the field of Science and Technology) began in 1980. Members of the Community jointly devote about 10 percent of their publicly funded research budgets to international cooperation, but less than 20 percent of this amount goes to Community research.

As is the case in most intergovernmental organizations, the decision-making process in the Community is cumbersome, partly on account of the fact that it is highly politicized and partly on account of the heavy bureaucracy and complicated procedures of the Commission. National interest and questions of prestige frequently prevent cooperative action or even coordination in fields which are economically or politically sensitive. Consensus formation is often difficult and always slow. This is probably inevitable until the Community becomes more cohesive than it is today. The European institutions are necessary, but even in the field of science they alone cannot impose rational solutions or get the common interest to triumph in the face of opposition from even one of the major partners. Too frequently criticism focuses on the institutions themselves; they are made the scapegoats for all the shortcomings and conflicts, all the failures to achieve progress. As a consequence, attention is turned away from the real issue, which is national or factional self-interest, often narrowly defined and viewed in a short-term perspective. It is not until governments adopt a broader vision and a longer-term perspective of national interest that the international organizations will be able to achieve the goals which were assigned to them by their statutes.

Scientists recognize, of course, that economy of scale dictates a much closer cooperation—particularly for the more expensive equipment and advanced techniques; even the larger European countries do not have the critical mass which would place them on a par with the great industrial powers. Public opinion also is in favor of pooling European resources if one accepts the results of a poll conducted by the Services of the Commission. As Table 6.1 shows, the authors of the survey conclude that "people are convinced that the European States should get together to pool their scientific research."[4]

It seems paradoxical that with the backing of the scientific community and the support of public opinion, progress toward cooperation should have been so checkered. Previous polls indicate that this is not a recent development: a survey conducted in 1974 shows that 59 percent of Europeans regard it as important or very important that the nine countries of the community endeavor jointly to solve scientific research problems.[5] And what should be noted is that in all countries "the number of those wanting European research is much greater than the number of those anxious to speed up the unification of Europe."[6]

The European University Institute

The first mention of an intergovernmental agency which would contribute to the construction of Europe in the fields of training and research was made at the Messina Conference of Foreign Ministers of The Six in June 1955. But the project was approved only at The Hague Summit Conference in December 1969, and the Convention setting up the European University Institute—a much more modest establishment than had originally been conceived—was not signed until April 1972. The Institute opened near Florence in the Autumn of 1976, twenty-one years after the idea was launched! The gestation period is obviously longer than for most Community organizations and suggests that research and higher education are not considered as particularly significant in the construction of Europe, in spite of the public opinion survey cited above.

The Institute is run as a graduate school in the humanities and European Studies and has departments of History and Civilization, Economics, Law, and Political and Social Sciences. During the academic year 1980-81, 110 students were preparing doctoral dissertations or conducting other advanced research under the supervision of an academic staff of 32. Members of the European Community contribute to the budget (according to an agreed scale), which for 1980 amounted to 5,752,626,000 Italian lire (approximately $6.7 million). The Institute is governed by a Council com-

TABLE 6.1

A EUROPEAN FUTURE FOR SCIENTIFIC RESEARCH?

Question: Scientific research is extremely expensive but it can bring advantages and prestige to the country where it goes on. Would you consider it preferable that . . .

	European States should get together to pool their research?	Each country should do research for itself?	Don't know	Total
	(Percent)	(Percent)	(Percent)	(Percent)
Community	79	14	7	100
Belgium	82	8	10	100
Denmark	67	16	17	100
Germany	73	19	3	100
France	85	9	6	100
Ireland	71	24	5	100
Italy	87	9	4	100
Luxembourg	83	6	11	100
Netherlands	83	9	8	100
United Kingdom	74	20	6	100
Index of Leadership[1]				
Non-Leaders (--)	67	20	13	100
(-)	80	14	6	100
(+)	84	12	4	100
Leaders (++)	86	11	3	100

NOTE: 1. The signs (--), (-), (+), and (++) indicate four categories or rating degrees of involvement from the general public (--) to active leadership(++).

SOURCE: Commission of the European Communities (Brussels), "Science and Public Opinion" (October 1977), p. 61.

posed of representatives of member governments, assisted by an Academic Council which is responsible for the teaching and research programs.

The European Organization for Nuclear Research (CERN)

The European Organization for Nuclear Research (CERN) is the first, largest, and probably the most successful of the cooperative ventures of its kind. It was created in 1954 to promote collaboration among Europeans in fundamental nuclear research. Its field is now defined as subnuclear, high-energy, or elementary particle physics. There are twelve Member States (Austria, Belgium, Denmark, France, Federal Republic of Germany, Greece, Italy, the Netherlands, Norway, Sweden, Switzerland, and the United Kingdom) and three observers (Poland, Turkey, and Yugoslavia). CERN is entirely funded by the governments of Member States and individual contributions are calculated on the basis of their net national revenues. The budget for 1980 was approximately $354 million. The organization is located near Geneva, but the territory on which large accelerators and other machines are installed extends into neighboring France. There is a permanent staff of about 3,500—physicists, engineers, and technicians—and there are usually 2,500 visiting fellows or scientific associates in residence. They come from all over the world, including the USSR, and generally form internatinal teams which conduct experiments jointly.

High-energy physics qualifies as "big" science since it requires the use of powerful accelerators and other expensive experimental apparatus. CERN operates at present a 600 MeV synchrotron-cyclotron (SC), a 28 GeV proton synchrotron (PS), the Intersecting Storage Rings (ISR), and a 400 GeV proton synchrotron (SPS), and is planning the LEP (large electron positron machine). The latter project involves the construction of a circular tunnel with a circumference of 30 km. Even the nonspecialist will realize the magnitude of the investment. It is obvious that it was in the general interest of Member States and of the scientific community to build these facilities together.

Over the years CERN has been able to maintain both its reputation and its dynamism. It has suffered less than most others from the usual handicaps of intergovernmental agencies. The reasons for its relative success are numerous, but this is not the place to analyze them in detail. However, let it simply be said that the second half of the 1950s, when CERN got under way, was a particularly propitious time: high-energy physics was at the peak of its prestige, and the public thought that nuclear energy would solve a number of the world's problems, the European economy was on the upward trend, and there was still great faith in what could be achieved by European integration. Another factor favorable to the development of CERN was the habit of cooperation between nuclear physicists from many countries, which developed in the United States during the War. More remarkable is the fact that the initial impetus has been maintained—of course, with some ups and downs—in less favorable circumstances, such as those which exist at present. This is no doubt largely due to the standing, skill, and imagination of those who have been responsible for steering the course of the Organization, the creativity and dedication of the engineers and physicists who designed and constructed the machines and who conceived and conducted the experiments. CERN has certainly become one of the most important laboratories and meeting places in its field in the world. But "big science" is coming in for harder times, not only because of the world recession, but also because it is felt in some quarters that too much emphasis has been placed and too much money spent on one sector and that other vital parts of science have been neglected. The trend away from particle physics and its expensive machines coinciding with spectacular developments in other disciplines might well be detrimental to CERN and favorable to European cooperation in other areas.

The European Molecular Biology Organization (EMBO)

On a much more modest scale, cooperation among European specialists evolved satisfactorily within the framework of the European Molecular Biology Organization (EMBO). This was at first a nonprofit organization registered in Geneva in 1963. In 1970 governments of twelve Western European countries, plus Israel, concluded an agreement which brought into existence the European Molecular Biology Conference (EMBC), a full-fledged intergovernmental agency with the purpose of providing secure funds for EMBO's general program and to prepare for the establishment of a European Molecular Biology Laboratory. The original aim of EMBO was simply to promote molecular biology in Europe and "so to attempt to regain for Europe some of the impetus and initiative that it had been progressively losing to the USA."[7] The general program provides for long- and short-term exchange fellowships, training courses, and workshops, and the construction of the laboratory. The latter was inaugurated in Heidelberg in May 1978. The budget for 1978—excluding, of course, the cost of construction of the laboratory—was approximately $2.8 million. The view has been expressed that the European Molecular Biology Laboratory, which is considerably smaller than some of the national laboratories, does not operate on a sufficiently large scale to become, like CERN, a real pole of attraction for the best scientists in the field.

The European Southern Observatory (ESO)

Although with a much more limited membership than the two organizations described above, the European Southern Observatory (ESO) presents an interesting case of a joint venture among a few European countries in the field of astronomy. By a convention concluded in October 1962, Belgium, Denmark, France, the Federal Republic of Germany, Italy, the Netherlands, Sweden, and Switzerland decided to plan and build together a powerful equipped observatory in the Southern Hemisphere. No facility existed to chart the southern skies equivalent to the large observatories in the Northern Hemisphere. After careful exploration, a site was selected on "La Silla" mountain in Chile, at 2,400m above sea level. The stable atmospheric conditions and the pure dry air are excellent for astronomical observations, with 62 percent of the nighttime fully clear. ESO staff members and members of other European institutes work there with the twelve available telescopes. The most powerful one is the 3.6m telescope, a fully computer-controlled instrument, which was completed in 1978 for a total cost (including building and dome) of about $33 million. The new scientific-technical center of ESO in Europe is located in Garching, near Munich. It has three main functions: the development of new telescopes and instruments, the processing of data obtained at La Silla, and the fostering of European cooperation in astronomy. The ESO operating budget for 1980 amounted to $23 million, of which $18 million were contributions from Member States. At present both Italy and Switzerland have decided to become full members of ESO.

OTHER ORGANIZATIONS, ASSOCIATIONS AND EXCHANGE PROGRAMS

In addition to the harmonization of policies and cooperation in science and technology conducted within the framework of the agencies referred to above, there are of course a large number of bilateral or limited multilateral arrangements which contribute to the growing network of intra-European exchanges, joint projects, and laboratories. Typical of the latter kind of establishments is the Laue-Langevin Institute (ILL) in Grenoble, which provides the scientific community with a unique neutron beam facility. Set up at first by an agreement between France and the Federal Republic of Germany, the ILL now also includes the United Kingdom as a full member. These limited membership organizations may have the virtue of administrative simplicity, although this is not proved, but they place the scientists from smaller nonmember countries in a position of inferiority.

Professional associations in the various disciplines and the scientific unions with a specifically European character—as opposed to the universal ones—are sometimes difficult to identify. They vary in size and academic standing. Some have a large membership of individual scientists, others are federations of national associations; some have a permanent secretariat and publish their own journal, others exist only on paper. Therefore, numbers in themselves are not very meaningful. The 1980 *Yearbook of International Organizations*[8] mentions over 150 such nongovernmental organizations (NGOs) in the natural and medical sciences alone; a more selective list, prepared by one of the large science funding agencies, includes 55 important associations of this type, ranging from the European Association for Cancer Research to the European Physical Society. These NGOs perform an important "forum function"; they serve as an effective channel of communication among specialists from the whole region and they contribute to creating a sense of solidarity among them. They have the advantage over the intergovernmental organizations of a more flexible structure and of being less politicized and bureaucratic, but most of them suffer from a chronic shortage of funds.

Exchange programs and fellowship schemes, by promoting intra-European mobility of scientists and scholars (we are not speaking here of student programs), contribute in no uncertain measure to the cohesion of the system. Multilateral exchange schemes are relatively rare. Among the most important are the EMBO long- and short-term fellowships, training programs and workshops, and the ESF Training Program in Brain and Behavior Research (ETPBBR).

NATO's Science Fellowship Program is mainly limited to basic science and has a transatlantic rather than European character.

> During the first 15 years of the Fellowship Program [1963-1976], most of the 10,153 fellows were from the United Kingdom, France, Italy, Turkey and Greece, in that order. The United States hosted about 50 percent of the fellows, followed by the United Kingdom (25 percent), France (10 percent), and Germany (7 percent). Movement from the smaller countries and in particular Greece and Turkey, tended to be outwards only. As regards fields of study, physics, chemistry and engineering occupy the most important places.[9]

NATO also organizes Advanced Study Institutes and runs a Research Grants Program and a Senior Scientists Program—all with the same general orientation.

Most countries offer a variety of unilateral study grants or fellowships for visiting scientists and scholars. The *Centre National de la Recherche Scientifique* (CNRS), for instance, offers four different types of fellowships for foreign scientists wishing to work in France. Bilateral arrangements are usually organized by national research councils, academies, or universities. The Royal Society's (UK) European Scientific Exchange Program consists of bilateral arrangements between the Society and sixteen other European countries and is one of the most effective schemes of its kind in Western Europe. The ESF report, referred to above, concludes that "sufficient exchange schemes and fellowship programs exist in most fields. However, in the social sciences and the humanities, it is felt that there is still insufficient movement between researchers."[10] It also thinks that it would be advantageous to encourage exchange schemes restricted to movement within Western Europe.

Several specialized institutes or laboratories, without having a specifically "European" status, also constitute strong poles of attraction for scientists from many countries. They contribute—as do the others—to strengthening the European network of researchers in a great many disciplines. The active participation in internationally conducted experiments as well as the discussions and exchanges which occur in such centers are both favorable to scientific innovation and to the establishment of confident relationships. Ultimately they bring into being communities of scientists which in turn help to consolidate European collaboration in all fields. We shall mention only two (among many) distinguished institutes which, although technically "national," perform such a role in Europe: the Institut des Hautes Etudes Scientifiques (IHES) at Bures-sur-Yvette, France, and the well-known Niels Bohr Institute in Copenhagen.

The IHES has become one of the leading institutions working at the frontiers of certain aspects of mathematics and theoretical physics. Each year the Institute receives around 150 visiting scientists, staying for periods ranging from a few weeks to two years. Between 1970 and 1979 the IHES received 743 visitors from forty-two countries. The total budget for 1980 was approximately $2 million, the main contributor being the French government. The European Science Foundation has been instrumental in helping to gain support for the Institute's international program. This has been, for the last five years, one of ESF's "Additional Activities," discussed below in greater detail.

The Niels Bohr Institute, which was established in 1920, remains one of the world's great centers for the study and discussion of theoretical physics. It played a role in the creation of CERN, and for the first five years the CERN Theoretical Study Group was located in Copenhagen. In 1958, Nordita, the Nordic Institute for Theoretical Atomic Physics, was brought into being by an agreement between the five Nordic countries in order to strengthen the participation of Scandinavian scientists in the international activities of the Niels Bohr Institute. The number of foreign visitors who stay for longer periods—usually about one year—to participate in the research work of the Institute has recently been about fifty a year. They come from both East and West, but the largest single contingent is from the USA. Many more physicists visit the Institute for shorter periods. An important element in the scientific program are the informal symposia on topics in the forefront of research—a tradition that goes back to the annual conferences held in the 1920s and 1930s which played a crucial role in the development of quantum physics at the time. The Niels Bohr Institute is part of the University of Copenhagen, but its international activities are funded by many different sources, both public and private.

FINANCES

The growing proportion of European R&D funds from the public sector which is alloted to international scientific organizations in Europe would suggest that their value is recognized by governments, national research funding agencies, and the respective scientific communities. The following extract from the 1980 *Annual Report of the European Science Foundation* speaks for itself:

Figure 6.1
TOTAL EXPENDITURE OF 36 MEMBER ORGANIZATIONS AND COSTS OF THE INTERNATIONAL ORGANIZATIONS CERN, ILL, ESO, AND ESA
(in millions of units of account)

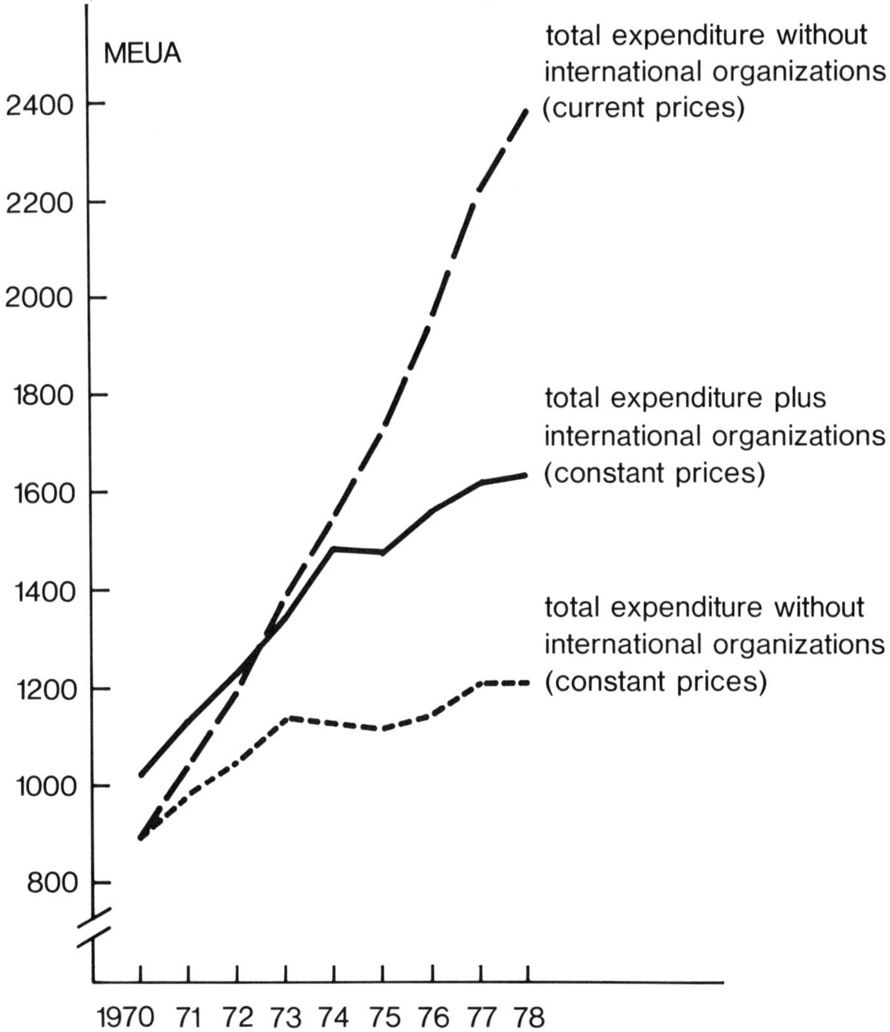

Source: European Science Foundation, Annual Report (Strasbourg, 1980), p. 69.

> Whereas the total sum available to ESF Member Organizations decreased from 1974 to 1975, contributions to ESA rose considerably and, in general, it can be said that international organizations' budgets increased at a higher rate than those of ESF Member Organizations. The total expenditure of Member Organizations rose from 1974 to 1978 by 35.5 percent, whereas the cost of international organizations, CERN, ILL, ESO and ESA increased by 231.1 percent in real terms over the same period.[11]

Figure 6.1 illustrates these trends during the 1970s. It is doubtful though whether they will continue to grow in the same way during the 1980s with the almost universal curtailment of national research expenditures.

In spite of these figures which appear encouraging, the fact remains that only a very small proportion of the total national R&D funds goes toward financing intra-European cooperation, joint projects, exchanges, or to the harmonization of science policies. Europe is still far from having reached, in the fields of scientific research and technology, the degree of integration which would enable it to maximize its considerable potential and therefore to compete on an equal footing with the major industrial powers of the world, such as the United States and the Soviet Union. Although evidently tangible results have been accomplished—the most outstanding ones are mentioned in this essay—and some progress has been made in certain disciplines, others have been almost totally neglected. Much remains to be done if Europe as a whole is to regain some of its former scientific prestige.

It is difficult to assess the proportion of private R&D funds which are devoted to intra-European cooperation, and, as is well known, foundations play a much less significant role in Europe than in North America. The Volkswagen, von Humboldt, CIBA, and Leverhulme foundations are among those which have contributed in a meaningful way to scientific cooperation in Europe. In the 1950s and 1960s, the Rockefeller and Ford foundations made important contributions to the mobility of European scientists, and their support of institutes and research centers was beneficial to research throughout the continent. Since these foundations have withdrawn from Europe, nothing has taken their place.

THE EUROPEAN SCIENCE FOUNDATION

Background

Every country in Europe has, in the course of time, worked out its own method of funding research and has set up the necessary machinery for this purpose according to its own cultural and political traditions; as a result, there are considerable differences in structure and decision-making processes. These different institutional patterns and procedures for planning and supporting R&D constitute an additional obstacle to cooperation and harmonization of science policies in Western Europe.

In the great majority of cases, science is *partly* funded directly by the government through a Ministry of Science or its equivalent, and through the technical departments (such as agriculture, fisheries, defense) and *partly* through research councils, or the like, with money from the government. In the UK there are five research councils (agriculture, medicine, environment research, science and engineering, and social science), but two Academies (The Royal Society and The British Academy) also play a role in research funding in their respective fields of competence. In the Federal Republic of Germany there are two main science funding agencies (the Deutsche Forschungsgemeinschaft and the Max-Planck-Gesellschaft), each with their own historical background and differing more by their modes of operation than by the disciplines they cover. In France, the Centre National de la Recherche Scientifique (CNRS) is the principal central funding agency, but medicine and atomic energy each have their own funding institution (Institut National de la Santé et de la Recherche Médicale [INSERM] and Institut de Recherche Fondamentale du Commissariat à l'Energie Atomique [CEA]). In the Netherlands, the distinction is made between applied and fundamental research (Nederlandse Organisatie voor Toegepast-Naturwetenschappelijk Onderzoek [TNO] and Nederlandse Organisatie voor Zuiver-Wetenschappelijk Onderzoek [ZWO]). In Belgium, Spain, Italy, and Switzerland, among others, research is funded by a single organization.

The research councils which we shall henceforth mainly be concerned with are, to a greater or lesser degree—depending on national traditions—independent from direct governmental interference. On the whole, they give an important voice in decision making to the scientists themselves, although major priorities remain issues everywhere.[12]

When the general trend toward integration gathered impetus in Europe, these national science agencies, which were growing in importance and resources, felt the need to collaborate. Bilateral agreements were negotiated on such matters as fellowships and exchanges, like the Royal Society's European Scientific Exchange Program mentioned above. Two multilateral organizations were also set up: the European Medical Research Councils (EMRC) in 1971 and the European Science Research Councils (ESRC) for the natural sciences in 1972. Their aim was to exchange information and to promote cooperation in their respective fields: for this purpose they periodically brought together science administrators and scientists. ESRC and EMRC have since become Standing Committees of the ESF.

In the latter part of the 1960s, however, more ambitious ideas were beginning to take shape, and various forces converged toward their implementation. The main driving force was no doubt a growing realization that if Europe wanted to remain significant in scientific research in the face of rapid developments in the USA, the USSR, and Japan, it just had no other option than to pool its resources. In 1973, "six countries (USA, USSR, Japan, the Federal Republic of Germany, France, the United Kingdom) employed 72 percent of the world's researchers and spent 83 percent of R and D funds. The USA and the USSR alone accounted for about 60 percent of the global R and D expenditure."[13] Incidentally, the relative position of Europe has not improved: in 1977, the nine Members of the European Community were spending 1.6 percent of their GNP on R&D, while the United States was spending 2.3 percent of its GNP. In Japan in 1975, there were 2.3 researchers per thousand inhabitants, whereas in Europe there were only 1.1 per thousand.[14]

Within the Community, there was a growing awareness of the fundamental importance of science and technology for the future of the European economy. The Commission, especially under the impulse of Altiero Spinelli and Ralf Dahrendorf, started to seek for ways of promoting closer cooperation among the Six, of harmonizing their R&D policies, and even of working toward a joint science policy. Different models were being simultaneously considered. Some favored the establishment of a kind of European Research Council, limited to the Six Member States, located in Brussels, funded by the Community budget, and working under its direct control; others favored a kind of loose federation of national research councils, which would be open to non-Member Countries. Still others, including Ralf Dahrendorf, wanted to see the establishment of a foundation which would be endowed with sufficient capital—initially provided in large part by the EC—to be independent from political pressures, and also to have enough income to operate effectively. A really large endowment was being considered. This foundation was to have had among its objective to work in various ways to initiate joint projects. For a variety of reasons, however, capital funds were not forthcoming, so that this type of institution which might have been a powerful tool for the elaboration of a real European scientific community, never saw the light of day. Nevertheless, the Community continued to encourage the creation of the European Science Foundation and a Council of Ministers resolution expressed the wish that the ESF should advise the Commission on matters concerning fundamental research. The Community itself worked out its own R&D program, which began in 1974 and which is very much oriented toward *applied science.* There was therefore from the outset a natural division of labor between the Commission and the ESF, which concentrated on basic research.

The Council of Europe had for many years been exploring the possibility of setting up an independent funding agency which would provide European science with the kind of seed money the large foundations had made available to scientists and scholars in the United States. This idea, unfortunately, never materialized. The Parliamentary Assembly of the Council of Europe also became interested in the project of a European Science Foundation, thus involving a broader audience and a larger number of countries. In an April 1972 recommendation, the Assembly invited governments of Member States to examine the functions, structure, and mode of funding of the Foundation. In a further recommendation in 1974, the Parliamentary

Assembly asked the Committee of Ministers to support the creation of the ESF.

In non-EC countries, namely in the UK and in Scandinavia, interest was also being expressed in providing intra-European cooperation in R&D with an institutional structure. They were, of course, in favor of an organization open to all European countries, which would remain flexible and as free as possible from political pressure, so they opted for NGO status. The Netherlands, as they had frequently done before, acted as a bridge between the EC Members and non-Member countries.

UNESCO also brought water to the mill by organizing, in June 1970, a Conference of Ministers of the European States Responsible for Science Policy. The working document prepared for the Conference by UNESCO stressed the need for European collaboration (both Eastern and Western Europe) in the basic sciences. This document concludes:

> As a first step, the Conference could resolve that a study be made of the possibility to associate, on a voluntary basis, the national organizations for fundamental research of the European Member States of UNESCO. Such a European Science Association might be called upon to design concrete and progressive measures for enlarged scientific cooperation in Europe, along the lines recommended by the Conference.[15]

It was in the wake of this Conference in 1972 that the meeting was convened in Aarhus (Denmark) by the Nordic Research Councils which set up the ESRC. After its meeting in Oxford in 1975, an agreement was reached whereby ESRC was to become the Standing Committee of ESF responsible for the natural sciences. The EMRC had come into existence the previous year, also on the initiative of the Scandinavian research councils, and followed the same pattern of close association with the ESF. It is worth noting that national institutions equally started expressing their support for more collaboration; in 1970, the Swedish Parliament passed a motion recommending that a joint organization of European Research Councils should be established.

Early History

These different but converging manifestations clearly suggest that there was a growing awareness throughout Europe of the need for some organization which would facilitate consultation between science agencies, which would promote cooperation and joint ventures and which might ultimately make coordination of research possible. The time was favorable for concrete initiatives; the formula finally adopted would, however, necessarily be the result of a compromise between the various proposals.

In February 1972, the research councils from the Nordic countries and the Nederlandse Organisatie voor Zuiver-Wetenschappelijk Onderzoek (ZWO) invited members of some other European research funding agencies to meet at Aarhus in order to examine ways and means of working out a more satisfactory coordination of research in Europe. The next step was taken by the Royal Society which convened in London in December of the same year a group of European scientists to exchange views on what form cooperation should take. The project became more precise at a meeting held at the Max-Planck-Gesellschaft in Munich in April 1973. The momentum was kept up and things moved rapidly, which indicates that the time was ripe. Professor Hubert Curien (France) was selected to chair a working party charged with the task of drafting a specific proposal to be submitted to all European research councils. Forty-seven of them met at Gif-sur-Yvette (France) in September 1973 at the invitation of the CNRS. There, the establishment of a European Science Foundation was agreed upon in principle, and at a further meeting in Saltsjöbaden (Sweden) in May 1974, it was decided that the Foundation would have its seat in Strasbourg. As is usually the case with international organizations, even the nongovernmental ones, the question of location of headquarters was a hotly debated topic. In the end, the choice was restricted to Leyden, proposed by the Netherlands, and Strasbourg, proposed by France. Each country offered facilities for the new organization, which led to some bargaining. Finally Strasbourg was selected, the arguments being that this city was at the crossroads of Europe but was not a capital, a natural point of contact between France and Germanic cultures, and that it was already the seat of the Council of Europe.

Establishment of the ESF

The European Science Foundation legally came into existence when its draft statutes were approved by an assembly of representatives of forty-two academies and research councils from fifteen different countries, which met in Strasbourg on 18 November 1974. The assembly also elected the President, the Vice-President, and appointed the Secretary General. The first President was to be Sir Brian (later Lord) Flowers, Rector of Imperial College (London), a distinguished physicist and science administrator. The first Secretary General to be selected was Dr. Friedrich Schneider, Secretary General of the Max-Planck Gesellschaft, and a well-known figure in German academic administration. So France obtained the headquarters, Britain the presidency, and Germany the secretary generalship; the normal balance was achieved, each of the larger countries obtaining an advantage. The two vice-presidencies went respectively to Professor Olivier Reverdin (Switzerland) and Professor Pavl Riis (Denmark); all the rules of equitable geographical distribution were respected!

The Statute, approved by the 1974 Assembly, stipulates that the ESF is "an international non-governmental non-profit association of organizations devoted to the promotion of basic research" (Article I). It is therefore, strictly speaking, not a "foundation" but an "association" set up under French law and duly registered as such in Strasbourg; nor is it a foundation in the broader sense since it has no capital endowment. The name remained on from the time when it was expected that the ESF would receive a large initial sum which would enable it to be financially independent.

The principal objectives of the Foundation are, according to the Statute, the following: to advance cooperation in basic research; to promote mobility of research workers; to assist in the free flow of information and ideas; and to facilitate the harmonization of the basic research activities by Member Organizations. Further objectives are: to facilitate cooperation in the use of existing facilities; to facilitate cooperation in assessing and executing appropriate projects of major importance; to facilitate cooperation in the provision of expensive specialized services; and to make grants for the support of concerted actions and collaborative schemes. The ESF Statute defines "science" in the broadest sense of the term, so as to include the humanities, social sciences, jurisprudence, and the natural, medical, and technical sciences. Emphasis is placed on basic research and not on applied sciences. This is a very broad mandate, and it is not surprising if the ESF has not in its short existence been able to progress on such a wide front. Obviously, without an independent income, the Foundation cannot fulfill the last objective in the list, namely, to make grants for research projects.

As the Statute says, the Foundation is "an association of organizations," the latter are the Member Organizations—the forty-two academies and research councils which attended the first Assembly, plus those which have been coopted since. "Any national organization of a European country which supports basic research from significant means assigned for that purpose mainly by the government of its country . . . is eligible for membership" (Art. XV). At present there are forty-eight Member Organizations in eighteen countries.[16] It will be noticed that the term "Europe" is not qualified, which implies that Eastern European countries can be admitted if they accept the terms. The Yugoslav research organization was a founding member of the ESF. Some have argued that "Europe" should not be interpreted in a purely "geographical" sense and that countries in a particular situation, such as Israel, could qualify for membership. Israel is a member of such "European" scientific organizations as EMBO.

The Foundation is funded by contributions from the Member Organizations. All members contribute to the "general budget," which covers the ordinary running costs and capital expenditure. Each national group of Member Organizations pays according to a scale based on the net national income of the country concerned. This scale is periodically revised by the Assembly. Special projects, or "Additional Activities," each have their own budget to which only the Member Organizations actively engaged in the project contribute (Art. XII). The Commission of the European Communities has contributed limited funds by contract for certain projects and some grants have been received from foundations in Britain and Germany. The general budget in round figures for 1981 amounted to FF 5,812,000 ($1 million) and the total of the special budgets for Additional Activities amounted to FF 4,600,000 ($800,000). The ESF remains, it will be seen, a modest organization.

Structure

The Assembly, which meets at least once a year, is the principal organ of the Foundation (Art. VI). It is composed of representatives appointed by each Member Organization. The European Communities may send a representative with an "advisory voice." It has become a practice to invite observers from other international organizations working in related fields and from some countries in which there are no Member Organizations. In 1980, for instance, the President of the National Academy of Science (of the USA) and the Vice-President of the Academy of Sciences (of the USSR) attended.

The Assembly determines the general policy and procedures of the Foundation, approves the report of the Executive Council, adopts the program and budgets, and approves the accounts. It also elects the President and Vice-Presidents for terms of three years. It elects the members of the Executive Council and appoints the Secretary General. The Electoral Commission, which is composed of one member from each country represented in the membership of the ESF, makes nominations for the election of the President and Vice-Presidents, as well as for each vacant seat on the Executive Council (Art. VII).

The Executive Council is responsible for running the Foundation. It consists of the President, the two Vice-Presidents, and eighteen members elected for a period of three years (Art. VIII). A representative of the EC attends in an advisory capacity. It has become an established practice that this representative should be the head of DG XII (the General Directorate for Science and Education of the Commission). The Executive Council is the place where the policy of the Foundation is really elaborated; it meets four or five times a year and operates as a team. It is rare that purely national interests determine attitudes and even less decisions, which are usually reached by consensus. The initial idea was that all major disciplines should be equally represented among the membership, but partly on account of the system of nomination, the perfect balance has unfortunately not been maintained. The humanities and social sciences have generally been underrepresented—which is frequently the case in similar types of international organizations—and physics is overrepresented. What is in fact more important than having a wide spread of disciplines on the Executive Council is that members should enjoy authority in their own country and command the respect of the scientific community as a whole. These two conditions have to be met for the decisions of the Executive Council to carry weight. Prestige substitutes for power. The ESF's standing and efficacy depends to a very large extent on the scientific reputation and personal authority of the President and the members of the Executive Council.

The President, the two Vice-Presidents, and the Secretary General constitute the Board, which, between meetings of the Executive Council, ensures the continuity of the Foundation's business (Art. IX). The office of the ESF is directed by the Secretary General, who, as we have seen, is appointed by the Assembly on the recommendation of the Executive Council for a term of five years (Art. X). He is assisted in his task by a small professional secretariat largely composed of staff members of Member Organizations seconded for limited periods of time. Bureaucracy has been kept to an absolute minimum and Parkinson's law disproved.

Activity of the Foundation

The scientific activities of the Foundation are in general planned and supervised by Standing Committees (Art. XI). There are, at the time of writing, six of them: one each for the Humanities, the Social Sciences, Astronomy, Space Science, Natural Sciences, and Medicine. The two latter ones enjoy a somewhat special status—keeping their own working rules—since ESRC and EMRC, as has already been mentioned, existed as separate bodies before the ESF was born. They also have a slightly different composition from the other Standing Committees, since their members are not only scientists but also science administrators. Members of the regular Standing Committees are nominated by Member Organizations and appointed by the Executive Council while the chairmen are appointed by the Assembly. These Standing Committees convene at regular intervals, discuss problems related to research in their respective fields, make suggestions for new ESF initiatives, and supervise those in progress. These can range all the way from small projects, meetings, seminars, or workshops which can be carried out within the general budget, to major "Additional Activities" which require approval by the Assembly and which have to be separately funded. The Standing Committees, in addition to serving the ESF directly, develop their own solidarity and become excellent channels of communication between European scholars, scientists, and officials of Member Organizations. However, with their present structure, they do not facilitate interdisciplinary or nonconventional projects in which the Foundation could play an innovative role. The work of the Standing Committees is periodically assessed, and they are only maintained in existence if it is felt that they have a further task to accomplish. This practice also applies to all ESF activities.

There are at present eight "Additional Activities" under way in the following areas: Brain and Behavior Research, Taxonomy, Chinese Studies, Byzantine Studies, Human and Cultural Aspects of Migration, Comparative Law, Synchrontron Radiation, and the International Program of the Institut des Hautes Etudes Scientifiques (at Bures-sur-Yvette). Several other possible "Additional Activities" are being explored and will be submitted in due course to the ESF Assembly for approval. The subjects they focus on range from Adult Language Acquisition and Toxicology to a major survey of the structure and composition of the earth's crust and upper mantle in Europe. More modest activities are being conducted within the general program of the Foundation by highly qualified experts collaborating through small international working groups or ad hoc committees in a great diversity of fields, including polymer research, nuclear physics, archaeology and the natural sciences, economics, of health, and forest ecosystems. Some of these may develop in time into full-fledged "Additional Activities"; others will lead to a set of workshops, a report, or a set of recommendations; those which do not prove useful will be discontinued.

The Foundation remains very flexible and adaptable in spite of its somewhat complicated structure. It is clearly neither a European research council nor primarily an establishment carrying out its own research. It has neither the funds nor the necessary national support to aspire to the first function—at least for the time being—and it could not possibly consider becoming a European research facility, dealing as it has to with so many disciplines. The ESF fulfills essentially a "forum" function: it constitutes a link and a means of intra-European communication between scientists. But, as all students of international organizations know, an institution, however well intentioned and equipped, will never be recognized as a legitimate forum where ideas can be exchanged, cooperation initiated, conflicts ameliorated, joint projects planned, and policies harmonized, if it merely offers an infrastructure of conference facilities and a secretariat. To play the role effectively, an institution has to enjoy the full confidence and respect of the community or communities it was set up to serve—in the case of the ESF, essentially the scientists, the Member Organizations, and also to some extent the governments. To acquire the necessary reputation and confidence, an organization cannot just sit back and wait for projects to be submitted; it has to be active, take initiatives, run a program—of course with the backing of its clientele—to prove its capability and its standards. Once its reputation is well established, it will be inundated with requests.

Bearing this principle in mind, the Foundation, once it was set up, immediately buckled down to work. Obviously, the choice of activities depended to some extent on circumstances. It would not be appropriate to describe here in any detail the past achievements or the present and planned activities; all this can be found in the successive *Annual Reports* of the ESF. It might, however, provide some insight into the modus operandi of the Foundation and the possibility and limitations of its action if we list the main ways in which it goes about its business, illustrating them with concrete examples. This is bound to be selective and schematic, omitting some of the less visible but not necessarily less important by-products or side-effects of specific projects, such as the gradual formation of closely knit European teams of specialists who have developed the habit of working together on a specific problem. These transnational communities are an obvious factor of integration.

First, the Foundation carries out cooperative studies. Its role in this case is mainly one of coordination and of facilitating contacts. For example, three separate projects are under way in sinology, in each case led by an outstanding scholar, and with the cooperation of experts from several countries. One project consists in the preparation of an analytical and descriptive bibliography of the Taoist canon, another of handbooks of Chinese literary works from 1900 to 1949, and the third project is an examination of the concept of the state in recent Chinese history. Cooperative projects of this type are also being conducted in Byzantine geography, comparative law, migration in Europe, and taxonomy. These studies usually lead to reports or monographs published by the Foundation. They can also lead to recommendations for action or further study.

Second, the ESF carries out surveys of areas where more intensive cooperation in Europe might prove fruitful. For example, in 1978 a working group was set up to determine whether there was a need to stimulate polymer science. As a first step, an inventory of this type of research performed at universities and institutes throughout eighteen European countries was prepared. It was published in 1980 as "Polymer Research in Europe: Universities and Non-Industrial Laboratories—1979 Survey," and led to the conclusion that it was urgent to improve communications between relatively small national groups working on a given topic. Thus, the Foundation started organizing a series of workshops, bringing together those scientists working in the most advanced sectors of the field. Similar surveys have been conducted in various aspects of astronomy, space science and archaeology.

Third, the ESF has a research-training function. The European Training Program in Brain and Behavior Research (ETPBBR) has been the Foundation's main activity of this type. It consists in a program of grants to individual scientists and scientific teams working in the neurosciences, the object being to promote international and interdisciplinary collaboration in this rapidly developing field. The program also includes winterschools, bringing together junior and senior scientists to discuss a different specific theme each time. In this activity, the ESF comes closer to operating as a European research council. A similar type of program is being envisaged in toxicology.

Fourth, the ESF can prepare the ground for the joint construction, by several European countries, of expensive scientific apparatus. Early in the life of the Foundation, a working group presided by Heinz Maier-Leibnitz observed that if Europe was to remain scientifically competitive, it should possess a powerful synchrotron radiation source. It was apparent that such a machine would be expensive and therefore that it would be cost-effective and also scientifically stimulating if it were conceived as a joint European venture. A committee was set up to examine the feasibility of such a European Synchrotron Radiation Facility (ESRF), which would be more powerful than any other at present in operation or being planned for the near future. The conclusions, which were submitted to the ESF Assembly in 1979, were published by the ESF in 1979 under the title "European Synchrotron Radiation Facility; The Feasibility Study." This study and the supporting scientific evidence published in three additional volumes resulted from close cooperation between more than 100 European scientists from various disciplines. The technical problems are solved and the indispensable character of the machine is recognized by a number of European scientific communities (materials science and chemistry, the life sciences, and fundamental physics). A synchrotron radiation community has been formed in Europe by involvement in the planning and designing stages.

The only remaining problem is implementation, and it is not an easy one. The ESF as an NGO cannot itself undertake the construction and operation of the machine. It would be able neither to raise the funds (estimated at about $150 million) nor enjoy the necessary authority. Nor would it really be its task. The project therefore must move to the intergovernmental level. An intergovernmental committee should take over the responsibility, but its establishment poses a number of practical, legal, political, and diplomatic problems which are not yet solved. It is too soon to judge the outcome. Obviously, the general economic situation is not conducive to such an investment; on the other hand, pressure from the scientists is building up. As we have mentioned earlier, support from governments is not unanimous. Some are very favorable to the ESRF; others would prefer a machine constructed on the basis of a bilateral agreement. Interests of the larger countries do not coincide with those of the smaller ones.

Among the complicated issues which will have to be settled by governments is the selection of a site for the ESRF, but evidently any choice will have technical as well as financial consequences: it is necessary for a close cooperation to be maintained between the intergovernmental committee and the ESF scientists. Rivalry concerning the site could well—strangely—have a positive effect on hesitant governments. In a project such as the ESRF, the Foundation is visibly fulfilling one of its fundamental *raisons d'être*.

Fifth, the Foundation helps to work out norms of scientific conduct in Europe. Through a liaison committee on recombinant DNA, for instance, the ESF closely followed scientific and legislative developments in Europe and North America. It issued a unanimously agreed-upon statement which was approved by the Assembly in November 1980 and which was widely diffused throughout the continent. The ESF followed a similar procedure concerning the Protection of Privacy and the Use of Personal Data for Research.

The ESF has become a recognized instrument of scientific collaboration in Europe. It enjoys the confidence and respect of scientists and scholars, and it is an acknowledged forum for contacts and communication among them and among the science funding agencies. It has conducted a series of worthwhile projects. However, its full potential as a tool for harmonizing European science policies and organizing cooperative projects is far from being fully exploited. What is lacking, as we have said before, is not an efficient institutional framework (the machinery is there), but the political will of governments to pool their resources.

OBSTACLES TO GREATER SCIENTIFIC COOPERATION IN EUROPE

Why has science, which by essence is international, not become one of the dynamic forces pressing for greater European cooperation, particularly when the scientists themselves and public opinion in general seem to be in favor of closer cooperation in this field? How have the character, dimensions, and costs of modern science not made it evident that European nations are too small to compete with each other? The most obvious lacuna which this rapid and by no means complete overview reveals is that in spite of the proliferation of international institutions which have come into being since 1945, in spite of all the efforts toward European unification and the achievement of the EC, there is so far no organization which has as its main task or principal objective to work toward an overall European R&D policy or even to attempt to harmonize effectively national science policies. One can only conclude from this that the *political will* to do so does not exist. Why should this be the case when so many factors appear to militate in favor of it? The answer to this question is complex because such a large number of factors interact. No attempt will be made to rank them by order of importance.

As Jean-Jacques Salomon has written:

> Science is by its very nature universal: the truths for which scientists quest are not particular to any nation. The same truths are sought the world over and are thus universally recognized. Moreover, science by its structure is international: research and discoveries—irrespective of the genius of individuals and peoples—represent a common and cumulative mission whose advancement depends on the efforts of scientists the world over, each bringing a stone to the edifice of scientific knowledge built up over the years, and each in his individual quest for truth depending on the truths revealed by others.[17]

This typically universal quality of science is not particularly conducive to limited regional forms of structured cooperation. Historically the learned societies and academies opened their doors widely to researchers from all countries and great international congresses of the nineteenth century were in no way restricted geographically. True, at the time, most scientific developments were taking place in Europe and in North America. The early intergovernmental scientific agencies, such as the International Bureau of Weights and Measures (BIPM) which was founded in 1875, were also intended to be universal. It is worth noting that then, as now, the scientific organizations came into existence *after* the diplomatic and political institutions and modeled their structure on them. Scientists everywhere, today as yesterday, are understandably reluctant to do anything which might restrict the free flow of communication between colleagues, wherever they may be working. This is axiomatic. One can understand therefore their reluctance to be strong advocates of regional organizations which in their view might in some way hamper the traditional openness of research. The most successful efforts of cooperation on a regional scale prove, however, that this fear is largely unfounded. Physicists from the USA, USSR, and from many other nonmember countries conduct their experiments in CERN, to the extent that it can be said that CERN is both a regional European organization and a truly international forum. It has favored spectacular progress in European science, but in the context of world developments. Sir Charles Carter expresses this conception very well when he writes that "one should give up the supposition that everything needs to have a European dimension, and to ask how, as part of a world-wide business of learning from each other, we could identify a few things most sensibly organized with our nearest neighbors."[18]

As we have pointed out, various scientific communities fully realize that it would not be cost-effective to construct several expensive machines in different European countries when by pooling intellectual and material resources, a single, better, and more powerful instrument could be placed at the disposal of the whole of the specialized community. The argument for joint action in "big" science where expensive tools are required is pretty obvious. However, as clearly resulted from the Council of Europe Helsinki Parliamentary Conference in June 1981, what is urgently needed is a European mechanism for establishing priorities and exploring areas in which cooperation would be most meaningful. Achievements so far—such as they are—have been somewhat haphazard rather than the result of careful planning at the European level. It is worth noting that it is a nongovernmental organization, the European Physical Society, which took the initiative of convening an international seminar on "The Great European Projects," in Rome in March 1979. The meeting examined projects in nuclear fusion, astrophysics, synchrotron radiation, and subnuclear physics.

Big and expensive machines alone do not of course justify regional cooperation. EMBO has proved that in less capital-intensive research, cooperation is possible, but that it is difficult to gather the funds to run a large enough laboratory to make it attractive to the best scientists. There are many other fields, for instance in the geosciences, where more joint European efforts would be of the utmost importance. What is sorely lacking to make such ventures possible is a fund which would enable modest sums to be made available, without strings attached, for exploring the relative merits of different projects, their feasibility, and ultimately to get the joint action launched. It was hoped by at least some of its founders that the ESF might in a modest way play such a role. Unfortunately this has so far not materialized, and one has once again to see the obstacle as the lack of motivation on the part of governments to set up or support machinery which they fear might, even in a limited measure, restrict their freedom of decision in matters concerning R&D.

This reticence is no doubt largely attributable to perceived national economic interests. At a time when scientific innovation constitutes more than ever before a determining factor in the economic potential of a nation, no government is prepared to run the risk of losing a possible advantage gained from research to its neighbors or competitors. For this reason, governments —and to a large extent government funded R&D agencies—wish to keep strict control over their own science policy. In many cases, when national and private interests coincide, powerful pressure groups just reinforce the restrictive attitudes of governments. Frequently, however, as in other areas of political decision making, the short-term interests win out against the long-term ones. Over these combined forces general public opinion or even the attitude of the scientific community itself have very little sway. The research community in the highly industrialized nations of the West remains numerically small, even if in relative terms it is influential. If it was unanimously in favor of greater European cooperation—which does not seem to be the case—it could only have a limited influence on decisions. As for public opinion, in spite of the polls, it does not feel itself sufficiently concerned to become actively involved. The battle is unequal. Breakthroughs can occur when the political and economic circumstances are favorable and where there is an effective leadership. Of course, the smaller countries have more to gain from cooperation than the large ones—hence their more positive attitude toward further integration in science as in other areas. *A contrario*, the big countries have a tradition of self-sufficiency, even if this is in practice no longer in fact the case in the contemporary world.

Military and security considerations also constitute an obstacle to close scientific cooperation in certain fields, as for instance in all matters concerning space, but of course to a lesser extent in Western Europe—which has a number of common strategic interests—than in other regions. But less tangible factors should not be neglected: national prestige, academic traditions, decision-making procedures, as well as language can all constitute serious stumbling blocks. These kind of obstacles count more in France, Britain, and the Federal Republic of Germany than they do in the smaller European countries. In passing it should be noted that subregional groupings, such as the one formed among the Nordic countries, have made considerable progress toward cooperation in R&D and the harmonization of science policy.

One of the arguments voiced against multilateral projects or organizations in the sciences is that they tend to be cumbersome and bureaucratic. While this criticism is undoubtedly true in some instances, there are a number of multilateral agencies which are functioning most efficiently within the existing parameters. Bilateral arrangements do not necessarily avoid these evils, and consensus is also difficult when there are only two partners. International cooperation in science, as in other areas, demands an institutional infrastructure. The effectiveness of these organizations depends mainly on the political will of the member governments. As we have said, the organizations cannot by themselves create consensus, but they are an indispensable forum for consensus formation and for its implementation.

NOTES

1. European Science Foundation (ESF), *Employment Prospects and Mobility of Scientists in Europe* (Brussels: Commission of the European Communities, 1980), p. 28.

2. Ibid., p. 29.

3. *The Times Higher Education Supplement* (London: June 12, 1981).

4. *Science and Public Opinion* (Brussels: Commission of the European Communities, October 1977), p. 86.

5. European Community Survey, *Eurobarometer*, no. 2 (Brussels: November 1974).

6. *Science and Public Opinion*, p. 50.

7. *European International Collaboration in Molecular Biology During the 1980's: The Case for the Continuation of the European Molecular Biology Conference and its General Program* (Heidelberg: European Molecular Biology Organization, 1978), p. 76.

8. Published by the Union des Associations Internationales (Brussels).

9. ESF, *Employment Prospects and Mobility*, p. 28.

10. Ibid., p. 43.

11. ESF, *Annual Report of the European Science Foundation—1980* (Strasbourg: ESF, 1980), p. 68.

12. See *Science Research Councils in Europe* (Stockholm: Working Group of the Science Research Councils, 1972); "Science Research Councils in Europe, II" (Stock-

holm: ESRC, 1975); "The Organization of Research in the Humanities in Western Europe" (Strasbourg: ESF, 1979).

13. Jan Annerset, *A Survey of World Research and Development Efforts* (Paris: OECD Development Center, 1979), p. 6.

14. See André Danzin, *Science et Renaissance de l'Europe* (Paris: Chotard et associés, Editeurs, 1979).

15. UNESCO, *Final Report of the Conference of Ministers of European States Responsible for Science Policy*, Paris, June 22-27, 1970.

16. The Member Organizations of the ESF are as follows: Austria—Fonds zur Förderung der wissenschaftlichen Forschung in Österreich, Österreichische Akademie der Wissenschaften; Belgium—Fonds National de la Recherche Scientifique (Nationaal Fonds voor Wetenschappelijk Onderzoek); Denmark—Statens Naturvidenskabelige Forskningsrad, Statens Laegevidenskabelige Forskningsrad, Statens Jordbrugs- og Veterinaer-videnskabelige Forskningsrad, Statens Samfundsvidenskabelige Forskningsrad, Statens Humanistiske Forskningsrad, Statens Tekniskvidenskabelige Forskningsrad, Det Kongelige Danske Videnskabernes Selskab; Finland—The Academy of Finland; France—Centre National de la Recherche Scientifique, Institut National de la Santé et de la Recherche Médicale, Institut de Recherche Fondamentale du Commissariat à L'Energie Atomique; Fed. Rep of Germany—Deutsche Forschungsgemeinschaft, Max-Planck-Gesellschaft, Konferenz der Akademien der Wissenschaften in der Bundesrepublik Deutschland; Greece—National Hellenic Research Foundation; Ireland—Medical Research Council, National Board for Science and Technology, Royal Irish Academy, Italy—Consiglio Nazionale delle Ricerche; Netherlands—Nederlandse Organisatie voor Zuiver-Wetenschappelijk Onderzoek, Koninklijke Nederlandse Akademie van Wetenschappen; Norway—Norges Almenvitenskaplige Forskningsrad, Det Norske Videnskapsakademi; Portugal—Junta Nacional de Investigação Científica e Tecnológica, Academia das Ciencias de Lisboa, Instituto Nacional de Investigação Cientifica; Spain—Consejo Superior de Investigaciones Cientificas; Sweden—Naturvetenskapliga Forskningsradet, Humanistisk-Samhällsvetenskapliga Forskningsradet, Medicinska Forskningsradet, Kungl. Vetenskapsakademien, Forskningsradsnämnden, Kungl. Vetterhets Historie och Antikvitets Akademien; Switzerland—Schweizerischer Nationalfonds zur Förderung der wissenschaftlichen Forschung; Turkey—Scientific and Technical Research Council; United Kingdom—The British Academy, The Royal Society, Agricultural Research Council, Medical Research Council, Science and Engineering Research Council, Natural Environment Research Council, Social Science Research Council; Yugoslavia—Savet Zajednica za Nauku Jugoslavije, Savet Akademija Nauke u Umjetnosti.

17. J. J. Salomon, *International Scientific Organizations* (Paris: OECD, 1965), p. 11.

18. Cited in *Science and Public Policy* 6 (London: April 1979), p. 144.

Joseph Rallo 7

THE EUROPEAN COMMUNITY AND THE MULTINATIONAL ENTERPRISE

The relationship between the multinational enterprise (MNE) and the state has been a subject of intense debate over the past twenty years. The threat posed by the MNE's mobility and operating practices directly affects a state's ability to pursue its independent economic policy objectives. Of particular concern is the demonstrated ability of the foreign MNE to dominate domestic industrial potential in vital areas of technological development. Individual state responses to such MNE activity differ in approach but not in objective. National regulation of the MNE is viewed as the key to future relations between the state and the foreign MNE. The question that remains is the manner in which such national objectives will be pursued given the transnational nature of the issue of MNE activities.

This chapter emphasizes the policy responses to the problem of MNE activity proposed by the members and institutions of the European Community (EC). As a major global economic actor engaged in pursuing harmonized industrial policies for their region, the EC and its members are in a unique position to effect a regulatory system for MNE activities. The potential of the EC to devise a regulatory system that transcends national borders is a key element in any code of conduct directed at curtailing the excesses of MNE activity. It is the ability of the Community to persuade its members of the need to implement such a regional regulatory policy that stands at the center of this essay.

Several themes overlap when discussing these proposals and serve to obscure the policy components that are basic to the Community's work. First is the gradual loss of member support for the objectives of regional political and economic integration. Second is the shift of policy responsibility from the Community-oriented Commission to the member-controlled European Council. Third is the undeniable fact that few of the Community's proposals in this area have ever been fully implemented. Finally, there is a close connection between the development of internal Community proposals and EC participation in the work of international organizations, specifically the Organization for Economic Cooperation and Development (OECD), in the area of MNE regulation.

This chapter addresses these themes and suggests how they coalesce to define a Community commitment to an effective regulatory policy for MNE activities. While the analysis is primarily descriptive, a specific statement emerges on the future direction of Community initiatives on the question of the MNE.

THE ISSUE OF MULTINATIONAL ENTERPRISE REGULATION

Although active discussion about MNE operations dates from the mid-1950s, the activities of these firms have been a feature of the international economic picture for a far longer period of time. In the eighteenth century, firms previously national in their scope of activities expanded their operations to take advantage of newly opened overseas markets. Aimed at securing raw materials for domestic manufacturing requirements, these operations were essentially exploitive, taking the form of mining or plantation concessions extracted from local officials.[1] While these operations continued into the 1900s in the less-defined markets of Africa and Latin America, significant changes in MNE activity were occurring by the early 1800s in rapidly expanding areas such as the United States. Foreign corporate investment in these markets was in the form of indirect or portfolio investment, with the foreign firm lending capital but leaving operational control in the hands of the local company. The foreign firm realized its return by a monetary profit rather than in the form of raw materials.[2] The limited nature of both concession and portfolio investment thus minimized the need for the foreign firm to seek to influence actively the policies of the host government in its favor.

It was with the 1906 establishment of a Singer Sewing Machine subsidiary in Britain that the relationship of investment to influence in the host market began to assume its modern proportions.[3] Singer's investment in an established market area was direct rather than portfolio. Instead of a simple financial return on its investment, Singer sought to operate in Britain's market under conditions previously applicable only to domestic British firms. From this point on, the nature of foreign corporate investment would no longer be simply economic in scope: to secure equal status with domestic firms, a foreign corporation had to participate actively in a market to protect its position, and to be effective such participation could not be limited to the location of its overseas industrial unit. Economic security depended on corporate access at the highest levels of government. An organization previously economic in structure became increasingly political as it sought to secure the status of its foreign investment.

This shift in the nature of corporate operations underlies the present debate over the permissible scope of MNE operations as they affect a host state's domestic economy. The host state's response increasingly has been to make the foreign MNE more responsive to the requirements of domestic planning objectives. The means to secure such corporate responsiveness has been the regulatory code of conduct defining the manner and extent of permissible MNE activities. For the members of the EC this national regulatory objective has been made more complex by the simultaneous development of the tenets of regional integration.

Regional proposals to regulate the operations of the foreign MNE are a response to the inability of a single state to address such transnational issues. The obstacles facing a single state which seeks to regulate the domestic effects of foreign corporate investment are suggested by the OECD's definition of the MNE: "A multinational enterprise is an enterprise which carries out operations, such as the production of goods or the provision of resources, in more than one country through component units which are subject to some measure of central control."[4] Therefore, to be effective any proposed regulatory code must address the transnational character of the issues raised by MNE activity. It is the nature of those issues termed here "corporate mobility" and "legal responsibility" that illustrates the state's inability to act unilaterally in this area.

Corporate mobility refers to the integrated MNE operational structure that is superimposed on an international economic system composed of individual states. Active in several states, the MNE's ability to direct its internal operations is not hampered by the normal formalities associated with crossing a border. A phone call or interoffice memo serves to transfer financial or managerial resources anywhere within the global corporate structure. While the excesses of "transfer pricing" have been well documented, corporate mobility remains a problem in even the more routine aspects of MNE-state relations.[5] Particularly troublesome is the MNE's ability to shift its vast currency reserves according to market trends which minimizes a state's ability to restore fiscal stability through domestically imposed monetary controls.[6]

The second problem posed by the operations of the MNE is termed that of legal responsibility. In its simplest form, responsibility refers to the question of which authority has the legal jurisdiction to assume control over a firm's activities. The state in which a firm is located has the jurisdiction to regulate those activities. In this manner, the home state and the host state (where the subsidiary is established) each have the jurisdiction to control a segment of that corporation's activities. The problem of legal responsibility arises because of the centralized nature of MNE activities where only the headquarters has the authority to establish operating rules for global activities. Thus the host state's potential to regulate the local activities of the foreign MNE is often chimerical given the limited potential for independent action entrusted to that local subsidiary.

These two concepts suggest the difficulties posed to the single state seeking to regulate unilaterally the internal effects of foreign MNE activity. Even the state's ability to deny the MNE access to its market in hope of gaining some leverage over the firm is often minimal, given the control by the firm over scarce technological and managerial resources desired by the state. This conflict may be viewed in terms of the manner in which both the MNE and the state utilize their ability to exercise that control potential. While the state's scope of control may be viewed vertically, that of the MNE is horizontal. To be effective, any proposed regulatory system must also be capable of exerting horizontal control. But a regulatory system based on national control of the MNE is incapable of meeting this requirement.

It is the nature of this control requirement that suggests the need for coordinated regulatory action between several states. The effectiveness of such a group regulatory proposal will naturally depend on the number and nature of the states privy to that agreement and on their ability to agree on common means and objectives for such regulation. This chapter is limited to assessing the regulatory proposals encompassed within the group of states forming the European Community.

The initial step toward EC integration was the establishment of the internal common market. The presence of that single market eliminated barriers to cross-border corporate movements within the region while simultaneously erecting a set of rules to govern the ability of a foreign firm to initially enter that market area. But once established in the region a firm could not then be arbitrarily prohibited from extending its activities to other states in the region. Thus the mechanics of regional integration actually served to lessen the ability of a member to limit the entry of foreign MNE's once that firm had gained access to any one of the other members of the group.

This facet of the mechanics of regional integration was the prime reason for the rapid establishment of US MNE subsidiaries in the EC just prior to the 1958 market completion deadline. This early penetration of the market area of the Community was later intensified by the industrial programs of Luxembourg and Ireland which actively encouraged such foreign investment as essential to their domestic economic policy objectives. Adherence to the objectives of integration thus increased the difficulties for a regional grouping when proposing a regulatory system to address the activities of the foreign MNE. It was the combined impact of these concerns that stimulated the series of Commission-sponsored measures on the MNE in the early 1970s.

COMMISSION PROPOSALS FOR THE REGULATION OF THE MULTINATIONAL ENTERPRISE IN THE COMMUNITY AREA

The EC is caught between two simultaneous yet inconsistent planning themes on the subject of MNE regulation. As both home and host to a multitude of MNE firms, the Community must seek to establish a leading role for itself in the development and maintenance of any system for the international economic regulation of such corporate activity. At the same time, the Community is involved with the economic planning requirements of regional integration. This latter commitment seeks to insulate the region from the larger international system in order to develop the Community's industrial potential to compete effectively in that external economic environment.

An understanding of these competing economic themes in Community planning is further complicated by the continually shifting patterns of member political support for the objectives of regional integration. Throughout this period, the members remained undecided on whether the final institutional configuration of the Community would be of a federal nature or would instead reflect some lesser level of regional cooperation. Responding to this uncertainty, Commission policy initiatives were phrased in terms of full integration even though member support for such action was far from assured.

Commission MNE proposals advanced in the late 1960s and early 1970s may be viewed as unifying in nature and objective. These industrial unification proposals were seen as the planning correlates to the more general objective of regional economic and political integration. In programmatic terms, unification required that Community institutions be responsible for initiating and implementing selective but comprehensive policy proposals. Unification proposals sought to substitute a single region-wide program under Community control in place of previously separate national programs. The essential aspect of this substitution required that program direction and monetary resources now under national control be ceded to appropriate Community institutions. Member support for both industrial unification policy and the objectives of regional political integration reached a high point at the 1972 Paris Summit where it was stated that a united Europe would be achieved by 1980.[7]

An unfortunate aspect of the Commission-sponsored MNE proposals is that they originated in this atypical period of Community history. Tentative to begin with, member commitment to the objectives of regional integration soon evaporated in the wake of events. The 1974 oil crisis was only one of the events that sorely tried the fragile commitment to political unification articulated in 1972. Members increasingly found themselves having to take a greater role in an international economic structure challenged by the oil crisis and the apparent inability of the United States to unilaterally reestablish that system. Underdeveloped Community institutions were unable to coerce members into presenting a unified response to these externally generated economic challenges. As a result, instead of focusing on intra-EC policy solutions, members now took a more active role in proposals of international organizations designed to reestablish a workable global economic system.

In keeping with their newfound international activism, Community members now demanded a greater share in the internal policymaking process defining and implementing the objectives of regional integration. Nowhere was this desire to share responsibility with Community institutions more evident than in the gradual transfer of policymaking control from the Council of Ministers to the European Council. An outgrowth of the 1976 report on *European Union* prepared by the then Belgium Prime Minister, Leo Tindemans, the European Council is composed of the heads of state or government of each member.[8] The Council meets several times a year to establish and refine Community policy objectives through the broad spectrum of planning activity. This direct intervention by the members has effectively narrowed the independent initiatory role of Community institutions and transformed their function from one of policy initiation to that of program implementation. European Council control over the scope of Community initiatives has also changed the objective of those measures from that of policy unification to one of program harmonization.

Program harmonization, like unification, establishes a single policy in effect throughout the Community in a designated planning sector. But unlike unification, harmonization leaves implementation and thus program control in the hands of member officials. A harmonized policy represents a coordinated sharing of responsibility by national and Community institutions and officials. While less extensive than unification, harmonization represents a commitment to coordinated action by a group of states far beyond that required by traditional international agreements. Even though program harmonization does not cede control from member to Community institutions, it does signal a unique pattern of policymaking possible only within a region still pursuing the objectives, albeit narrowed, of integration.

This shift in internal planning objectives serves to blur the already fuzzy area of Community initiatives in the area of MNE policy. To explain Community MNE proposals through an analysis of such internal shift would simply lead to the conclusion that these initiatives have suffered because of member ambiguity over the objectives of regional integration. Instead, this chapter demonstrates that the Community's emergent MNE policy is an affirmative response by members to the problems posed by the international firm. The Community and its members now recognize the need to establish a regulatory system whose scope of control extends beyond the boundaries of the regional grouping. Such a system must include the United States and Japan, neither of which is involved in the internal planning dynamics of integration. The requirements of an effective internationally oriented regulatory system must therefore be made to mesh with the internal dynamics of Community planning. Policy unification which seeks to isolate the region from the international system is not capable of fulfilling this requirement. Program harmonization which coordinates Community planning while still allowing members to engage in extraregional regulatory schemes does provide this needed flexibility.

PROPOSALS TO COMPLETE THE ESTABLISHMENT OF THE SINGLE INTERNAL MARKET

Corporate Disclosure of Information: The Seventh Directive on Group Accounts

The previous discussion on the fragmented nature of legal responsibility suggested the obstacles present when national authorities seek information on the local activities of a foreign MNE. While national officials may gain access to the records of locally incorporated firms, they do not have the same capability with respect to the records of that firm's foreign parent. Thus any effort to regulate those foreign-initiated activities is seriously impaired by the inability to gather the information essential to begin even preliminary inquiries. The solution to this impasse lies in the ability to extend the jurisdictional power of the state beyond its national boundaries. Two Commission proposals were designed to redress this problem by harmonizing the disclosure and reporting standards that affect a foreign MNE active within the Community area.

The first proposal was presented in a 1973 Commission paper titled *Multinational Undertakings and Community Regulation* and contained two major objectives.[9] First: enlarge the ability of national and Community officials to gain access to data on the operating procedures of firms active in the region "in order to allow all interested parties to arrive at their own judgment of the policies carried on by the various undertakings."[10] Second: define how much information a foreign MNE could be forced to disclose under these new standards. It was this latter objective that posed the far greater problem.

National capability to require disclosure initially depends on the definition of the corporation adopted by the legal system in effect in that state. The presence of both civil and common law systems in the Community posed the initial barrier to disclosure requirements because of the way each tradition defined the corporate personality. The common law system, in effect in the UK and Ireland, adheres to a restrictive definition of the corporation. Under common law, the country where a parent firm is incorporated has the jurisdiction to require disclosure over that corporation, its domestically incorporated subsidiaries, and its branches wherever located. Corporate subsidiaries incorporated in another country, even though under the operational control of the parent, are not subject to the disclosure requirements in effect in that parent's home state. Rather, only the country where that subsidiary is incorporated has the ability to determine what that firm must disclose. This common law distinction between influence and incorporation thus inhibits a state's ability to treat the operations of parent and foreign subsidiary as one unit for disclosure purposes.

The civil law system in France, West Germany, Italy, and Denmark is in sharp contrast and is far more flexible than common law in its treatment of the corporate personality. The civil law looks beyond the mere fact of incorporation and instead treats all companies that are subject to central management by the dominant influence of one firm over another as an economic unit for purposes of disclosure. The effect of this focus on influence rather than incorporation permits a greater amount of MNE operations to come within the reach of a single state's regulatory system.

In keeping with its objective of enlarging the jurisdictional reach of Community disclosure requirements, the original 1973 Commission proposal adopted the broader civil law definition of corporate personality.[11] Although Industrial Commissioner Davignon was aware of the definitional differences present in member legal systems, he continued to support the use of the more flexible civil law approach. This commitment was reemphasized in the Directive on disclosure submitted to the Council of Ministers on May 4, 1976.[12] When implemented, this Seventh Directive on Group Accounts would require all MNE firms registered or incorporated in the Community to publish information concerning their activities and those of all affiliated companies wherever located. MNEs with incorporation outside the Community would also be subject to these disclosure provisions "as far as their activities through companies established in the Community are concerned."[13] The antitrust provisions of the EC supply adequate precedent for subjecting the activities of foreign firms whose operations affect the Community to the jurisdiction of its authorities.[14] For example, while the activities of IBM-Europe would be reported as a unit, the disclosure provisions would not extend to include information from the US parent based in New York. The provisions of this Directive do not go beyond these precedents and for that reason passage of the measure in the near future appears certain.

A New Form of Corporation: The European Company

Perhaps the best-known harmonization proposal in the area of corporate activity is the Regulation to establish a European Company (SE). Proposed in 1970 and amended in 1975, the Regulation is a complex set of provisions governing the activities of large firms that operate within the Community area.[15] Both EC and foreign MNEs may apply for SE status. The Regulation's most innovative feature is that the law and institutions of the Community rather than those of a single member would govern an SE's activities. In its most basic sense, the Regulation was an effort to harmonize the existing corporate laws of the members by choosing from existing legislation a mixture that was to serve both as a goal and as a compromise in the creation of the unified internal market: a goal since implementation of the Regulation would grant to relevant Community institutions the control responsibility previously exercised only by national officials and a compromise since adoption of SE status is a voluntary decision on the part of a firm. Thus the more radical step of substituting a Community-controlled corporate system for the present nationally based structure would not be fully realized even with passage of the Regulation. Although the Regulation has not yet been adopted, Commission staffers remain optimistic on the question of passage in the near future.[16]

Three reasons may be suggested for the inability of the Regulation to have gained passage through the relevant Community institutions. First is the sheer complexity of the Regulation's provisions. Encompassing scores of pages of rather technical provisions, it complicates rather than encourages a firm's ability to carry out its operations within the Community area. Second, the Regulation adopts the controversial West German codetermination provisions of shared worker-management responsibility for corporate activities. Few firms wish to have to operate under provisions which have yet to prove their viability outside the limited West German corporate environment. Third, the Regulation adopts the broad civil law definition of corporate personality and disclosure requirements contained in the Directive on Group Accounts. Since a firm may still operate throughout the Community area by simply incorporating in one of the members, there has been little incentive to add an additional burden by taking on the responsibilities contained within the Regulation's provisions.

PROPOSALS TO INCREASE THE COMPETITIVE ABILITY OF EXISTING COMMUNITY FIRMS

A Community Export Program

The provisions of the customs union contained in the Rome Treaty of 1956 govern the terms of entry for foreign goods into the Community market area.[17] Foreign-produced goods are subject to variable price levies to assure that they are sold at prices equivalent to those charged for similar Community products.[18] A resurgent Community industry benefited greatly from the protection afforded by this unified EC program in the area of imports. The Commission sought to implement a similar unified Community export program as part of its emerging MNE regulatory policy.

The EC Treaty assigns to Community institutions the role of establishing a single export policy along the lines of the customs union for imports.[19] The obstacle in establishing a Community export policy is the existence of individual national programs designed to secure as large a portion as possible of any potential sales market for their own domestic firms. This member-firm relationship goes far beyond mere market fragmentation. Direct government assistance to domestic firms binds those companies more closely to national rather than to Community planning objectives.[20] Similarly, the preferential treatment offered to foreign firms is designed to mesh their investment and technological resources with domestic industrial capability.[21] These separate national export policies prevent the development of a single Community program while at the same time grant foreign firms access to the regional market. One aspect of the Commission's export policy proposal was to seek to redress this imbalance in favor of Community-oriented objectives.

The introduction of a coherent Community export policy would also provide distinct advantages to European firms operating in foreign markets. Part of the success attributed to US and Japanese MNEs in attracting foreign contracts is their ability to offer comprehensive financing and insurance terms in a single currency and at fixed rates. This capability is due in great measure to government agencies, such as the US Export-Import Bank (EXIM), which underwrite these business contracts at very favorable rates.[22] In contrast, the lack of a single European currency and the inability to offer coordinated financing terms often leave Community MNEs at a competitive disadvantage when soliciting customers in foreign markets.[23]

The Commission sought to correct this competitive imbalance by instituting an export policy designed to unify the independent export programs of Community members.[24] The Commission began its work in the mid-1960s in the areas of interest rates and insurance programs. But its original objective of substituting a single Community policy for separate national systems soon had to be abandoned in view of the diversity in legal and financial traditions present within each of the members. This diversity and its attendant problems only increased with the admission of the common law nations of the UK and Ireland to the Community in 1973. The Commission then abandoned any efforts to unify Community export policy in favor of a harmonized approach to the issue. The Commission's new emphasis was to dismantle existing regional impediments to an increased Community industrial capability to penetrate foreign markets.[25] In keeping with the mandate of harmonization policy, this effort was pursued at both the Community and international levels.

Beginning with the *gentleman's agreement* on export credits signed in Puerto Rico on June 28, 1976, several of the Community members now sought to stabilize their own programs by recourse to international agreements.[26] The Puerto Rican agreement was signed by the United States, Japan, and the major EC members—France, Italy, West Germany, and the United Kingdom. This agreement, establishing rate structures for national export credits, was then made applicable to the entire Community area by a decision of the Council of Ministers.[27] This aspect of Community export credit policy was thus harmonized because of the work completed at the international level. Recently, the July 1981 Ottawa Summit reaffirmed this continuing relationship between internal Community policy and work at the international level through a wide range of economic issues.[28]

The European Export Bank

One of the cornerstones in completing the Community structure was the effort to establish a single economic and monetary system for the region.[29] The present European Monetary System (EMS), in place since 1979, is a result of the earlier work on the Economic and Monetary Union (EMU).[30] The benefits associated with EMU, such as a single currency and financial structure, were particularly relevant in the export trade sector of Community corporate activity. The Commission proposal for a European Export Bank (EEB) was now designed to establish an institutional structure capable of enhancing the ability of Community firms to compete with foreign MNEs in the international market.

The EEB Regulation substitutes a single Community-run financing system in place of existing and separate member banking facilities throughout the entire export sector of corporate activity.[31] Unlike the existing European Investment Bank (EIB), the EEB was a Community structure whose capital and management were not subject to the control of the members.[32] Adoption of the EEB would require members to channel their export assistance funds and programs through the Bank which, in turn, would dispense such resources in a manner consistent with the objectives of a unified Community export program.

The EEB Regulation was strongly supported by diverse export-oriented industrial and banking groups within the Community. Both the Confederation of British Industry (CBI) and the Union of Industries in the European Community (UNICE) felt the introduction of the EEB would allow European firms to offer competitive terms similar to those being extended to purchasers by both US and Japanese MNEs.[33] Reflecting its widespread appeal in Community export circles, the EEB proposal was included in Commission budget requests from 1976 to 1978, even though the Regulation itself had yet to be acted on by the Council of Ministers.

The present status of the EEB is somewhat unclear. In keeping with the general shift to program harmonization within the Community, the EEB Regulation has been amended to make the Bank a department of the EIB and thus under the effective control of the members.[34] Although under the control of the EIB, the EEB is nonetheless still viewed as playing a leading financial role in any emerging Community export policy. But the exact nature of that role is ultimately dependent on the final development of a Community policy in the entire area of export and MNE-related issues.

Public Contracts and Preferential Treatment of National Firms

Preferential treatment of firms in bidding for public government contracts is a widely used means to indirectly channel national projects to selected domestic companies. The major industrial role played by member governments in the Community and the substantial number of such public contracts allow national officials to have a great impact on the ability of Community companies to compete effectively for such projects.[35] The ability of each government to establish the provisions for bidding allows it to word those provisions so that only selected domestic firms have an opportunity to enter that bidding process.[36] This longstanding practice among Community members greatly contributed to the existing fragmentation of the EC's industrial potential. The existence of separate national procurement policies maintained a domestic firm's dependence on its government's largesse and inhibited its ability to expand operations into other more lucrative markets. Ironically, the beneficiaries of this fragmented Community situation were the foreign MNEs who were able to attract the contracts too large or complex for less sophisticated EC national firms to handle.

In the late 1960s, the French government was the first to suggest that this tradition of separate national procurement contracts be replaced by a Community-wide system based on free access to the bidding process by all European firms.[37] This suggestion was adopted by the Commission in a 1971 Directive which outlined the procedures designed to eliminate national preference from the procurement system.[38] Basic to these new procedures were the requirements of publication and advance written notice of contract terms and product specifications. While the system would apply to practically all national contracts, the Commission was particularly interested in providing the capability for Community firms to compete in the high-technology sectors of commercial activity. Thus the provisions were worded to allow non-EC-based MNEs to enter the bidding process if, in turn, the home governments of those firms would reciprocate in their own procurement programs. This latter provision was directly aimed at the Buy America Act which, by granting preferential treatment to bids placed by US firms, effectively excluded Community firms from lucrative high-technology defense and civilian contracts in that market area.[39] The 1971 Commission Directive was adopted by the Council of Ministers on December 20, 1976 and came into effect in 1980.[40]

Although the Directive on public contracts has harmonized effectively the Community's policy in this area, it has been unable to assist EC firms in their direct competition with foreign MNEs. Because of the difficulties presented by the issue of legal responsibility, a foreign MNE may simply incorporate a subsidiary in the Community area and thereby become eligible to enter the bidding process for public contracts. Since there is no framework extending Community reciprocity terms to non-EC nations, the public contracts let by countries such as the United States and Japan still remain closed to European firms. For this reason, the thrust of the Commission's recent work in the area of procurement program harmonization has been pursued at the international rather than the Community level. The bulk of this work has been concentrated within the framework of both the General Agreement on Tariffs and Trade (GATT) and the OECD.

The 1947 GATT agreements which reestablished the international economic system after the Second World War specifically had exempted the sensitive area of national public contracts from its provisions.[41] Thus national programs to assist selected domestic firms became the norm in Western Europe, Japan, and the United States.[42] Efforts to eliminate such restrictive national barriers began in the 1960s and continued through the 1970s. An agreement to drop such barriers was finally completed in 1980 with the signing of the Multilateral Trade Agreements (MTA).[43] The MTA provisions require that firms from any OECD member be allowed to bid on an equal basis for all national public contracts let by government agencies. More than likely final ratification and implementation of the MTA will produce certain exceptions to the scope of these provisions. But whatever the sweep of those exceptions, the Community's efforts to gain reciprocity in access to non-EC public contracts have been successful. More important, the flexibility inherent in the Community's switch to program harmonization rather than unification has again proved its worth in the region's efforts to develop a comprehensive yet effective policy concerning the activities of the foreign MNE.

PROPOSALS TO RESTRUCTURE THE HIGH-TECHNOLOGY SECTORS OF COMMUNITY INDUSTRY

One of the components of Commission proposals in the area of MNE policy has been the effort to increase the capability of European firms to meet effectively the competition offered by foreign companies in the more open global marketplace. The bulk of these efforts have been the measures previously discussed which were designed to increase the competitive potential of European firms by eliminating intra-Community barriers to industrial expansion. But with respect to the high-technology sector of industry, itself uniquely the province of MNEs, the Commission has sought to go beyond the mere lifting of such trade barriers. In the twin sectors of data processing and aerospace, the Commission has sought to increase the competitive potential of Community firms by unifying separate national firms into a Community-controlled regional industrial structure. Mirroring the goal of political unification by 1980, Action Programs in these two sectors were designed to produce a single Community data processing and aerospace industry by that same date. Although the objectives of these Action Programs have been severely modified in keeping with the trend toward program harmonization, the market conditions that first prompted the Commission to develop its proposals remain essentially unchanged to date. The essential aspect of these market conditions is the almost complete control by US MNEs of both Community and global sales in these vital industrial sectors. Since an integral aspect of the Community's MNE policy is to secure an equitable share of the world market for its own firms, it becomes essential to determining if EC program harmonization in these sectors is capable of attaining that objective.

1975 Action Program for the European Aeronautical Sector

Except for certain heavily subsidized military aircraft ventures such as the French Mirage or the joint UK, West German, and Italian Multi-Role Combat Aircraft (MRCA), no other modern European aerospace project has been commercially successful.[44] The Community's members, like the rest of the noncommunist world, purchase US-produced aircraft for almost all of their civilian needs. While individual sectors of Community industry are competitive, it is the fragmentation of its total industry that prevents EC firms from securing what might be termed an equitable percentage of the available world market. Several factors combine to inhibit the competitive potential of the Community's aerospace manufacturers.

One factor is the compartmentalized nature of state aid directed toward these firms which inhibits an optimal utilization of the research and development (R&D) funds they receive. Second, unlike US government contracts, European public contracts do not require a sharing of the newly generated technological information within the entire national industry. Third, the major financial and control role played by Community governments hampers a firm's ability to limit its losses by recourse to traditional cost-effective business techniques. Aerospace worker productivity in Community industries is generally about one-half to two-thirds that of the US counterparts because of the inability of these firms to lay off workers when market conditions require such action.[45] Fourth, the short production runs of Community planes—designed to sell only within a national market—tend to raise questions about the availability of parts and service over the normal multiyear lifespan of a craft. Finally, and independent of the previously mentioned problems, is the disproportional government aid avail-

TABLE 7.1

NATIONAL GOVERNMENT AID TO THE EUROPEAN AEROSPACE INDUSTRY

(in million u.a. for 1975)
($1=1.25 u.a.)

Research and Development	Civil	Military
FRG	47.7	462.9
Belgium	1.8	.1
France	148.4	359.6
Italy	1.6	21.2
Netherlands	.9	1.8
UK	119.5	305.6
Total	319.9	1151.2

SOURCE: EC Commission, Directorate General for Internal Market and Industrial Affairs--Data on the Aeronautical Sector, 2 August 1977 (Brussels: SEC [77] 2939), Table 43.

able to both Community and US aerospace manufacturers. At its highest point in 1975, US government assistance to its aerospace industry was about 11,000 million units of account ($1=1.25 u.a.). As Table 7.1 indicates, this US figure can be compared to a combined European aid total of about 1,500 million u.a.[46] It was the composite impact of these market conditions that first prompted the Commission's proposal to restructure the entire European aerospace industry.

First submitted to the Council of Ministers in 1975, the Commission's Action Program was designed to unify the Community's aerospace industry so that it could compete effectively on the global market.[47] The Program is quite explicit in its objectives. Responsibility for the entire Community aerospace industry was to be removed from national control, and cooperation between national firms, as exhibited within the Airbus consortia, would no longer be acceptable. The controlling section of the Program stated that "sponsorship of the aircraft industry should be exercised by the Community."[48] The Commission also emphasized that its ability to produce a competitive Community aerospace industry was closely tied to full implementation of all related proposals in the area of exports and national procurement policy.

The Commission's objective of a single unified Community-controlled aerospace industry has not come to pass. In keeping with the overall shift to program harmonization, the Community's goals for this industrial sector have been similarly modified. Industrial Commissioner Davignon endorsed this change by noting that his new goal is one of harmonizing national aerospace efforts within a loose Community structure.[49] Shared collaboration between Community firms, particularly evidenced by the Airbus consortia, has begun to challenge the hold of US MNEs on the global aerospace market. European manufacturers also have sought out US firms to form partnerships for the commercial production of civilian aerospace craft.[50] But the ability of a harmonized Community aerospace policy to effectively wrest a substantial portion of the available global market from US MNEs is a question still in the process of being answered.

1976 Commission Proposal for the Development of Informatics

The Community's data processing market shares many similarities with conditions present in the aerospace sector of manufacturing. Despite the continuation of substantial governmental grants and supports, the Community's data processing industry remains minimally competitive in the global market. Although fragmentation of the Community's industrial potential is a major reason for this inability to compete, two additional market conditions serve to underscore the secondary status of EC data processing firms.

First is the dominant global and European position held by the US firm of IBM. While IBM's global presence allows it to exploit innovations in this most creative of technological fields, it is IBM's ability to self-generate R&D funds that allows it to maintain its competitive lead over other US as well as European and Japanese firms. In 1974, typical of the period in question, IBM alone spent $890 million on R&D while its closest European competitor, International Computers Limited (UK), spent $36 million.[51]

The second factor that inhibits the ability of European firms to break into the data processing market is the manner in which computer-related items are marketed. Most hardware is leased from a manufacturer, with profits coming from sales of software packages designed to fit the diverse operational needs of clients. IBM's technological lead in the area of software and the fact that its packages are incompatible with any other hardware produces what is termed a "captive market" where renters of IBM equipment must purchase that firm's software in order to properly utilize the system's potential.[52]

This domination by IBM thus severely limits the available share of the market that might be sought by Community manufacturers. One recent

TABLE 7.2

PUBLIC SECTOR DATA PROCESSING MARKET HELD BY

EUROPEAN MANUFACTURERS[1]

Country	Firm	Percentage of Public Sector Held By Firm
UK[a]	ICL	47.2 (an average of all public depts.)
	IBM	24.0 (an average of all public depts.)
Denmark[b]	Eur. firms	9.0
	IBM	85.0
W. Germany[c]	Ger./Eur. firms	44.0
	IBM	56.0
France[d]	CII	34.0
	Other Fr.	2.0
	Honeywell-Bull	9.0 (now will be added to CII figures after 1975 merger)
	IBM	36.0
Belgium[e]	Siemens	46.6
	Philips	17.2
	IBM	23.0

NOTE: 1. This material was supplied during an interview with Commission staff member R. Coleman on March 26, 1979, in Brussels, Belgium.

SOURCE:
a. UK delegation to the Commission.
b. 1979 study by Danish Statistical Institute.
c. Deutscher Bundestag 7. Wahlperiode Drucksache 7/4553, 7-1-1976.
d. "L'Informatique dans les Entreprises publiques au Ier Janvier 1975." Ministere de l'Industrie et de la Recherche--Direction Générale de l'Industrie.
e. Courrier Hedbdomadaire of CRISP--May 1975

estimate suggests that of the $5 billion to be spent annually on data processing, all but $0.5 billion would be accounted for by US MNEs.[53] IBM's recent share of the world market, as shown in Table 7.2, hovered around 57 percent, with its closest competitor, the US firm of Honeywell, claiming about 9 percent.[54] It was this combination of a lucrative but closed global data processing market that prompted Commission proposals in the mid

1970s designed to enhance the ability of Community firms to gain their fair share of international sales and contracts.

The Commission's original 1974 proposal for the data processing sector acknowledged the rather unique competitive conditions that exist in this global market.[55] Paralleling its Action Program for Aeronautics, the Commission sought the establishment of a "fully viable and competitive European computer based industry by 1980."[56] But unlike its aerospace proposals, which originally sought a unified Community industry, this data processing plan sought only to harmonize existing member programs through a process of "limited collaboration" between nationally run firms.[57]

There were several reasons why these Commission proposals sought to enhance rather than replace existing and nationally supported data processing firms. First, Community data processing manufacturers already held a market share that hovered near the industrially set profit mark of 8 to 10 percent of the available market.[58] This potential viability of Community firms becomes even stronger when one separates the percentage of national public contracts for computer-related sales held by these companies. Second, the potential availability of Community and national funding is much less than that present in the aerospace sector. Thus even if the Commission were to aggregate all sources of available national funds, the total would fall far short of that required to support an industrial capability that could compete effectively on the global market. Therefore the Commission proposal concentrated on first capturing as large a portion as possible of the European market before pursuing more global ambitions. From the outset the development and pursuit of a Community data processing policy was to be a joint effort blending financial and managerial resources from both national and EC sources.[59]

This harmonized approach to the data processing sector, in sharp contrast to the Commission's path pursued in aerospace, has accounted for the greater level of member support accorded to this series of proposals. The original 1974 proposed outline for joint Community-member financing of this sector was accepted by the Council of Ministers in mid-1974.[60] Selective programs jointly financed have been approved and implemented in recent years. Among these ventures have been a computerized medical bank and a legal retrieval system for information on both Community and member legislation and court rulings.[61] This system of joint Community member control over the pace and scope of data processing proposals was formalized with the introduction of the Consultative Committee which by qualified majority vote now passes on proposals in this entire sector of industrial activity.[62] In 1976 the Commission updated and expanded its proposals on the Community's data processing needs and capabilities well into the decade of the 1980s.[63] Although members have blocked selected Community proposals when they interfere with parallel national projects, there continues to be a shared and growing commitment to the development of an EC data processing capability consistent with the tenets of program harmonization.[64]

THE FUTURE DIRECTION OF THE EUROPEAN COMMUNITY'S WORK ON THE ISSUE OF MULTINATIONAL ENTERPRISE POLICY

The previous sections analyzed the scope of EC MNE-related programs while seeking to identify the policymaking pattern present in each proposal. Two alternative patterns—unification and harmonization—were identified as central to this analysis. The objective of unification measures was to insulate the region from the international system through economic programs based on the goal of a politically united Europe. In contrast, harmonization proposals sought economic progress through a coordination of Community and existing member programs with work being conducted at the international level. Typically, the key to the ability to implement any new economic programs resolved around the issue of political integration.

Program harmonization has emerged as the basis for EC MNE policymaking precisely because it accommodates itself to the Community's present lack of commitment to political integration. Additionally, harmonization has gained support because of its ability to coordinate member and Community activity with work conducted at the international level. It is only at this international level that successful resolution of the issue of MNE control will be achieved. The future course of Community policy in this area will be a combination of internally harmonized measures meshing with work pursued within selected international groupings.

The question of MNE regulatory policy is unique in its ability to underscore the close relationship between internal Community planning and the need to secure an EC presence in agreements undertaken at international levels. This relationship demonstrates clearly the inadequacy of policy unification as a planning theme in this program sector. An understanding of MNE-related policies strengthens the argument, first proposed by Ernst Haas, that increasingly the issues posed to Community planners will not be susceptible to regionally limited solutions.[65] Instead, Community policy must be framed by reference to broader international considerations. The previous sections developed the interrelationship between Community and international agreements in an effort to illustrate this sentiment.

But the development of a Community MNE policy must be viewed in terms more positive than a mere passive accommodation to events occurring external to the EC grouping. In actuality, Commission members pressed for work to be conducted at the international level as an active supplement to the policies they were proposing for the internal Community area. The Commission's original proposals throughout the area of Community MNE policy spoke in terms of unification rather than harmonization precisely because of the parallel work being conducted within GATT and the OECD. If the measures that ultimately passed these two bodies had retained their original wording, the effect would have been to support the Commission's bid for a unified Community response to the issue of the MNE notwithstanding member opposition. In effect, the Commission's bid to further the Community's integrating objectives sought to utilize agreement in these international groups as a lever to force member discipline in support of regional integration. While ultimately unsuccessful, the Commission's continued use of international agreements to support internal program changes for the Community remains important to any assessment of the future direction of EC activity in the area of MNE policy.

Although this interpretation of the Commission's use of international agreements to pursue regional integration might appear forced, there is ample evidence to support this conclusion. The starting point in the evidence is the generally neglected 1973 proposal entitled *Multinational Undertakings and Community Regulation.* Drafted and supported by the then Industrial Commissioner Altiero Spinelli, the proposal outlined the reasons why member control over the activities of the MNE was incapable of addressing the issues posed by this transnational corporate actor. Spinelli's well-known views on the need for a united Europe were translated by this document into a blueprint for Community control over vast sectors of member industrial policy and planning.[66] Integral to that blueprint was the parallel development of measures at the OECD level designed to reach the issues of corporate mobility and legal responsibility that strictly Community regulations could not touch.

The Commission's 1973 proposal stated explicitly that the parallel acceptance of binding measures at both EC and OECD level was the only way in which the Community proposals would be capable of controlling intraregional MNE activities:

> It is quite obvious that the activities of the Community will be fully effective only to the extent that identically inspired rules are imposed at world level with a view to ensuring a homogeneous framework for the operations of multinational undertakings whatever their origin and their geographical field of activity.[67]

The Commission's 1973 regulatory proposals and those finally passed within the OECD's 1976 Code of Conduct for International Firms are in fact identical in their scope and focus.[68] It is this regulatory system, first accepted in 1976 and reaffirmed in 1979, that now forms the basis for the international measures directed at the activities of the MNE throughout the membership of the OECD and the EC.[69]

Acceptance of this binding regulatory code at the OECD level would have produced two immediate outcomes for Commission planners. First, with an identical regulatory system in place covering both the OECD and the EC membership, the specific MNE issues of procurement reciprocity, legal responsibility, and corporate mobility would be solved. Second, and more important for the Commission's objectives, the increased competition afforded to EC firms by this newly opened market situation would have generated internal Community support for increased unification in export, public contract, and other industrial reorganization measures sponsored by the Commission. The Commission's efforts to pursue internal industrial reforms in line with the objectives of regional integration would thus have been augmented by these efforts undertaken at the international level.

It was the inability of the OECD to accept a binding regulatory system that ultimately forced the Commission to revise its own internal measures in the area of MNE policy. Partially due to the pressure brought on the US administration by American defense contractors to maintain their preferred domestic position for public contracts, the OECD membership accepted a regulatory code with voluntary rather than binding measures.[70] While there is substantial evidence to suggest that compliance with even these voluntary measures has been quite successful, the change undercut the Commission's ability to use this new system to force Community members to adopt a more European view of the issues.[71] Without the leverage afforded by a binding OECD regulatory system, Commission staffers found that they had to increasingly accommodate themselves to the desire on the part of their membership to become directly involved with work at the international level. It is this reason that ultimately explains the Commission's switch from unification to harmonization in their objectives for the issue of MNE regulatory policy.

The future for Community initiatives in the area of MNE policy will be based on this relationship between internal harmonization proposals and work conducted at the international level. Because harmonization proposals do not threaten member control and authority, there is great optimism about the Commission's ability to implement MNE-related measures based on joint EC-member responsibility. At the same time, agreement at the international level continues to look promising, given the vagaries of the global system and the need for new regulatory measures throughout the vital economic policy sector. Finally, the Community has begun to assert itself on selected international issues in keeping with its perceived position as a major global actor. Given the extensive foundation already in place, it is more than likely that major agreements at the international level will continue to be in the general area of economic and MNE-related issues. One can suggest persuasively that the reason why the Community will be able to take an active part in such work is due to the revamping of its own internal policy goals away from the objectives of regional political integration.

Ironically, the future role of the Community in international economic affairs appears promising, due in large measure to this inability to achieve the goal of "political unification by 1980."

NOTES

1. Mira Wilkins, *The Emergence of the Multinational Enterprise* (Cambridge, Mass.: Harvard University Press, 1970).

2. Lawrence Franko, *The European MNs* (London: Harper and Row, 1976).

3. Wilkins, *Emergence of the Multinational Enterprise*, p. 11.

4. OECD, Report of the Committee of Experts on Restrictive Business Practices, *Restrictive Business Practices of Multinational Enterprises* (1977), p. 7.

5. N. Clark, "MN Corporations-Transfer of Technology and Dependence," *Development and Change* 6 (Fall 1975): 5-21.

6. U.S. Congress, House Committee on International Relations, *The Multinationals: The View From Europe*, pursuant to H.R. 315, 94th Congress, 1st session (1975), pp. 69-72.

7. *EC Bulletin* (October 1972), pp. 9-26.

8. *EC Bulletin*, Report by Leo Tindemans to the European Council, January 1976 (Brussels: EC Bulletin Supplement 1/1976).

9. EC Commission, *Multinational Undertakings and Community Regulation*, 8 November 1973 (Brussels: EC Bulletin Supplement 15/73).

10. Ibid., p. 13.

11. EC Commission, *Lavori Della CCE Che Possono Riguardare Le Societa Multinazionali*, 17 Gennaio 1977 (Brussels: III/164/77-I), pp. 1-44.

12. EC Commission, *Proposal for a Seventh Directive Concerning Group Accounts*, 4 May 1976 (Brussels: EC Bulletin Supplement 7/32).

13. Ibid., p. 19.

14. *Treaty of Rome*, Articles 85 and 86.

15. EC Commission, *Proposition d'un Statut des Sociétés Anonymes Européennes* (Brussels: EC Bulletin Supplement 8/1970); revised: EC Commission, *Statute for European Companies*, submitted to the Council of Ministers April 1975 (Brussels: EC Bulletin Supplement 4/75).

16. Interview, Mr. Kirschner, Staff, *Directorate for Approximation of Laws, Right of Establishment and Services*, EC Commission, 27 March 1979, Brussels, Belgium.

17. *Treaty of Rome*, Articles 12-37.

18. Kenneth Dam, "The European Common Market in Agriculture," *Columbia Law Review* 67 (1967): 209.

19. *Treaty of Rome*, Articles 113 (1) and 114.

20. European Parliament Working Document, *Report on the Harmonization of Export Aid Systems*, 8 June 1977, Doc. 129-77, PE 47.346/fin., pp. 7-11.

21. EC Commission, *Report on Irish Economic Law*, vol. 7 (Brussels: Approximation of Legislation Series, 1977-20), pp. 17-33.

22. *Export Import Bank Act of 1945*, 12 U.S.C. Section 635-635n (1970).

23. European Parliament Working Document, *Report on the Proposal for a Regulation Setting up a European Export Bank*, 4 May 1977, Doc. 66/77, PE 42.970/fin., pp. 45-46.
24. European Parliament Working Document, *Report on the Harmonization of Export Aid Systems*.
25. Reply to question No. 811/75, *Official Journal*, No. C99, 3 May 1976, p. 37.
26. "Export Credits: One for All, or Each for Himself," *The Economist*, 5 February 1977, p. 61.
27. European Parliament Working Document, *Report on the Harmonization of Export Aid Systems*, p. 10.
28. *EC Bulletin*, November 1975, pp. 88-90; "Strains in the Alliance," *Newsweek*, 27 July 1981, pp. 14-17.
29. *European Community*, March 1971, pp. 12-15.
30. EC Commission, *12th General Report on the Activities of the European Communities 1978* (Brussels: Commission Reports, February 1979), pp. 69-76.
31. European Parliament Working Document, *Report on the Proposal for a Regulation Setting up a European Export Bank*.
32. "Protocol on the Statute of the European Investment Bank," in Eric Stein, Peter Hay, and Michel Waelbroeck, eds., *Documents for European Community Law and Institutions in Perspective* (New York: Bobbs-Merrill, Inc., 1976), pp. 92-99.
33. European Parliament Working Document, *Report on the Proposal for a Regulation Setting up a European Export Bank*, pp. 38-39.
34. *Debates of the European Parliament*, 12 September 1978, p. 110.
35. *EC Bulletin*, September 1972, pp. 77-84, points 66-67.
36. EC Commission, *Economic Law of the Member States of the European Communities in an Economic and Monetary Union*, no. 20 (Brussels: Competition-Approximation of Legislation Series, 1973), pp. 39-41.
37. R. Toulemon, "Stage Reached in Work on Industrial Policy in the Community," *Venice Conference Proceedings*, Venice, Italy, (April 1972), pp. 22-24.
38. *EC Bulletin*, May 1971, p. 45.
39. 41 U.S.C., Sections 10a-10c (1976).
40. *EC Bulletin*, December 1976, pp. 22-23, points 1401-1405.
41. *General Agreement on Tariffs and Trade*, October 30, 1947, Treaties and other International Acts Series. No. 1700, 55 United Nations Treaty Series, 187.
42. General Accounting Office, *Governmental Buy-National Practices of the United States and other Countries – An Assessment*, 7 (1976).
43. US Congress, House, *Agreements Reached in the Toyko Round of the Multilateral Trade Negotiations pursuant to H.R. 153*, 96th Congress, 1st Session, 1979.
44. "Can Europe Agree to Show America How?," *The Economist*, 3 August 1974, pp. 32-33.
45. "US Airlines Ahead in Productivity," *The Times* (London), 30 March 1977, p. 23.
46. EC Commission, *Action Programme for the European Aeronautical Sector*, 3 October 1975 (Brussels: EC Bulletin Supplement 11/1975), p. 21.
47. Ibid., p. 133.
48. Ibid., p. 11.
49. "Come Fly With Me," *The Economist*, 3 June 1978, p. 60.

50. "McDonnell Fokker in Plane Pact," *The New York Times*, 5 May 1981, p. D1.

51. EC Commission, *A Four Year Programme for the Development of Informatics in the Community*, COM (76) 524 final, 29 October 1976 (Brussels: EC Commission), vol. I, p. 13.

52. European Parliament Working Documents, *Report from the Commission to the Council on a Community Policy on Data Processing*, 2 July 1974, Doc. 153/74, PE. 36.983/fin., pp. 8-10.

53. EC Commission, *6th Report on Competition Policy 1976* (Brussels: Commission Reports, April 1977, pp. 121-122.

54. *3rd Data Processing Programme of the Federal Government* (West Germany), 1976-1979.

55. European Parliament Working Document, *Report from the Commission to the Council on a Community Policy on Data Processing*, pp. 1-32.

56. Ibid., p. 5.

57. Ibid., p. 29.

58. Ibid., pp. 8-10.

59. *Official Journal* of the European Communities, "Council Resolution on a Community Policy on Data Processing," no. C 86/1, 20 July 1974.

60. Ibid.

61. *Official Journal* of the European Communities, no. L 223/11, 16 August 1976.

62. European Parliament Working Document, *Report on the Communication from the Commission to the Council (Doc. 21/75) Containing Initial Proposals for Priority Projects in Data Processing*, 31 August 1975, Doc. 199-75, PE 40.502/fin. pp. 25-28.

63. *Informatics Study*, vol. III, p. 127.

64. "Babel Still Rules," *The Economist*, 6 August 1977, p. 44.

65. Ernst Haas, *The Obsolescence of Regional Integration Theory* (Berkeley: Institute of International Studies, University of California, 1975).

66. "Unite and Rule," *Forum: Council of Europe*, February 1980, p. 10.

67. EC Commission, *Multinational Undertakings and Community Regulations*, p. 8.

68. Activities of the OECD in 1976, Report of the Secretary-General, *Declaration of International Investment and Multinational Enterprises*, 21 June 1976, Annex A, pp. 97-107.

69. OECD, International Investment and Multinational Enterprises, *Review of the 1976 Declaration and Decisions*, 1979.

70. *Debates of the European Parliament*, 19 April 1977, pp. 28-53.

71. OECD, International Investment and Multinational Enterprises, *Review of the 1976 Declaration and Decisions*, p. 40, point 77.

Harmen Lehment 8

THE EUROPEAN MONETARY SYSTEM

THE ROAD TO THE EUROPEAN MONETARY SYSTEM

When the Bretton Woods system of "fixed but adjustable" parities finally collapsed in March 1973,[1] a number of European countries (Belgium, Denmark, France, Germany, Luxembourg, the Netherlands, Norway, and Sweden) decided on a joint floating of their currencies. The exchange rates of their currencies remained fixed against each other (with the possibility of discretionary parity changes), but were free to vary against third currencies. Since the exchange rate of these currencies moved closely together, showing a snake-type picture in exchange-rate diagrams, the floating bloc also became famous as the "snake."

During the life of the "snake" several adjustments in central rates were made. The German mark (DM) was revalued several times, whereas the Scandinavian countries were subject to a number of devaluations. Moreover, there were changes in membership: France left the "snake" in January 1974, returned in July 1975, and left again in March 1976; Sweden left in August 1977 and Norway followed in December 1978, shortly before the "snake" was replaced by the European Monetary System (EMS).

In order to understand the political and economic motives that led to this replacement, it is helpful to take a brief look at the development of exchange rates vis-à-vis the currencies that did not belong to the "snake." In respect to the currencies of countries which were members of the European Community (EC) but not of the snake, sharp exchange-rate changes had taken place in 1976 when the Italian lira and the pound sterling depreciated against the snake-currencies by more than 30 percent. A similar although less strong devaluation was recorded for the French franc after its second departure from the snake. All three currencies, however, recovered substantially in the subsequent period. In 1978 exchange-rate changes between these currencies and the snake currencies were relatively moderate, thus providing no urgent reason for a reform of the monetary system, although the idea to prevent similar exchange-rate developments among EC currencies as those of 1976 may have been conducive to the introduction of the EMS. It was, however, not the main reason.

The decisive event for the creation of the EMS was the so-called dollar crisis that started in autumn 1977. The substantial depreciation of the dollar and a weakening confidence in the ability of the Carter administration to protect the internal and external value of the US currency caused the political heads of France and Germany, Giscard and Schmidt, to start an initiative for a European "zone of exchange-rate stability." An additional French consideration was that France, as a leading EC country, should also be a member of the exchange-rate arrangement that already existed between several EC currencies. Since the French membership in the "snake" had been dissolved two times, a new system—offering more favorable conditions for a French participation than the snake—was regarded as a promising new chance.

One driving force behind the German initiative for the EMS has been the intent to dampen the revaluation pressure on the DM.[2] This pressure resulted from the dollar crisis and was seen as a threat for the competitive position of German producers. With an EC-wide exchange-rate system, it was hoped, international portfolio diversification away from dollar assets would no longer have its predominant counterpart in an additional demand for DM-assets, but would be spread more evenly over the European countries;[3] some officials even argued that the EMS might help to strengthen the dollar.[4] A second consideration was that the EMS might have a disciplinary effect on European countries with a relatively high inflation rate and, hence, prevent a repetition of the 1976 experience when an overly expansionary policy in some countries led to sharp exchange-rate changes within the European Community.

A common motive for the initiative may also have been that the EMS was regarded as a step toward a currency union in the EC area, the final stage being "one money for Europe." The plan for a European currency union had originally been launched by the later prime minister of France, Raymond Barre, in 1968 when he was vice-president of the EC Commission. In December 1969 the heads of state and government of the EC member countries formally proclaimed an Economic and Monetary Union as a long-run aim of the Community. Several reasons were given for this initiative:[5] First, the common market had been completed so that the Community was looking for new integration targets. Second, the parity changes of the French franc and the DM in 1969 had led to substantial problems for the common agricultural policy; the EC governments, therefore, were looking for a system which would prevent further parity changes. Third, the problem of the "dollar-overhang" and the resulting need for a devaluation of the US dollar became more and more visible; a common exchange-rate policy of the EC countries was regarded as necessary in order to support parity changes vis-à-vis the dollar.

In October 1970 a study group headed by the Luxembourg prime minister, Pierre Werner, presented a report containing suggestions for further steps toward a currency union. The group recommended (1) to gradually "freeze" the exchange rates among the member countries; (2) to establish a European fund for Monetary Cooperation; (3) to centralize monetary policy; and (4) to introduce – at the final stage – a common currency. Apart from these suggestions, the report included several (although rather vague) suggestions for a harmonization of fiscal policy, for cooperation in respect to regional and structural policy, for the liberalization of intra-European capital movements, and for institutional reforms.

Of the four steps toward currency union that had been envisaged by the so-called Werner plan, only one – the introduction of the European Fund for Monetary Cooperation – was reflected in the decision that led to the joint float of the European currencies in Spring 1973. The "snake" system did not freeze exchange rates; on the contrary, central rates among member currencies were changed frequently. Moreover, there was no attempt to centralize monetary policy or to even introduce a common currency. Some observers regarded the introduction of the EMS as a new chance proceeding toward a European Currency Union along the lines of the Werner plan although currency unification did not appear as a target in the official documents.

The outline of the EMS was presented and discussed at the meeting of the European Council of Heads of State or Government in Bremen on 6 and 7 July 1978. After some revisions and supplements, the main lines of the system were adopted by the European Council at its meeting in Brussels on 4 and 5 December 1978. The system was formally introduced on 13 March 1979.

THE MAIN ELEMENTS OF THE EMS

There are three main elements of the EMS: (1) an adjustable peg system for most EC currencies; (2) an extension of credit facilities through the European Monetary Cooperation Fund (EMCF); and (3) the introduction of a European Currency Unit (ECU).[6]

The first main element of the EMS is the introduction of an adjustable peg system for all EC currencies with the exception of the United Kingdom. The UK did not join the exchange-rate arrangement and continues with an independent floating of its currency. Greece, which only joined the EC in January 1981, is also not a participant in the exchange-rate arrangement. Exchange rates in the EMS are not completely fixed, but are allowed to fluctuate around a margin of 2.25 percent on both sides of the central rate; for Italy the respective margin is 6 percent in order to account for the fact that the relatively high Italian inflation rate tends to require more exchange-rate flexibility. The central rates are determined on a bilateral basis against each of the currencies. The matrix showing the value of the currencies in terms of the other currencies has become popular under the name of the "parity grid." The central rates are not irreversibly fixed, but can be changed if all member countries agree.

The second main element is the extension of credit facilities provided by the European Monetary Cooperation Fund (EMCF). The role of this Fund, which also existed under the "snake" arrangement, is to give credit assistance to central banks whose currency faces devaluation pressure in the EMS. The financial means of the EMCF amounts to 20 percent of the member countries' gold and gross dollar reserves which the Fund receives from the national central banks on the basis of revolving swaps: that is, the currency reserves are given to the EMCF on the basis of a quasi credit, the final control over the currency reserves remaining with the national member states.

The Bremen plan and the Brussels agreement also envisaged the setup of a European Monetary Fund (EMF) after two years as a replacement of the EMCF. The intention was to supplement the financial means of the EMF by transferring national currencies of an amount similar to that of the gold and dollar transfer. The second stage, however, which would have been due to start in March 1981, was postponed to an indefinite date. A main reason was that the transfer of national currencies to a European Fund was seen as a threat to the control of the domestic money stock in the various member countries.

The third main element is the introduction of a European Currency Unit (ECU). The ECU is defined as a basket of the national member countries and is in this respect not new. Before the establishment of the EMS there existed a European Unit of Account (EUA) which served as a basis for payments in the EC and which represented exactly the same currency basket as the ECU. The composition of the basket is as follows: 0.828 German marks, 0.0885 pound sterling, 1.15 French francs, 109 Italian lire, 0.286 Dutch guilder, 3.66 Belgian francs, 0.14 Luxembourg francs, 0.217 Danish krone, and 0.00759 Irish pound.

The functions of the ECU are the following: (1) a denominator for the exchange-rate mechanism and for operations in both the intervention and the credit mechanism—for example, if a member country receives an assistance credit, the volume of this credit is expressed in terms of ECU; (2) a means of settlement between monetary authorities of the EC—for example, a central bank can repay part of its liabilities against other central banks by transferring ECUs which it received as the counterpart of the deposit of gold and dollar reserves at the EMCF; the ECU is, therefore, practically a claim to gold and dollar reserves held by the EMCF; and (3) the basis of the so-called divergence indicator which has been constructed to detect potential future tensions between member currencies.

As a side point it may be interesting to note that ECU was the name of a medieval French coin—a fact that made the name of the new currency unit quite popular, especially, of course, in France. Apart from these main elements, the Brussels resolution provided for the potential participation of non-EC countries in the EMS and the coordination of exchange-rate policies vis-à-vis third countries.

TECHNICAL PROBLEMS OF THE EMS: THE DIVERGENCE INDICATOR—A MISCONSTRUCTION

The EMS was received with substantial criticism in both "weak currency" and "strong currency" countries. The criticism was directed both at the technical aspects and the economic consequences of the system. The main technical flaw of the system was seen in the failure of the divergence indicator to serve as a reliable signal for future tensions in the system.

The divergence indicator is the result of a compromise between those EC governments (Germany, Benelux) which favored a determination of central rates on a bilateral basis and the governments (France, Italy) which had suggested to fix central rates in terms of the ECU. The compromise was such that central rates were set on a bilateral basis, but that exchange rates vis-à-vis the ECU were introduced as an indicator for tensions in the system. A currency reaches its divergence threshold when its value against the central ECU rate changes by three-quarters of 2.25 percent, multiplied with the share of the other currencies in the basket in order to adjust for the different weights of national currencies. Without this adjustment, currencies with a large weight in the basket would be less likely to reach the threshold than currencies with a small weight: when the share in the basket is 30 percent, an appreciation against all the other member currencies by 3 percent raises the ECU values by $0.70 \times 3 = 2.1$ percent; when the share is 10 percent the respective change will be $0.90 \times 3 = 2.7$ percent.

The proponents of this indicator argued that as a general rule the divergence threshold is reached before bilateral limits are reached. It is relatively easy to show, however, that there are cases when the divergence indicator will fail to flash.[7] Consider the following example: bilateral intervention points between the Dutch and the Belgian currencies are reached if the Dutch guilder appreciates against a third currency by 1.125 and if the Belgian franc depreciates by the same amount so that the bilateral change amounts to 2.25 percent. Since the value of the ECU is hardly altered by these exchange-rate changes (both currencies have about the same weight in the basket so that the appreciation of the guilder balances the effect of the franc depreciation on the value of the ECU), the change in ECU exchange rates of the two currencies amounts to about 1.125 percent in the positive and the negative direction respectively. This is less than the change of about 1.50 which would be necessary to reach the divergence threshold. Thus, bilateral intervention points can be reached before the divergence threshold is reached. As a matter of fact, this case has occured several times in the EMS: the Danish krone and the German mark reached their bilateral limits in 1979 without being close to their thresholds.

But even when the divergence indicator works—when the threshold is reached before the bilateral points are reached—the policy reaction is indeterminate. The authorities concerned can choose from a large menu of measures listed in the Brussels agreement: (a) diversified intervention; (b) measures of domestic monetary policy; (c) changes in central rates; (d) other measures of economic policy; (e) do nothing, but explain to the other authorities why nothing is done. Since the divergence indicator cannot trigger any specific policy measures, it may be regarded as a superfluous construction.[8] It may be interesting to note that neither the Danish nor the Belgian authorities reacted when their currencies reached the thresholds in 1979: the krone stood below its threshold for four weeks, the Belgian franc for more than three months.

ECONOMIC PROBLEMS OF THE EMS

The EMS has several economic problems: a conflict between internal and external stability; its credit facilities are a potential source of inflation; the discipline argument is weak; there are costs of discretionary exchange rate adjustments; and the ECU is not a vehicle for European currency unification.

Conflicts between exchange-rate stability and internal stability have been the main reason for the collapse of the Bretton Woods system.[9] Several critics argued that similar conflicts would be likely to arise in the EMS. As an illustration for the potential conflicts in the adjustable peg system of the EMS, one may consider the experience in the "snake," and especially that of France when it left the system for the second time in March 1976. In February 1976 the French franc fell to its lower intervention point—mainly as a result of a relatively expansionary monetary policy. In such a case there are usually three options to defend the exchange rate.

The first option is that the Bank of France switches to a restrictive monetary policy. A restrictive open-market policy—reducing the supply of French francs—would tend to raise French interest rates and support the exchange rate of the franc in currency markets. The French authorities, however, were not willing to pursue such a policy because they held the view that this measure would lead to a stabilization crisis and an increase of unemployment in France. The second option is a more expansionary monetary policy by the other "snake" members in order to prevent a further rise in the value of their currencies vis-à-vis the franc. The authorities of these countries, however, resisted such a policy on the grounds that it would lead to a rekindling of inflation. The third option consists of a combination of monetary restriction in France and monetary expansion in the other countries. These exchange market interventions would simultaneously reduce the supply of francs and increase the supply of other currencies. Interventions to support the franc were substantial in February/March 1976. But it became clear after a short time that this policy could not be continued, since France resisted a further reduction of its money supply through interventions while the other countries, likewise, were not willing to accept a lasting additional expansion of their money supplies.

The only choice remaining was, therefore, between devaluation of the franc or a withdrawal of the French currency from the exchange-rate arrangement. In March 1976 the French government decided for the latter alternative. This example shows that fixed exchange rates imply a fundamental dilemma for the monetary authorities: since the exchange rate is the relative price of two currencies, central banks can influence the exchange rate by raising or reducing the amount of currency in circulation. These respective measures, however, have also an expansionary or restrictive impact on domestic demand for goods and services. If these changes in demand are undesired because they lead to more inflation or additional unemployment, the central bank has no choice other than to sacrifice either the exchange-rate target or the internal target.

The basic question for each system of fixed exchange rates and, hence, also for the EMS is: which of the countries shall adjust its money supply in order to defend the rates of the system? If the "weak currency" countries adjust, the result may be a stabilization crisis in these countries; if the "strong currency" countries adjust, the result tends to be a higher inflation rate. While EMS critics from high-inflation countries were especially concerned about the possible negative employment effects of the system, critics from low-inflation countries expressed their concern about the inflationary dangers of the system. The main reason for this concern was seen in the construction of the system of credit facilities in the EMS.

The credit facilities in the EMS are considerably larger than those in the "snake." The central argument for the extension of financial means was the intent to strengthen the position of central banks in their defense of exchange rates. The conviction, however, that a larger volume of credit facilities will improve the performance of the EMS as compared to the snake rests on a fundamental misunderstanding. The previous discussion of the French withdrawal from the "snake" has shown that a system of fixed exchange rates does not run into problems because the member countries *cannot* defend the exchange rates, but because governments *are not willing* to defend exchange rates.[10] They are unwilling because the required measures would run counter to domestic policy targets. An extension of credit facilities, however, does not remove this conflict.

The inflationary threats of the credit facilities can be illustrated by the following example. Suppose that the Italian lira comes under pressure against a strong currency such as the DM. To defend the lira the Italian authorities can apply for financial assistance. If the assistance is paid in DM and used for interventions in the exchange market, the German money supply tends to increase; this increase will not automatically be reversed if the Italian authorities repay the credit, since settlement may be effected by transferring dollars or ECUs. If the increase in the German money supply which results from the operation of the Italian authorities is not desired by the German central bank, the German authorities may try to neutralize the increase by, say, a restrictive open market policy. Such measures to reduce the DM supply, however, also tend to strengthen the position of the DM vis-à-vis the lira in the exchange market, thus producing a situation of counteracting exchange-rate policies: the interventions of the Italian authorities support the lira, while the neutralizing operations by the German authorities tend to weaken the lira. In such circumstances, the German central bank may come under substantial pressure to stop the neutralizing operations; if it yields to this pressure, the likely result will be more inflation in Germany.

Some proponents of the EMS argued that the new monetary system would have a stabilizing impact on prices in member countries with a relatively high inflation rate. The argument was based on the experience in the "snake," where the smaller member countries had pursued a relatively restrictive monetary policy which led to a reduction of inflation rates in the years 1976-78. Inflation rates, however, were also reduced substantially during this period in countries such as Italy and the United Kingdom which had not been members of the "snake." Thus, a successful stabilization policy does not necessarily require the disciplinary effects of a fixed exchange-rate system. Moreover, the experience of the Bretton Woods system and the snake raises severe doubts about the effectiveness of such disciplinary elements. Governments can hardly be forced anymore by an exchange-rate system to pursue a policy which they regard as overly restrictive. In contrast to the 1950s and 1960s, a country can now sidestep the disciplinary effects of the system quite easily by devaluing its currency without raising a storm of international protest.

The disciplinary force of the EMS is also weakened by the creation of large credit facilities. If a country pursues a relatively expansionary monetary policy, which causes pressure on the exchange rate of its currency, it has access to assistance credits which permit it to postpone the return to a stable policy. An additional problem results from the fact that the interest rate on assistance credits in the EMS is below the market rate, so that an overly expansionary policy is even "rewarded" by favorable lending conditions. The experience of previous adjustable peg systems also casts substantial doubts on the conviction that the EMS will prove to be successful because of the political prestige involved—especially on the part of the German and French governments who were the proponents of the system. Exchange-rate policy certainly holds a top position when it comes to list the areas where political prestige in the past has suffered most. One may recall the official denials of exchange-rate changes in the Bretton Woods era shortly before they actually took place, or the common belief that the return of France to the "snake" in 1975 involved so much prestige that a second leave would be impossible—it occured only a few months later.

The information and adjustment costs resulting from discretionary changes of central rates in an adjustable peg system are probably larger than the costs resulting from automatic exchange-rate changes in a system of flexible rates. Thus, under the Bretton Woods system parity adjustments were often delayed and caused distortions in the international production structure. The prolonged undervaluation of the DM in the late 1960s which caused an overexpansion of industrial capacity in Germany, may be mentioned as one example.[11] Moreover, discretionary exchange rate changes may give rise to large speculative attacks. If private agents expect a revision of parities—say, a devaluation—they will immediately sell this currency in the exchange market where central banks have to buy it in order to defend the old parity. When the parity change has occured, the private agents can repurchase the currency and thereby avoiding a loss from devaluation which is, instead borne by the monetary authorities whose assets are depreciated by the parity adjustment.

Compared to the "snake," the EMS provides less favorable conditions for a further step toward a currency union. The main reason is that the EMS comprises both a larger and a less homogeneous group of countries.[12] Attempts to narrow the margins for exchange-rate fluctuations among member currencies, while considered as a future task in the Brussels agreement, will be more difficult to realize than in the "snake" where national inflation rates of the remaining member countries (Germany, Benelux, and Denmark) did not differ as widely as inflation rates in the EMS. A centralization of monetary policy and the introduction of a common currency, two central elements of the Werner plan, are not even mentioned in the EMS agreement.

The ECU might be regarded as conducive to European currency unification if it represented an attractive parallel currency which could displace national member currencies in a competitive process.[13] In its present form, however, the ECU is no currency of its own but—similar to the Special Drawing Rights (SDR) issued by the International Monetary Fund—only a basket of various existing currencies. Since such a basket contains also currencies with relatively high rates of inflation (for example, the lira) it is less stable in value than the least-inflation currency in the basket (for example, the DM). Since the ECU is less attractive than other currencies, it is therefore most likely that the ECU will not be able to outcompete the existing currencies and thus share the fate of other basket currencies such as the SDRs.[14]

THE RECENT EXPERIENCE WITH THE EMS

The main task of the EMS has been to provide a zone of monetary stability: less frequent and relatively small exchange-rate changes among the member currencies and a convergence of inflation rates at a low level. If one applies these criteria as a basis for an evaluation of the performance of the EMS in its first two years, one finds that exchange-rate adjustments have been quite moderate. There have been only three realignments of the central rates: (1) in September 1979 the DM was revalued against the other EMS currencies by 2 percent; at the same occasion the Danish krone was devalued by 3 percent vis-à-vis the other currencies; (2) in November 1979 the Danish krone was devalued again, this time by 4.76 percent; and (3) in March 1981 the Italian lira was devalued by 6 percent.

The first realignment already made it clear that exchange-rate adjustments in the EMS is subject to similar problems as in the "snake" or the Bretton Woods system. The first realignment only came about after massive exchange market interventions of several central banks.[15] The decision about the new central rates turned out to be a major political problem. As in the previous adjustable peg systems, a revaluation or devaluation was considered as a matter of political prestige. Politicians of weak-currency countries were eager to avoid a devaluation of their currency and apparently preferred an appreciation on part of the other countries, although from an economic point of view a devaluation of say, 5 percent of country A's currency vis-à-vis country B's currency is the same as 5 percent appreciation of B's currency against A's currency.

A second problem is that some countries have made the attempt to support their exchange rates through capital controls and even trade restrictions against other EC countries, as Italy did in 1981. In the light of these developments, it cannot be excluded that the European Monetary system, rather than being a vehicle for a closer European integration, leads to disintegration by destroying the main achievement of the European Community: free trade among its member countries.

With regard to inflation rates, there has been no convergence. The maximum difference among the inflation rates in the EMS countries, which had been at 9.5 percent at the end of 1978, increased to 15.4 percent in April 1981. The increase of inflation rates and inflation differentials has, however, mainly been due to the monetary expansion in 1978 and cannot be regarded as a result of the EMS. As can be seen from the last column in Table 8.1, monetary expansion measured in terms of M1 has slowed down substantially during the last two years; the differences in the growth rate of M1 are also smaller than before the introduction of the EMS, although the maximum difference of 14.6 percent (between Italy and Belgium) is still very large.

The fears that the EMS might prevent a restrictive monetary policy in the member countries with a low inflation rate has—at least so far—not materialized. It should, however, also be noted that the recent reduction of monetary expansion rates can hardly be attributed to the EMS. Thus, a strong monetary deceleration has also occured in the United Kingdom, which does not participate in the exchange rate system of the EMS. Moreover, a restrictive monetary policy is a normal reaction of central banks to a rise in inflation and can also be observed in a system of flexible exchange rates. The change of nominal exchange rates largely reflects the parity changes in the EMS. The DM has appreciated against the other EMS currencies, but has depreciated against the pound sterling which does not participate in the exchange-rate arrangement.

Looking at the development of real exchange rates (changes in nominal exchange rates adjusted for inflation differentials on the basis of consumer prices) one finds, as shown in Table 8.2, that the DM shows a slight revaluation vis-à-vis the Belgian, Danish, and Dutch currencies. On the other hand, the nominal revaluation of the DM against the French, Irish, and Italian currencies has been much smaller than the inflation differential so that there has been a substantial real depreciation of the DM vis-à-vis these currencies by 15.7 percent, 30.8 percent, and 29.7 percent, respectively. This means that the competitive position of the French, Irish, and Italian industry has become worse in recent years. Such a result applies even more for the United Kingdom, which shows a real appreciation against the DM by more than 50 percent since the end of 1978.

To summarize, the exchange-rate adjustments in the first two years have not been sufficient to offset the inflation differentials in the member countries. This especially holds for the exchange rate for the French franc, the Irish pound, and the Italian lira. This indicates that a substantial need for exchange-rate adjustment has built up, which tends to become stronger over time since the inflation rates in these countries continue to stay fairly above the Community average. One can therefore expect that future exchange-rate realignments have to be stronger than those which could be observed in

TABLE 8.1

DEVELOPMENT OF PRICES AND MONEY SUPPLY IN THE EC

COUNTRY	12-month rate of change of consumer prices		12-month rate of change of money supply (M1)	
	December 1978	April 1981	December 1978	April 1981
Belgium	3.9	7.4	6.9	0.3[a]
Denmark	7.1	8.9	15.9	9.4
France	9.7	12.7	11.1	8.2
Germany	2.4	5.6	14.3	1.6
Ireland	7.9	21.0	24.8	12.9[a]
Italy	11.9	19.8	26.0	14.9
Netherlands	3.9	6.2	4.7	5.5
United Kingdom	8.4	12.3	15.2	8.1
maximum difference	9.5	15.4	21.3	14.6

[a] = December 1980

Source: OECD, Main Economic Indicators (Paris), various issues.

TABLE 8.2

CHANGES IN THE EXTERNAL VALUE OF THE D-MARK VIS-A-VIS OTHER EC-CURRENCIES FROM DECEMBER 1978 TO APRIL 1981

Currency	nominal changes (%)	real changes[a] (%)
Belg. Franc	+ 3.3	+ 2.0
Dan. Kroner	+ 12.9	+ 4.1
French Franc	+ 2.9	- 15.7
Irish Pound	+ 3.0	- 30.8
Ital. Lira	+ 11.3	- 29.7
Dutch Guilder	+ 2.4	+ 1.4
Pound Sterling	- 26.0	- 55.6

[a] = Calculated on base of consumer prices

Source: OECD, Main Economic Indicators (Paris), various issues. Deutsche Bundesbank, Monatsberichte (Frankfurt/Main), various issues.

the first two years. The question, therefore, is: Can the EMS react to the increased exchange-rate pressure with sufficient flexibility? Or will it share the fate of its predecessors: the Bretton Woods system (which finally had collapsed) and the "snake" (where countries with a relatively high rate of inflation left the exchange rate arrangement)? The real test is still to come.

NOTES

1. For a detailed analysis of the causes that led to the breakdown of the Bretton Woods system, see Charles A. Coombs, *The Arena of International Finance* (New York: Wiley, 1976); Otman Emminger, *The D-Mark in the Conflict Between Internal and External Equilibrium, 1948-1975*, Essays in International Finance, No. 122 (Princeton, N.J.: Princeton University Press, 1977); and Robert Solomon, *The International Monetary System, 1945-1976: An Insider's View* (New York: Harper and Row, 1977).

2. Harmen Lehment, "Der Bremer Plan für ein Europäisches Währungssystem: Zurück nach Bretton Woods," Kieler Diskussionsbeitrage No. 59 (Kiel: Institut für Weltwirtschaft, October 1978).

3. Jacques van Ypersele, "The Future of the Monetary System," *Revue de la Banque* 45 (1981): 179-196.

4. For a divergent view, see Tripartite Group, *International Linkages and Flexible Exchange Rates* (Washington, D.C.: The Brookings Institution, 1979).

5. Roland Vaubel, "Probleme der internationale Währungspolitik and Währungsordnung," in Hans H. Glismann et al., *Weltwirtschaftslehre*, vol. 3 (Munich: dtv, 1980): 193-288.

6. Commission of the European Communities, *The European Monetary System*, European Economy no. 3 (Brussels: EC Commission, July 1979).

7. Roland Vaubel, "The Return to the New European Monetary System: Objectives, Incentives, Perspectives," in Karl Brunner and Allan Meltzer, eds., *Monetary Institutions and the Policy Process* (Amsterdam: North Holland, 1980), pp. 178-222.

8. Peter Oppenheimer, "The Economics of EMS," in J. R. Sargent, ed., *Europe and the Dollar in the World-Wide Disequilibrium* (Rockville, Md.: Alphen/Rijn, 1981), pp. 309-327. Other economists like Thygesen see the main importance of the divergence indicator in the fact that it represents an objective indicator as a trigger for policy coordination, even it it does not contain a clear rule on what the coordination should look like. See Niels Thygesen, "The Emerging European Monetary System: Precursors, First Steps and Policy Options," *Bulletin* (de la Banque Nationale de Belgique) 54 (1979): 87-125.

9. Emminger, *The D-Mark in the Conflict Between Internal and External Equilibrium, 1948-1975.*

10. Lehment, "Der Bremer Plan für ein Euröpaisches Währungssystem."

11. Klaus-Werner Schatz, *Wachstum und Strukturwandel der Westdeutschen Wirtschaft im internationalen Verbund*, Kieler Studien No. 128 (Tübingen: Mohr, 1974).

12. The importance of homogeneity as a condition for a monetary union is stressed by W. Max Cordan, *Monetary Integration*, Essays in International Finance no. 93 (Princeton, N.J.: Princeton University Press, 1972).

13. Roland Vaubel, *Strategies for Currency Unification: The Economic of Currency Competition and the Case for a European Parallel Currency*, Kieler Studien No. 156 (Tübingen: Mohr, 1978).

14. Michele Fratianni, "The European Monetary System: A Return to an Adjustable-Peg Arrangement," in Karl Brunner and Allan Meltzer, eds., *Monetary Institutions and the Policy Process* (Amsterdam: North Holland, 1980), pp. 139-172.

15. Harmen Lehment, "Die Devisenmarktinterventionen der Deutschen Bundesbank und ihre Bedeutung fur die Geldmengenentwicklung 1973-1980," in Gottfried Bombach, Bernhard Gahlen, and Alfred Ott, eds., *Zur Theorie und Politik internationaler Wirtschaftsbeziehungen* (Tübingen: Mohr, 1981), pp. 355-382.

Leon Hurwitz 9

PARTISAN IDEOLOGY OR NATIONAL INTEREST? AN ANALYSIS OF THE MEMBERS OF THE EUROPEAN PARLIAMENT

INTRODUCTION

Objectives

A milestone in the European integrative process was reached in June 1979 when approximately 112 million voters went to the polls across the nine-country European Community and elected 410 representatives (24 Greek members were added subsequently) to the first directly elected supranational Parliament in history – the European Parliament (EP). To be sure, the election of the European Parliament did not generate the same level of interest for the European publics as it did for us political scientists and voter turnout varied widely from nation to nation. The turnout ranged from a low of 33 percent in the United Kingdom (32.6 percent in Great Britain and 57 percent in Northern Ireland) to a high of 91 percent in Belgium; for the EC as a whole; 62 percent of the electorate participated.[1]

As Ronald Inglehart and Jacques-René Rabier write, this 62 percent was a respectable figure when compared to American behavior but was a rather disappointing performance for these European countries when approximately 85 percent of the electorate normally votes in national elections.

Nevertheless, these 434 representatives are from ten separate, sovereign states – each with its own culture, national identity and political values –

Sections of this essay were originally presented at the International Conference on the Centennial of Mosca's *Theory of the Ruling Class* held at Northern Illinois University in September 1981. I would like to thank Moshe Czudnowski for his comments on the earlier version and for his kind permission to reproduce certain sections.

and they have formed six major transnational party "groups" in the Parliament. Prior to 1979, the representatives were chosen by, from, and were responsible to, their respective national parliaments. The new Parliament, directly responsible to the EC's population and voter constituencies, possesses a political legitimacy that the former appointed Parliament never had. This does not by itself give the Parliament any more real effective power vis-à-vis the Commission and the Council of Ministers (its real power, in fact, is quite low—most of its "decisions" are only statements of intent without any force in Community law) but it at least strengthens the Parliament's potential to have more influence at the European level in the future.

This essay has three limited objectives: (1) to offer some comments on the general level of conflict/consensus in the European Parliament as a whole; (2) to note the degree of voting cohesiveness within each of the delegations and the transnational party groups; and (3) to identify the degree to which the members of the EP vote along partisan ideological lines compared to national interest lines. The fact that some beginnings have been made to formulate transnational party platforms across the EC and that the groupings have been established in the Parliament leads to the hypothesis that transnational party affiliation will be a stronger explanatory variable for the observed voting differences than will national identity (for example, a socialist will agree more with other socialists, regardless of country, than with fellow nationals of different parties).

The findings will allow some comments regarding possible future conflict /consensus within the Parliament, depending upon the scope of bloc-like behavior and voting similarities. Strong transnational party groups may encourage Community interest groups to use their electoral weight to bargain for changes. A more balanced representation of interests at the European level might then be secured for, until now, the most influential interest groups have been producers and employers. Cohesive parties in Parliament —at least those on the left—may be more sympathetic to trade unions and consumer and environmental groups.

Finally, the essay will permit some comments on the scope of the erosion of long-held national mind-sets by Europeans and the emergence of truly transnational attitudes. It would be significant for the future of Europe if the representatives in Parliament actually behave (vote) as *European* Socialists or Christian Democrats than as, say, Germans, Danes, or Italians. This would intimate that nationalism is breaking down and, while not necessarily decreasing levels of conflict in the short run (ideological conflict would be simply substituted for nationalism), elite consensus and cooperation appear to be more readily attainable when based upon explicit and bargainable political goals rather than when based upon the subconsciousness of national identity.

In order to place the European Parliament within the general context of the European Community, the section below presents a brief discussion of the EP's history, function, and structure.

The European Parliament[2]

The European Parliament began life in 1952 as the Common Assembly, established by the 1950 Treaty of Paris. This Treaty, better known as the European Coal and Steel Community (ECSC) Treaty, was signed by France, West Germany, Italy, Belgium, The Netherlands, and Luxembourg. The ECSC was the immediate forerunner of the Treaty of Rome which established the European Economic Community (EEC), subsequently referred to as the European Community (EC). The original Common Assembly had seventy-eight members, each chosen by, from, and responsible to, their own respective national parliament. Compared to the Council of Europe's Consultative Assembly, which was (and still is) only a forum for debate, the ECSC's Common Assembly had real, albeit limited, political responsibilities and power. This power was due to its mandate of supervising the activities of the ECSC's executive – the High Authority.

The most important power that the Common Assembly had within the ECSC was the ability to force the High Authority to resign (a vote of censure). Even though the current Parliament has the authority to force the resignation of the EC Commission, the original Assembly had a relatively greater role within the ECSC than does the EP within the EC.[3] The High Authority was responsible for most of the real decision making within the ECSC and thus, by threatening a vote of censure, the Assembly could exert some control over the High Authority. The current Parliament, by contrast, has no influence over the primary decision-making unit within the EC – it is the Council of Ministers and not the Commission who holds effective power in the EC. The Commission may be "responsible" to the Parliament but the Council of Ministers is responsible to the member state governments.

From the very first session of the original Assembly, the members did not opt to sit and operate as did most other intergovernmental organizations; that is, as national delegations. The members sat by party groups, not by country groups, and in 1953 some political groups were recognized (the Christian Democrats, the Liberals, and the Socialists).

The organizational context changed somewhat with the signing of the EEC and Euratom Treaties in 1956. Rather than having a separate parliamentary assembly for each Community – the ECSC, EEC, and Euratom – it was decided that the original Assembly would function within all three Communities. The Common Assembly was transformed into the European Parliamentary Assembly in 1957 and its membership, still chosen by the national parliaments, was enlarged to 142. The European Parliamentary

Assembly was transformed into the European Parliament in 1962 and when Britain, Denmark and Ireland joined the EC in January 1973, its membership was again increased to 198.

As noted above, the members of the EP were chosen by, from, and responsible to, their own respective national parliaments even though Article 138 of the EEC Treaty stated that the "Assembly [Parliament] shall draw up proposals for elections by direct universal suffrage in accordance with a uniform procedure in all Member States." This Article was ignored by the Council of Ministers and the member governments for twenty years. It was not until 1976 that the Council decided that direct elections should be held for the EP. An agreement on a "uniform procedure in all member states" was not reached, however, and each country established its own electoral process. There is some doubt whether such a uniform procedure can be worked out by the time of the next direct elections. The membership increased to 410 and direct elections were held in June 1979. The Parliament's membership has subsequently increased by 24 to 434 with the accession of Greece to the EC.

The European Parliament since direct elections has attempted to move out of its traditional role as a "consultative" assembly and into a position of having the ability to influence the decision-making process within the EC. There are some areas where the Council of Ministers must consult the Parliament before a decision is reached but there is absolutely no obligation or requirement that the Council accept any of the Parliament's advice. That is to say, consultation has rarely led to influence in the past. As Michael Palmer comments:

> Only too often members of the European Parliament have had the impression that the Council has hardly even bothered to open the envelope and read the text of Parliament's opinion when it arrives at the Council's mail registry before announcing a decision prepared by the Permanent Representatives and the expert Committees well in advance.[4]

It is only with certain parts of the Community budget that Parliament's opinion is binding on the Council and it has the power to reject the budget by a majority vote of the 434 members. In December 1979 Parliament rejected the Community's 1980 draft budget in its first real show of strength following direct elections—the rejection was based on the refusal of the Council to accept the admendments proposed by Parliament in the Common Agricultural Policy (CAP) and the Regional Fund sectors. The amounts of money in question were not large and an eventual compromise was reached. But Parliament made its point: it acted with (rare) determination and was able to exert some influence over the budgetary process.

The Parliament's influence over the budget should not be exaggerated or overestimated, however. The following remarks by Lord Bruce of Donington, Parliament's rapporteur on the Community accounts, illustrate that Parliament still has a long way to go before achieving effective control of the Community's budget. Lord Bruce comments that after the budget procedure has been concluded,

> the Commission and the Council proceed to do as they please. On the basis of spurious legal arguments and as a result of inertia, Parliament's admendments are almost systematically *not* implemented. Vast movements of funds within the budget knock it out of recognition as regards to budget as originally adopted. *Sums are added, subtracted and transferred with the barest Parliamentary involvement* and the sums concerned are far greater than the minute amounts over which Parliament went into battle during the original procedure. [Parliament's admendments]... *show more clearly than anything else that Parliament is left to fight for control of the petty cash while the Commission and Council are free to determine without any democratic control the use or misuse of thousands of millions of units of account.*[5]

Each member of the European Parliament receives an annual salary equal to that of a member of his or her national parliament.[6] The national governments fund this salary rather than the EC itself. There is a wide discrepancy in the salaries paid: from a low of approximately $18,800 (Ireland) and $21,000 (UK) to an approximate high of $43,000 (Germany) and $48,000 (France). This state of affairs is due to the Council's inability to agree on a single salary level for all members. The Parliament itself has begun to work out a proposal to establish such a level—most members agree that the principle of "equal pay for equal work" should also apply to themselves—but a solution has yet to be attained.

One additional problem with the parliament—and the EC as a whole—concerns the "seat" of business or, in other words, the "capital" of the EC. The present arrangements defy the logic of efficiency, moral and financial prudence but they do, however, satisfy the logic of national prestige. At present, the Council of Ministers, the Commission and the Committee of Permanent Representatives are based in Brussels (although they frequently meet in other cities); the Commission's Information Service, the Court of Justice, the Court of Auditors, the European Investment Bank, and the administrative headquarters of the Parliament are in Luxembourg; the actual sessions of the European Parliament rotate among Brussels, Luxembourg and Strasbourg.[7]

The obvious and logical conclusion is that the three main EC institutions—the Council, the Commission, and the Parliament—should be located together and share the same seat or "capital." But vested national interests make it hard to change the status quo. Belgium has a strong interest to maintain the Council and Commission, along with the 12,000 or so officials who work for the EC. The French and Luxembourg governments also wish to maintain a Community presence in Strasbourg and Luxembourg City, respectively. The situation is such that each city—Strasbourg, Luxembourg, and Brussels—has constructed new buildings for the Parliament. Each is trying to outdo the other in the availability of accommodations (and, unfortunately, on the amount of complimentary food and drink offered the members of the EP). The Council of Ministers constantly postpone the decision as to the permanent seat or capital and it appears as if the traveling road show will continue for the foreseeable future.

The inability of the European Parliament to determine for itself some basic housekeeping questions—salary, elections, place of business—only underscores its real lack of power and influence in the political decision-making process. Nonetheless, the Parliament exists, it does vote on a wide range of resolutions, its influence may increase in the future, it is an institution which may provide popular democratic control over the European Community. The following section presents a brief description of the methodology employed in analyzing the voting behavior of the members of the European Parliament.

METHODOLOGY

The accepted techniques of legislative roll-call analysis are employed to note the general level of conflict/consensus in the European Parliament as a whole as well as to note the degree to which the members of the EP vote along partisan ideological-national interest lines. Three basic procedures are employed: Riker's Coefficient of Significance, the Rice-Beyle Index of Voting Cohesion, and Rice's Index of Voting Likeness Between Groups.

Riker's Coefficient of Significance[8]

Riker's Coefficient of Significance is used for two purposes: (1) to generate some data relating to the general level of conflict/consensus in the European Parliament as a whole and (2) as a means of selecting a sample of the roll calls for additional analysis. Riker's Coefficient of Significance is an empirical index mathematically derived from the level of participation (the number of legislators present and voting on any specific roll call) and the level of conflict (the degree to which the outcome of a specific roll call is contested). The most "significant" roll call in any voting body would be where every member was present and voting with the maximum possible conflict (only one vote would separate the two sides); the least "significant" roll call would be where only a quorum voted all the same way.

Riker's Coefficient of Significance is expressed as follows:

$$v(aij) = n - qij - m + 2 + \left(\frac{n - ri + 1}{n - t + 2}\right), \text{ where}$$

aij = any possible outcome,
v(aij) = value of aij,
n = number of members of the legislature,
ri = number of voting on a roll call in which the outcome is aij,
qij = number on the losing side of aij,
m = minimum necessary for victory when ri participate, and
t = a quorum.

With the above expression, the higher the value of aij, the lower the significance; the lower the value of aij, the higher the significance. But these values also depend upon the size of the legislature and different voting bodies will have different values—the least significant outcome for the U.S. House of Representatives (325) is much different than the least significant outcome for the U.S. Senate (77); the European Parliament's least significant outcome is 309 and its most significant outcome is two. To remedy this situation—to make the measure comparable from one voting body to another and to make the measure have a common sense direction (the higher the score, the more significance; the lower the score, the less significance)—Riker introduces a second step in the calculations:

$$S = 1 - \frac{V(aij) - V(all)}{V(adg) - V(all)}, \text{ where}$$

V(aij) = the value of any specific outcome,
V(adg) = the value of the least significant outcome;
V(all) = the value of the most significant outcome;
S ranges from 0 (the least significant outcome) to 1 (the most significant outcome).

The addition of S is much better: now a high score (1) means more significance; a low score (0) means less significance. Also, the size of the voting body no longer influences the results and the S values can be compared across different voting bodies of differing numbers of members.

Riker's Coefficient of Significance has several applications,[9] but, as mentioned above, this essay makes limited use of the measure. The actual S values are employed to comment on the general level of conflict/consensus in the European Parliament as a whole and, second, an arbitrary cutoff point will be set in order to select a sample of the Parliament's roll calls for additional analysis (that is, only the "more" significant roll calls will be examined—a vote in which the outcome is 295 to 3 presents little information on the explanatory value of partisan ideology/national identity since practically everyone agrees with everyone else).

The Rice-Beyle Index of Voting Cohesion (IVC)

There are a number of studies in the literature dealing with the identification of voting blocs or groups and the measurement of such blocs' degree of cohesion behavior or voting agreement in legislative bodies.[10] But since this particular study need not identify by any methodological or empirical procedure the existence of any specific group—that the nine country delegations and that the six major transnational party groupings in the EP each constitute (or should constitute) a group is an *a priori* theoretical determination—this analysis is not required to examine the voting behavior of *all* the MEP pairs (83,845 separate pairs for each roll call). Rather, only the voting behavior of the MEP pairs found within each of the predetermined nine country groups and six transnational party groups need to be examined.

The Rice-Beyle method, as presented and amended by Arend Lijphart, is utilized to note the degree of voting cohesiveness within these different EP groups.[11] The Rice-Beyle Method, as presented by Lijphart, produces an index of voting agreement between pairs of voters by pairing every voter within each group to every other voter in the same group on every vote.[12] The basic Index of Voting Cohesion (IVC) is a result of the following expression:

$$IVC = \frac{f + \frac{1}{2} g}{t} \times 100 \text{ percent, where}$$

IVC = ranges between 0 (denoting maximum disagreement) and 100 (denoting maximum cohesion);

f = the number of votes in which each A-B pair of voters vote in an identical manner (A and B both vote pro, con, or abstain);

g = the number of votes in which each A-B pair of voters display partial cohesion (A votes pro or con, B abstains); and

t = the total number of votes in which each A-B pair participates.

Aggregated IVCs are calculated by summing the individual IVCs within each group and dividing by the number of A-B pairs: $IVC = \Sigma IVC_i / n$. For aggregated IVCs where the number of votes are not identical, $IVC = \Sigma (IVC_i \times [t_i / \Sigma t])$.

Some discussion is necessary regarding abstentions and absences in the above expression. Abstentions in the context of the European Parliament have their own particular structure and meaning and cannot simply be seen as a negative vote or be excluded from the calculations. Abstentions are in a sense "neutral" votes—neither for nor against the resolution—and abstentions are thus perceived as partial agreement and scored at one-half maximum cohesion. Present and voting members cast abstentions as a formally recorded position, and although the reasons for taking this middle ground are numerous and often contradictory, the fact remains that the recorded position is neither for nor against, and thus the assigned one-half maximum cohesion value.

Absences, as differentiated from recorded abstentions, are treated as abstentions after Russett.[13] This categorization rests upon the beliefs that such absences represent a willful and conscious decision not to participate, to remain neutral. The members of the European Parliament are not hampered or constrained by residence or registration requirements or by most of the other reasons which lower voter turnout in national elections. The job of the members is to vote, and absences cannot be seen as unavoidable misfortune. Nonvoting (absences), therefore, is seen as an abstention and is coded accordingly.

Rice's Index of Voting Likeness Between Groups (IVL)[14]

The degree of voting similarity between and among this study's various subgroups (the nine national delegations and the six major transnational party groupings) is noted by utilizing the Index of Likeness Between Groups, devised by Stuart A. Rice. The Index of Voting Likeness Between Groups (IVL) is expressed as follows:

IVL $= 100 - |A - B|$, where
A = percentage of subgroup A voting pro on resolution Z,
B = percentage of subgroup B voting pro on resolution Z,
$|A - B|$ = absolute value of $A - B$, and where IVL ranges between 0 (maximum disagreement) and 100 (maximum voting similarity).

Aggregated IVLs are calculated as $IVL = \Sigma\, IVL_i z/i$. For aggregated IVLs where the number of votes are not identical, $IVL = \Sigma\, (IVL_i z) \times i / \Sigma\, z$.

The temporal scope of this paper is from July 1979 (the first session subsequent to direct elections) to December 1980. The data were generated from an examination of the European Parliament's plenary roll-call votes as reported in the *Official Journal* of the European Communities. No precise count of all the votes taken in the EP was made because many of them were by hand/voice/standing or passed "without objection." These types of votes are not amenable to the proposed methodology and only those votes that identified how each individual member of the EP voted could be examined —a total of 103 roll calls were so identified.

Riker's Coefficient of Significance was calculated for each of these 103 and the (very arbitrary) cutoff point was set at .4 or above. Only nineteen roll calls were at .4 or above, and these were examined by noting how each individual member voted (pro, con, abstain, absent) in order to calculate the IVCs and the IVLs. The 410 members of the European Parliament were also placed into national contingents as well as into the transnational party groupings.[15]

DATA PRESENTATION AND ANALYSIS

Riker's Coefficient of Significance

The application of Riker's Coefficient of Significance to the 103 roll-call votes shows that the general level of elite consensus is quite high within the European Parliament or, conversely, that there is a relatively low level of conflict. The actual results on the 0-to-1 scale range from a low of .06 to a high of .63 with .30 as the mean. Although no really good comparative data exist, it appears to this writer—based upon an intuitive judgment of the figures and upon the examination of the nature of the roll calls—that the mean of .30 is quite low. The elites in the European Parliament simply do not exhibit conflict in their aggregate voting behavior.

The reason for this level of high aggregate consensus/low conflict is reasonably obvious: the European Parliament is still not yet an "important" legislative body with real political power. The EP's "decisions" are only statements of intent or desire without any binding force in Community law, and the organization appears to function more like a social club with sporadic attendance than as a legislative body. The formal limits on its power has reduced the Parliament to passing resolutions expressing sorrow and concern over floods in France. Political conflict is not woven from this fabric, and it is not surprising that people of goodwill—even from nine different countries and fifty-five political parties—agree on such matters.

The elites in the European Parliament evidence a high level of general consensus, but this does not necessarily mean that consensus will increase *if* the Parliament can expand its formal powers vis-à-vis the Commission and the Council of Ministers and begin to legislate rather than request.

Only those roll calls that were at .4 or above on Riker's scale were selected for additional analysis (n=19). The following discussion of the voting behavior within and between the various groups thus isolates what kind of conflict exists from what is otherwise a rather high level of consensus.

Level of Voting Cohesion (IVC)

As noted above, the IVC, by pairing every member of a specified group to every other member of the group on every vote, can generate data on the general level of voting cohesion-degree of "bloc-like" behavior. These calculations have been done for three different categories: (1) the nine national delegations, (2) the six transnational party groupings, and (3) the thirteen largest specific country/party subgroups.

Table 9.1 ("Index of Voting Cohesion by Country Delegation") contains the IVCs for the nine separate country delegations which, it is to be remembered, are fractionalized into the six transnational party groupings. Do the values reported in Table 9.1 evidence "cohesive" or "bloc-like" groups? This is a difficult question to answer. As was the situation above with Riker's Coefficient, no good comparative data exist on the use and interpretation of the IVCs and whatever cutoff point established between cohesive/noncohesive would be arbitrary at best.

The above comments notwithstanding, however, the reported IVCs *do* appear to be rather low—none are at the 80+ level and this level (80+)

would seem to be a reasonable cutoff point for the definition of a "bloc." Only one country delegation (United Kingdom) is at the 70+ level: this is a direct result, as can be seen in Table 9.3, of the makeup of the British EP delegation. Of the 81 UK MEPs, 61 are Conservative with an IVC of 85.23. The remaining eight country delegations range between 68.76 (Ireland) and 56.55 (The Netherlands).

The only conclusion reached here is that the country delegations are not cohesive and do not exhibit a high degree of bloc-like behavior.

Table 9.2 ("Index of Voting Cohesion by Transnational Party Group") contains the IVCs for the six separate transnational party groups, which, it is to be remembered, are fractionalized into the nine country delegations. But the interpretation of these IVCs is subject to the same caveat above: no good comparative data exist and cutoff points would be arbitrary.

Nonetheless, the transnational party groups' IVCs are *higher* (more cohesive) than the national IVCs. They range from a high of 81.75 (ED) to a low of 65.04 (SOC). The parties may not be "highly" cohesive entities with everyone voting the identical way, but they are at least "more" cohesive than the country delegations. This lends some support to the hypothesis that transnational party affiliation is more important than national identity in explaining EP voting behavior and that we may be witnessing the beginnings of strong European transnational political parties.

Table 9.3 ("Index of Voting Cohesion by Country-Party Subgroup") presents the IVCs for the thirteen largest country-party subgroups. Again, while it is difficult to define these subgroups as blocs, the reported IVC values are—not surprisingly—generally higher than those contained in Tables 9.1 and 9.2. The range is from 87.96 (the nineteen French Communists) to 71.18 (the sixteen French Liberal Democrats).

In looking at Tables 9.1, 9.2, and 9.3 as a whole, it can be seen that with only four exceptions, the IVC values are highest for the specific country-party subgroup, and lowest for the country group. The four exceptions are the French Progressive Democrats, the French Socialists, the British Socialists, and the Belgian European Peoples Party.

The identified groups in the European Parliament are relatively cohesive, with the party groupings a bit more "bloc-like" than the national delegations. The following sections employ the Index of Voting Likeness (IVL) to note the degree to which the MEPs vote along partisan ideological lines compared to national-interest lines.

Voting Likeness Between Groups—Country Comparisons

Table 9.4, "Index of Voting Likeness—Country Comparisons," contains the IVLs for each of the nine countries compared to the other eight. Table 9.4 shows that the Belgian contingent to the European Parliament has the

TABLE 9.1

INDEX OF VOTING COHESION (IVC)

BY COUNTRY DELEGATION

Country	N	IVC
United Kingdom	81	76.45
Ireland	15	68.76
France	81	65.50
Denmark	17	64.43
Italy	81	62.48
Belgium	23	61.92
Luxembourg	6	59.99
Germany	81	59.20
The Netherlands	25	56.55

TABLE 9.2

INDEX OF VOTING COHESION (IVC)

BY TRANSNATIONAL PARTY GROUP

Group	N	IVC
European Democrat (ED)	64	81.75
Progressive Democrat (PD)	22	78.57
European Peoples Party (PPE)	107	76.88
Communist/Allies (COM)	44	69.66
Liberal Democrat (LIB)	40	67.48
Socialist (SOC)	113	65.04

TABLE 9.3

INDEX OF VOTING COHESION (IVC)

BY COUNTRY-PARTY SUBGROUP

Group[a]	N	IVC
French COM	19	87.96
British ED	61	85.23
German SOC	35	81.48
German PPE	42	78.24
Dutch PPE	10	77.95
Italian PPE	29	77.78
Italian COM	23	77.19
French PD	16	77.06
French SOC	21	74.83
British SOC	17	74.72
Belgian PPE	10	73.33
Italian SOC	13	71.51
French LIB	16	71.18

[a] Only those subgroups where N $\geqq$ 10 are included.

highest mean IVL (81.39) across the remaining eight. At the other extreme is the contingent from the United Kingdom with a mean IVL of 59.09 across the remaining eight country groups. Belgium's score is not surprising to those among us who have studied the European integrative process over the years. The Eurobarometers have shown that Belgium consistently has given the idea of integration strong support—the Belgian representatives to the European Parliament are ready to agree with their colleagues on most issues. The IVL for the United Kingdom (59.09) is quite low, calling into question the degree of British attachment to the Community. But these comments on the United Kingdom must be qualified: approximately sixty-one of the eighty-one members from the UK are Conservatives and it is this latter group that exhibits a different aggregate voting behavior within the EP. The British score is low because the Conservatives are different from the other transnational party groupings within the Parliament.

TABLE 9.4

INDEX OF VOTING LIKENESS (IVL) -- COUNTRY COMPARISONS

	All	Belgium	Germany	Netherl.	Italy	Luxemb.	France	Denmark	Ireland	UK
Belgium	81.39	--	87.86	86.95	89.33	82.37	84.14	79.46	81.30	59.77
Germany	80.22		--	91.35	81.39	82.87	75.49	77.78	74.89	70.11
Netherlands	79.90			--	81.87	81.85	77.28	76.33	74.38	68.40
Italy	79.36				--	79.17	82.70	82.90	78.50	59.03
Luxembourg	77.01					--	77.68	74.76	79.33	58.08
France	76.98						--	82.25	87.53	48.79
Denmark	76.13							--	74.41	61.12
Ireland	74.76								--	47.75
UK	59.09									--

Table 9.4 also shows that there are some high (and low) IVL scores for specific individual A-B country pairs. The three highest pairs are Germany-Netherlands (91.35), Belgium-Italy (89.33), and Belgium-Germany (87.86). These three pairs evidence similar voting behavior in the aggregate and these elites show a rather high level of intercountry group consensus. The three lowest individual A-B pairs all contain, not surprisingly, the United Kingdom: Ireland-UK (47.75), France-UK (48.79), and Luxembourg-UK (58.08). If these country pairs were composed solely of national delegations, the evidence would appear that severe conflict exists between these specific pairs. But these country groups are composed of different parties which cross-cut the countries; it is this party difference which accounts for the rather low IVL scores.

Table 9.4 contains one last interesting pattern. The three "new" members of the EC (Denmark, Ireland, and the United Kingdom), as a group, has a significantly lower mean IVL toward the remaining eight than do the "original" six members (69.99 compared to 79.13). The new three still appear to be "different" from the original six, although, as above, these comments only apply to the national voting behavior in the aggregate. As Table 9.6 below will show, specific parties within these three (the UK Socialists, for example) exhibit a higher level of voting agreement with fellow party members of different countries than those shown by the entire national group. The Danes as a *national* group may not agree very much with other national groups, but the specific parties within the Danish contingent do agree with the other members of the transnational party group within Parliament.

Voting Likeness Between Groups — Party Comparisons

Table 9.5, "Index of Voting Likeness — Party Comparisons," contains the IVLs for each of the six major transnational party groupings within the European Parliament.

The scores are lower than those for the country groups and show that the level of consensus among party groups is less than among the aggregate country groups. The Liberals have the highest score at 71.10 while the European Democrats (that is, the British Conservatives) have the lowest at 52.40. The Liberals and the European People's Party (the Christian Democrats) have the highest score (87.7) for individual pairs while the Progressive Democrats-European Democrats have the lowest (41.0).

The figures in Table 9.5 must be interpreted with caution, however. The IVL is really a surrogate measure for lack of internal cohesion: the higher the mean score for each party, the closer that party is to a 50 percent yes vote. The Liberals, for example, are indecisive as a *group* and, therefore, their 71.1 value means they split their vote (yes-no) vis-à-vis other parties. The European Democrats, on the other hand, are much more cohesive internally and thus the lower IVL score.

TABLE 9.5

INDEX OF VOTING LIKENESS (IVL) -- PARTY COMPARISONS

	All	Liberals	European People's Party	Progressive Democrats	Communist and Allies	Socialist	European Democrats
Liberals	71.10	---	87.70	84.80	70.90	62.50	49.60
PPE	68.02		---	77.00	65.60	56.30	53.50
PD	67.56			---	72.80	62.20	41.00
Communist	65.02				---	67.40	48.40
Socialist	63.58					---	69.50
ED	52.40						---

TABLE 9.6

INDEX OF VOTING LIKENESS (IVL) -- COUNTRY AND PARTY COMPARISONS

Group[a]	N[b]	IVL to Rest of Party[c]	IVL to Rest of Country[d]	Difference
German PPE	42	95.74	47.43	+48.31
German SOC	35	70.26	42.63	+27.63
Netherlands PPE	10	93.05	65.60	+27.45
Italian PPE	29	91.70	64.86	+26.84
Belgian PPE	10	91.78	71.26	+20.52
French PD	16	88.09	80.55	+ 7.54
French LIB	16	87.63	82.88	+ 4.75
Italian SOC	13	78.99	76.83	+ 2.16
UK SOC	17	78.29	76.18	+ 2.11
French COM	19	63.70	69.59	- 5.89
Italian COM	23	64.71	71.46	- 6.75
French SOC	21	62.04	78.57	-16.53

a . The UK Conservatives are not included in this table. The UK Conservatives represent 61 of the 64 members of the European Democrat group in Parliament. The remaining 3 EDs are simply too small a group to compare to the 61 UK EDs.
b . Only those groups with at least 10 members are analyzed.
c . This IVL is calculated by comparing the specific group's voting to the same transnational party group less the specific group's members.
d . This IVL is calculated by comparing the specific group's voting to the same country group less the specific group's members.

Partisan Ideology or National Interest?

The previous sections attempted to give a brief overview of the aggregate levels of voting cohesiveness and voting agreement for each of the country groups and party groups considered separately. This section now combines them and tries to identify whether partisan ideology or national interest is stronger. Table 9.6 gives the data for the twelve largest specific country/party groups.

The hypothesis put forth at the beginning of this paper—partisan political ideology (defined as membership in one of the transnational party groups in the European Parliament) will be a stronger explanatory variable for the observed voting differences than will national interest (defined by country of representation)—is seen to be "correct" in nine of the twelve specific groups analyzed. The differences in IVL values between party identification and national identification for the nine "confirmed" cases range from a high of 48.31 (the German PPE) to a low of 2.11 (the UK Socialists). The three groups which do not agree with the hypothesis are the French Communists (−5.89), the Italian Communists (−6.75), and the French Socialists

(—16.53). These latter three groups show a higher level of voting agreement with the rest of their country representatives than with the rest of their transnational party group in the European Parliament.

The data in Table 9.6 could be explained at length, but this section will only discuss a couple of the more interesting results. The most striking aspect of Table 9.6 is the degree to which the Germans (at least seventy-seven of eighty-one) exhibit the least amount of "nationalism." The group of forty-two German members of the PPE has an IVL value of 47.43 against the remaining German members of the Parliament—a 48.31 IVL difference when compared to their IVL against the other PPE members in Parliament; the thirty-five German members of the Socialist group has a 42.63 VIL score against the remaining German members—a 27.63 difference compared to other Socialists. The Germans appear to be approaching the votes in Parliament *not* as Germans but as members of transnational party groups—the partisan ideology of Christian Democracy (PPE) and of Socialism has, at least for the Germans, surpassed the national interest mind-set.

But as the Germans are de-emphasizing nationalism, the French and the Italians, especially the Communists and the French Socialists, appear to value national identity more than transnational party ideology. This is doubly striking since our conventional wisdom has the parties of the Left as more monolithic, coherent, and more internationally oriented. The French Socialists' IVL to the rest of the French delegation is 16.53 points higher than to the rest of the Socialist group in the European Parliament. This paper is only a preliminary study, and I have no adequate explanation of the French Socialists' behavior at this time.

The degree to which the French and Italian Communists agree more with other French-Italian representatives than with other European Communists is also striking. The reason for this can be isolated, but, as above, cannot as yet be explained adequately. The low IVLs for the rest of party is directly attributable to the Italy-France pair (Italy and France have forty-two of the forty-four members of the Parliament's Communist and Allies group). The French Communists show a low IVL with other Communists because they have a low IVL with the Italian Communists; just the obverse is true with the Italian Communists. This may locate where the difference is, but it only poses an additional question: Why do the French and Italian Communists show the rather low level of voting agreement?

One possible preliminary reason could be the very real differences in the political outlook and behavior of these two parties, both in their respective domestic environments and their international positions. The French have been much more Moscow-oriented than the Italians; the Italians are the leading voice for Eurocommunism. The low level of intracommunist voting agreement in the European Parliament can be observed; an explanation of their behavior, however, requires further research.

CONCLUSIONS

The transnational political groups in the European Parliament do attempt to work out common positions on the major policy issues, but the degree of internal cohesiveness—although higher for the political groups than for the country delegations—does not reach significant levels. It is all too obvious that members frequently vote counter to the majority view. The very fact of direct elections may contribute to this comparative independence of the individual MEP; no longer responsible to the party hierarchy in the home parliament, the MEP has much more leeway when he is now responsible to an amorphous electorate.

But it is not very realistic to expect a very high degree of cohesiveness or degree of bloc-like behavior from members of a political group who have been elected, not as a member of a *European* political party, but rather as a member of one of fifty-five separate *national* parties. The political groups are not (yet) transnational political parties. The groups are only broad coalitions/alliances composed of different national parties.

The transnational political groups in the European Parliament may develop into transnational parties in the future, but in order to do so, they will first have to present candidates for the EP across the ten member states under a single label and with a single, common platform. At present, there are three parties linked at the European level—the Socialists, European Peoples Party, and the Liberals. These federations attempted to coordinate the 1979 campaign and they attempt to maintain links between the EP groups and the national political parties. But these federations still cannot be called transnational political parties.

What does this study say about elite behavior, conflict and consensus, partisan ideology and national interest, the European Parliament, and the European integrative process? Unfortunately, not a great deal. The very nature of the European Parliament—its lack of any real political power, its atmosphere of a congenial club, the nonbinding roll-calls, the emphasis upon symbolic politics rather than upon the substance—all these factors combine and detract from the significance of whatever the representatives do or do not do in the Parliament.

But after these limiting conditions are accepted, the representatives in the European Parliament do show a remarkable degree of transnational party agreement and a de-emphasis of national interest. Most of these people act (vote) as members of transnational party groups, for they have a higher level of voting agreement with their party compared to fellow nationals. It just may be that the traditional national mind-sets are breaking down, strengthening the integrative process. These transnational parties can serve as new political forces in Europe when and if the European Parliament enlarges its power vis-à-vis the Commission and the Council of Ministers. This enlargement does not appear to be imminent, but the groundwork has been laid.

NOTES

1. Figures are from Ronald Inglehart and Jacques-René Rabier, "Europe Elects a Parliament: Cognitive Mobilization, Political Mobilization, and Pro-European Attitudes as Influences on Voter Turnout," chapter 2 (pp. 27-51) of Leon Hurwitz, ed., *Contemporary Perspectives on European Integration Attitudes, Non-Governmental Behavior, and Collective Decision Making* (Westport, Conn. and London, England: Greenwood Press/Aldwych Press, 1980); esp. table 2.1, "Rates of Electoral Participation for the Election of the European Parliament and for the Most Recent National Election," p. 29.

2. There are several good surveys of the European Parliament in the literature. The best is perhaps Michael Palmer, *The European Parliament: What It Is, What It Does, How It Works* (Oxford: Pergamon Press, 1981). See also D. Coombes, *The Future of the European Parliament* (London: PSI, 1979); J. Fitzmaurice, *The European Parliament* (Farnborough, UK: Saxon House, 1978); Val Herman and Juliet Lodge, *The European Parliament and the European Community* (London: Macmillan, 1978); R. Jackson and J. Fitzmaurice, *The European Parliament: A Guide to the European Elections* (London: Penguin, 1979); and J. Pridham and P. Pridham, *Towards Transnational Parties in the European Community* (London: PSI, 1979).

3. Palmer, *The European Parliament*, p. 20.

4. Ibid., p. 31.

5. Lord Bruce of Donington, as cited in ibid., pp. 40-41. Author's emphasis.

6. Dual mandate members – members of both the EP *and* the national parliament – receive one salary only. Only dual mandate members from Ireland receive a double salary. Dual mandate members (about 125) however, receive the full allotment of per diem allowances (about $100 per day), travel allowances (an average of approximately 32¢ per km or about 53¢ per mile), and close to $40,000 per year for research and secretarial assistance. The EP funds the allowances.

7. In 1979 it cost the EP approximately $25 million (about 15 percent of its total budget) just to pay for the constant shuffle of staff, equipment, and documents between Luxembourg, Strasbourg, and Brussels. In 1981 this cost escalated to $40 million.

8. William H. Riker, "A Method for Determining the Significance of Roll Calls in Voting Bodies," in John C. Wahlke and Heinz Eulau, eds., *Legislative Behavior: A Reader in Theory and Research* (Glencoe, Ill.: The Free Press, 1959), pp. 377-384.

9. Some applications of Riker's Coefficient, applications that are not pursued in this essay, would be an examination of the salience of issues over time (either for each voting category and/or by session) and the level of conflict/issue salience across different legislatures. The computation of the coefficient is quite tedious, but there is a FORTRAN program – VOTES – that makes it a bit easier.

10. There is an extensive literature in this area. An excellent discussion of several techniques is by Arend Lijphart, "The Analysis of Bloc Voting in the General

Assembly: A Critique and a Proposal," *American Political Science Review* 57 (December 1963): 902-917. For a more detailed description of some empirical measures, see the following: Hayward R. Alker, Jr., "Dimensions of Conflict within the General Assembly," *American Political Science Review* 58 (September 1964): 642-647; Hayward R. Alker, Jr. and Bruce Russett, *World Politics in the General Assembly* (New Haven: Yale University Press, 1965); Thomas Hovet, Jr., *Bloc Politics in the United Nations* (Cambridge, Mass.: Harvard University Press, 1960); Hanna Newcombe et al., "United Nations Voting Patterns," *International Organization* 24 (Winter 1970): 100-121; Leroy N. Rieselbach, "Quantitative Techniques for Studying Voting Behavior in the UN General Assembly," *International Organization* 14 (Spring 1960): 291-306; and Bruce M. Russett, "Discovering Voting Groups in the United Nations," *American Political Science Review* 60 (June 1966): 327-339.

11. Lijphart, "The Analysis of Bloc Voting in the General Assembly," pp. 909-910.

12. The original notation terms the generated values the Index of Agreement (IA). I have opted for the term Index of Voting Cohesion (IVC), as the former might falsely connote a measure of the frequency that an A-B pair of voters (or an aggregated group of A-B pairs) agreed (a pro vote) with the resolutions under examination. IVC is employed in order to avoid any possible confusion; cohesion refers to the degree that each A-B pair vote in an identical manner (both pro, both con, or both abstain). See Leon Hurwitz, "The EEC in the United Nations: The Voting Behaviour of Eight Countries, 1948-1973," *Journal of Common Market Studies* 13 (March 1975): 224-243; and "The EEC and Decolonization: The Voting Behaviour of the Nine in the UN General Assembly," *Political Studies* 24 (December 1976): 435-447.

13. Russett, "Discovering Voting Groups in the General Assembly," p. 329.

14. Stuart A. Rice, *Quantitative Methods in Politics* (New York: Knopf, 1928) as discussed by Rieselbach, "Quantitative Techniques."

15. The 24 Greek members are not included in the present study. The 9 country delegations, excluding Greece, and their strengths, are Belgium (24 for 5.8 percent), Denmark (15 for 3.9 percent), Ireland (15 for 3.6 percent), Luxembourg (6 for 1.5 percent), Netherlands (25 for 6.1 percent), and Germany, France, Italy, United Kingdom (each has 81 for 19.7 percent). The transnational party groupings in the EP and their approximate strengths are: Socialist (113 for 27.5 percent), Christian Democrats/European People's Party (107 for 26.1 percent), Conservatives/European Democrats (64 for 15.6 percent), Communist and Allies (44 for 10.7 percent), Liberal and Democrat (40 for 9.8 percent), European Progressive Democrats (22 for 5.4 percent), and Others (Independents and Non-Attached: 20 for 4.9 percent). There are approximately 55 national political parties represented in the EP.

Jonathan Miller 10

A EUROPEAN BILL OF RIGHTS?

The initial purpose of the European Community, as set forth in the Treaty of Rome, is that of economic integration between the Member States. The Preamble to the Treaty speaks of the desire of the contracting parties "to guarantee steady expansion [of their economies], balanced trade and fair competition" and to strive "for the progressive abolition of restrictions on international trade." Article 2 states that the Community shall have as its task the establishment of a common market and the promotion of four overriding goals: "the harmonious development of economic activities"; "a continous and balanced expansion"; "an increase in [economic] stability"; "an accelerated raising of the standard of living"; and finally "closer relations between the States belonging to it." The latter phrase is a reference to the penultimate and ultimate goals of the Community in the form of economic *and* political union. How this end is to be reached is outlined in Article 3 which speaks of a common customs tariff and a common commercial policy toward third countries; free movement of services, capital and people; a common transport and agriculture policy; the promotion of free competition between the Member States; and in order to ensure the above, "the approximation of the laws of the Member States."

This view of the *raison d'être* of the EC was expressed a decade later by the United Kingdom in its White Paper on the proposed membership of the Community:

> Community Law operates only on the fields covered by the Treaties, that is broadly: Customs duties; agriculture; free movement of labour, services and capital; transport,; monopolies and restrictive practices; state aid for industry; and the regulation of the Coal and Steel and Nuclear Energy Industries. By far the greatest part of our domestic law would remain unchanged. Nothing in Community Law would, for

example, materially affect the general principles of our criminal law, or those of the law of contract or tort or its Scottish equivalent, nor would it affect the land law, the relations of landlord and tenant, housing and town and country planning law, matrimonial law or the law of inheritance.[1]

Indeed such is the emphasis in the Treaty on economic, as opposed to civil, considerations, that a Community lawyer was able to write: "The absence of a catalogue of fundamental rights in the Community seems to be the outstanding feature of the Community Treaties."[2] In order to obtain the economic objectives of the Treaty, Article 5 places an obligation upon the Member States to carry out the purposes of the Treaty and to abstain from initiating policies which could undermine the workings of the Community. Moreover, so that these objectives do not languish merely as a pious hope rather than constitutional reality, the Court of Justice of the European Communities clearly has spelled out the relationship between the Member States and the Community and between the national law of the said States and the new "Community law." In *Costa v. E.N.E.L.* the European Court boldly stated:

As opposed to other international treaties, the Treaty instituting the EEC has created its own order which was integrated with the national order of the Member States the moment the Treaty came into force; as such it is binding upon them. In fact by creating a Community of unlimited duration, having its own institutions, its own personality and its own capacity in law, apart from having international standing and more particularly, real powers resulting from a limitation of competence or a transfer of powers from the States to the Community, the member-States, albeit within limited spheres, have restricted their Sovereign rights . . . [and] the executive strength of Community laws cannot vary from one state to another in favour of later internal laws without endangering the realisation of the aims envisaged by the Treaty.[3]

It can be seen, therefore, that not only is Community law superior to national law and liable to prevail over inconsistent subsequent national law; it is also part of the national legal systems, bestowing in certain circumstances rights and obligations upon individuals. And in case any doubt might have lingered in the minds of the Member States, the Court again stated:

Every national court must, in a case within its jurisdiction, apply Community law in its entirety and protect rights which the latter confers on individuals and must accordingly set aside any provisions of national law which may conflict with it, whether prior or subsequent to the Community rule.[4]

Thus far what has been established is the emphasis on financial and trade matters in the minds of the original six members of the Community responsible for drafting the Treaty. It would be wrong, however, to suppose from this observation that the Treaty has remained wholly silent on matters which concern the political and economic protection of the citizen and which have been rather carelessly lumped together by the phrase "human rights."[5] Within the Treaty of Rome there exist Articles which relate to the rights of the individual and these together with the doctrine of the supremacy of Community law and the conferment of legal rights upon individuals[6] are, it is submitted, destined to play an increasing role in the jurisprudence, not only of the Community, but also the Member States.

In the first place, the Preamble to the Treaty speaks of the objectives of the Member States to achieve a progressive improvement in the living and working conditions of their respective populations, and a common desire to raise the standard of living of the more backward regions of Europe. One is further informed of the aspirations of the Community to ensure their development and prosperity in accordance with the principles of the Charter of the United Nations. Though what exactly this means is unclear as the principles of the UN referred to under the heading of Article 2 of the Charter merely make reference to the relations between the sovereign states of the world, with the aim of preserving world peace. For those references to human rights within the Charter one is forced to look elsewhere.

Of much more significance than the Preamble are those references to human rights which are to be found distributed throughout the main body of the Treaty, albeit in an uneven and somewhat random manner. Article 2 refers to an acceleration of living standards as one of the Community's goals. Article 3 makes reference to the establishment of a European Social Fund with the aim of enhancing employment opportunities among the workers of the Community and in order to facilitate a rise in their standard of living. Moreover one is told (Article 39) that among the objectives of the common agricultural policy (CAP) is a "fair standard of living for the agricultural community." Article 117 speaks of the agreement and necessity of the Member States "to promote improved working conditions and an improved standard of living for workers, so as to make possible their harmonization while the improvement is being maintained." Furthermore, by Article 118 the Commission is given the task of coordinating the activities of the Member States in areas covered by employment and labor law, social security, collective bargaining and the right of association, and what might loosely be termed health and safety at work.

When grouped together, the above provisions might well be classified as economic and social as opposed to civil and political rights. Although they are not unique to the Treaty of Rome, being found, for example, in the Universal Declaration of Human Rights, they nevertheless provide an additional formulation of social rights as compared to the European Convention on Human Rights with its emphasis on the minimum civil and political rights acceptable to the nations of the Council of Europe.

One of the foremost aims of the Community is freedom of movement of persons, services, and capital,[7] and it is the first of these categories that deserves consideration when enumerating the rights listed under the Treaty. In order to ensure the free movement of workers, it is necessary to prohibit any discriminatory practices, and to this effect Article 7 places a general prohibition on any discrimination based on grounds of nationality. More specifically, Article 48(i) speaks of the necessity of abolishing discrimination in employment based on the nationality of the individual worker, and of the securing of free movement of labor "by the end of the transitional period at the latest."[8] Moreover, the free movement of workers within the Community is also to include self-employed persons (Article 52), and in order to facilitate this objective the Council is required, after receiving a proposal from the Commission and after consulting the Assembly, to issue directives for the mutual recognition of diplomas, certificates, and other evidence of formal qualifications (Article 57).

It would be wrong, however, to assume from the above Articles that the EC Treaty gives an unlimited right of entry and residence to the populations of the Member States irrespective of the wishes and policy considerations of the individual states. Two cases, originating in the United Kingdom and pronounced upon by the European Court of Justice (E.C.J.) under a preliminary ruling, serve to illustrate the Court's thinking in this matter.[9]

The first case, *Van Duyn v. Home Office*, arose out of a statement made in 1968 in the House of Commons by the Minister of Health. He pronounced that the Government was of the belief that the practice of Scientology was socially harmful and that foreign nationals would not be issued work permits for employment at Scientology establishments. Following the UK's accession to the EC in 1973, this policy continued; although, as before, no legal restrictions were placed upon the practice of Scientology in the UK, nor were British nationals prevented from taking up employment with the organization. The plaintiff, Miss Van Duyn, who was a Dutch national, was offered employment with the Church of Scientology at its college in the UK. She was, however, refused entry into the country on the basis that the Secretary of State considered it "undesirable to give anyone leave to enter the United Kingdom on the business or in the employment of that organization."

The matter was referred to the European Court of Justice on the questions of (1) whether Article 48 of the EC Treaty and Article 3(1) of EC Directive 64/221[10] permitted a Member State to refuse a person leave to enter its territory on the basis that he was associated with an organization whose activities that state held to be contrary to the public good; and (2) whether the voluntary act of Van Duyn associating with the Church of Scientology and taking part in its activities could be held to be a matter of personal conduct within the meaning of the EC Directive. The Court ruled in the affirmative on both questions. Moreover, the Court argued that although UK nationals were free to study and practice Scientology and to work at the organization's institutions, the UK was nevertheless not practicing discrimination contrary to the terms of the EC Treaty and that:

> Where the competent authorities of a member State have clearly defined their standpoint as regard the activities of a particular organisation and where, considering it to be socially harmful, they have taken administrative measures to counteract these activities, the member State cannot be required, before it can rely on the concept of public policy, to make such activities unlawful, if recourse to such a measure is not thought appropriate in the circumstances.[11]

In the case of *R. v. Bouchereau,* which concerned a French national who was the subject of a deportation order from the UK as a result of his being convicted, for a second time, of possession of dangerous drugs, the Court elaborated further on the term "public policy" and the justification for restrictions on the free movement of persons within the Community. The Court was of the opinion that the restrictions on the free movement of persons on the basis of public policy, as set out in Article 48, presupposed the existence "of a genuine and sufficiently serious threat affecting one of the fundamental interests of society." The Court was careful to point out, however, that this threat to society had to be something more than the disturbance of society which was a necessary consequence of law breaking. Moreover the Court approved the reasoning in the *Van Duyn* case:

> The particular circumstances justifying recourse to the concept of public policy may vary from one country to another and from one period to another and it is therefore necessary in this matter to allow the competent national authorities an area of discretion within the limits imposed by the Treaty and the provisions adopted for its implementation.[12]

Article 119 of the Treaty, which sets out the principle of equal pay for equal work between the sexes and whose ambit was extensively discussed by the E.C.J. in *Defrenne v. Sabena Airlines,*[13] is of major contribution to community law in the area of fundamental rights. Gabrielle Defrenne was appointed a Sabena Air stewardess in December 1951. In October 1963 a new contract was offered her as an air hostess chief steward. She subsequently left employment in February 1968 in accordance with Sabena's standard contract of employment for crews, which stated that female employees should terminate their employment as members of air crews from the time they reach forty years of age. On ceasing that employment, Mlle Defrenne was in recepit of severance pay. Subsequently, after consideration by the Belgian courts of Mlle Defrenne's claim that she had suffered in terms of salary, termination of service allowance, and pension on account of the fact that male and female members of the air crew carrying out the same work were not in receipt of equal pay, *two specific questions were referred to the E.C.J.* First, does Article 119 of the Treaty, by itself, introduce into the national law of Member States of the EC the principle of equal pay for equal work and does it thus, independently of any enactment by Member States, entitle nationals to go before national courts in order to claim equal pay? And second, is Article 119 applicable in the national law of Member States by virtue of rules enacted by Community institutions and if so from what dates?

Thus the question of the direct applicability of Article 119 was placed before the Court, and it was because of the extensive repercussions of this possible holding that the Governments of the Republic of Ireland and the United Kingdom asked to present observations to the Court. Counsel for both the UK and the Republic of Ireland argued that to hold Article 119 directly applicable since 1 January 1973 might adversely affect the economies of the two countries. The UK stated that under the terms of the Equal Pay Act (1970), complete equality in the area of financial remunerations would not be achieved until the end of 1975. In Ireland the situation was similar, as the Anti-Discrimination (Pay) Act of 1974 would not be in force until 31 December 1975. In the course of their judgment, the Court held that the principle of equal pay for equal work, which was clearly set out in Article 119, could be invoked before the national courts. The Court asserted its right

> to protect the rights which Article 119 bestows on individuals, particularly in cases of discrimination resulting directly from legislative enactments, from collective bargaining agreements or from the practice of distinguishing between male and female pay for identical work as long as such work is performed in the same shop or service, private or public.[14]

On the question of from which date Article 119 was to be applied, the answer was that the Article was to have been enforced in the original Member States from 1 January 1962 and in the new Member States from 1 January 1973. The Court did say, however—in order not to cause economic dislocation among the Member States and with the exception of similar cases or cases now pending—that Article 119 could not be used to support claims for back-payments over periods prior to the Court's decision. The Court than discussed the necessity of regarding Article 119 as directly applicable. First, the Court held that mindful of the varying degrees of social and economic progress which the Member States had achieved, it would be disadvantageous to those countries and undertakings which had implemented the principle of equal pay if other countries were not to do so. The Court also asserted that Article 119 was an instrument for the implementation of the social policy objectives of the Community and that the Community also had its rationale in the promotion of the living standards of the Member States. "Equal pay for equal work" the Court asserted, was fundamental to the Community.

This was not, however, the definitive pronouncement on this matter, as Mlle Defrenne embarked on further litigation[15] in order to try and show that the scope of Article 119 included, not only the principles of equal pay for equal work, but also that of equal working conditions for men and women. This was an argument that the Court was unwilling to accept. In its judgment, the Court stressed the precise nature of Article 119 (as opposed to Articles 117 and 118) and that to include general working conditions would jeopardize the direct applicability of the Article. Moreover, the further contention of the plaintiff that there exists a general principle of Community law prohibiting any form of sexual discrimination in the work place was not given judicial sanction. The Court repeated its often-held view that fundamental human rights form part of the general principles of Community law and that the elimination of sexual discrimination was one of these fundamental rights. But the Court went on to say that in the period under question Community law did not prohibit discriminatory practices in working conditions, except as set forth in Article 119.

The remaining miscellaneous articles in the Treaty dealing with the protection of human rights include the following: the obligation on Member States to progressively adjust any state commercial monopolies so as to ensure that at the end of the transitional period *no discrimination existed between nations of Member States* with relation to the procurement and marketing of goods; the right to damages or other form of compensation set forth in Article 215; and, finally, the Treaty makes provisions for the involvement of the individual citizens of the Community in the government of the same. The last point is to be achieved in part by the activities of the European Parliament (EP) whose membership consists of representatives of the population of the Community and whose function, bestowed upon it by the Treaty, is one of supervision and advice.

The Treaty also contains a provision whereby the European Parliament is exhorted to draw up proposals for elections by direct universal suffrage. This was not in fact achieved until June 1979, and the provision of Article 138, by which the EP was to consist of delegates designated by their respective Parliaments from among their members in accordance with the procedure laid down by each Member State, was envisaged as a temporary procedure only. The rules for the direct election to the EP require that they shall be held "in accordance with a uniform procedure in all member States," but in fact, owing to different attitudes among the Member States, this was not carried out by the date of the first election. Thus the Constitutional Court of the Federal Republic of Germany[16] was able to hold that the 5 percent rule in the German European Elections Act, whereby candidates for the European Parliament are not declared successful unless their party list achieves at least 5 percent of the total vote, was constitutionally valid as part of an "unwritten" constitutional law even though it was not universally adopted by other members of the Community.

In addition to the fact that the Treaty of Rome contains the above articles, there has also been some important development in the jurisprudence of the European Court. This has helped to establish that the protection of human rights is one of the fundamental objects of the Community. In the initial period after the establishment of the EC, the European Court failed to deal with this issue, and those who look to the earlier cases for a lead in this matter will be disappointed.[17] However, with the growth in the activities of the Community and the unequivocal endorsement of the supremacy of Community law, apprehensions were aroused in the Member States about the impact of the EC law on the rights of the individual citizens. It was against this background that the European Court felt able to assert in *Stauder v. Ulm:* "Thus interpreted, the decision in question does not contain any element that might jeopardise *the fundamental rights of the individual contained in the general principles of the law of the Community of which the Court must ensure the observance.*"[18]

Of more significance than this assertion is the problem which arose in the *Internationale Handelsgessellschaft* case over the questions of a possible conflict between a national constitutional law which seeks to protect fundamental human rights and Community law overriding these constitutional provisions. In the case in question, a German company forfeited its deposit (required by Community law) owing to its failure to obtain the necessary license for the export of cereal. The company subsequently instituted litigation in the Federal Republic of Germany, arguing that the deposit which was required was excessive for the needs of the Community to regulate the cereal market, and that the deposit system infringed Articles 2(1) and 14, respectively, of the German Constitution which protected freedom of action, economic liberty, and proportionality (that the deposit required was excessive for the common organization of the markets in cereals).

The German Federal Constitutional Court held, by a majority, that in cases where there was a conflict between the fundamental rights guaranteed in the German Constitution and Community law, then the rights set forth in the German Constitution must take precedence. Moreover, this was especially so in the view of the German Court, as the Community had no charter of fundamental rights nor any guarantee that individual rights would be protected. The E.C.J., of course, refused to accept this line of reasoning and was of the opinion that if member countries were permitted to invoke their national laws when they desired so to do, then the unity of the Community would be at risk and the legal system of the Community would suffer. The Court went on to add: "Therefore the validity of a Community instrument or its effect within a Member State cannot be affected by allegations that it strikes at either the fundamental rights as formulated in that State's constitution or the principles of a national constitutional structure."[19]

The Court, however, did not let the matter rest there, as they then proceeded to argue the possibility that some "analogous guarantee" inherent in Community law might have been infringed. And in a passage which has opened the door to a more adventurous interpretation of Community law, the Court held:

> Respect of our fundamental rights has an integral part in the general principles of law which the Court of Justice ensures respect. The protection of such rights, while inspired by the constitutional principles common to the Member States, must be ensured within the framework of the Community's structure and objective.[20]

On the facts of the case, however, the Court held that the deposit system did not infringe the fundamental human rights protected by the legal order of the Community.

Following the above decision, the European Court has proceeded to enlarge upon this doctrine. In *Nold v. EC Commission*, the applicant argued that as a result of trading restrictions imposed by the Commission, the said institution was thereby acting in violation of fundamental rights protected not only by the Constitution of the Federal Republic of Germany and the constitutions of the Member States, but also those rights protected by various international treaties and declarations in general and the European Convention on Human Rights (ECHR) in particular. This was an argument that the Court was ready to consider, and in the reasoning of its judgment, it repeated its previously held view that fundamental rights were an integral part of the general principles of law which it would seek to protect and enforce. Furthermore, the Court said that in the protection of these rights, it was required to take into account the constitutional traditions shared by all the Member States and was thus willing to strike down measures which it considered were at odds with the fundamental rights guaranteed by the constitutions of the Member States.[21]

On the second question of the relationship of the international treaties and the European Convention to Community law, the Court took the view that they can supply indications which may be taken into account within the framework of Community law. Therefore, while the Court was willing to use the imperative and argue that it was required to take into account the constitutional traditions of the Member States, it was only willing to hold that international treaties, including the ECHR, could supply indications of which rights may be taken into account. This is not altogether surprising, bearing in mind the emphasis which the ECHR places on civil and political rights as opposed to the economic and social rights which are mentioned in the Treaty of Rome. Moreover, it was not until France ratified the ECHR on 3 May 1974 that all the then members of the EC had ratified the Convention.[22] Nevertheless, both the Preamble to the ECHR and the Treaty of Rome speak in the first case of the desire to achieve greater unity between the members of the Council of Europe and in the second instance of "an ever closer union among the people of Europe." It is therefore to be supposed that the unity of the EC countries would be imperfect without some form of agreement on the definition and protection of fundamental rights.

Following from the dicta in the above cases, the argument was taken a step further in *Prais v. Council.*[23] In this instance, the Secretariat of the Council of Ministers of the EC had given notice of an open competition for the recruitment of a legal translator who possessed English as her mother tongue. The plaintiff was informed that she had been accepted by her Examining Board and that she was to take her written examination on 16 May 1975. Following this notice, the plaintiff informed the Council that she was unable to sit for the examination as the examination fell on the first day of a Jewish religious holiday when it is forbidden to travel or write. She therefore requested that she be allowed to take the examination on another day, but the Council was unwilling to accept this proposal as they considered it vital that all the candidates sit for the examination on the same day.

In her proceedings before the E.C.J., the plaintiff based her claim on the ground that the religious discrimination which she alleged she suffered was prohibited by Community law as being contrary to the fundamental rights of the individual. She also relied on the Articles of the ECHR in general and on Article 9(2) in particular,[24] basing this submission on the fact that since the ECHR had been ratified by all the Member States, then the rights set forth in the same document are to be seen to be included in the Community's fundamental rights. In its submission, the Council accepted that the right of freedom of religion as set forth in the European Convention forms part of the fundamental rights recognized in the Community, and the Court accepted this. However, on the facts of the case, the Court held that the Community is not required when fixing an examination date to make certain that this date does not coincide with a religious festival. The onus, the Court said, is on the candidate to inform the authority of the dates upon which she will not be able to take the examination prior to her having received a notification of the examination date.

In a subsequent case, *Hauer v. Land Rheinland-Pfalz,*[25] the Court again considered the role which both the ECHR and the provisions of national constitutions can have in formulating the Community's fundamental rights and in reviewing Community legislation in the light of this criteria. This case involved a Community regulation which prohibited, over a period of time, the planting of new vineyards—a regulation which the applicant argued was a violation of his right to property set forth in the German constitution. In the course of its judgment, the Court stated that although this was not a case where property rights had in fact been violated, nevertheless, such a right is guaranteed in the Community legal order in accordance with the ideas which are common to the Member States and that such a right is also reflected in the First Protocol to the ECHR.

Thus far, when considering whether the Community law has developed the notion of fundamental rights, attention has been paid to the enactments of the European Community. An equally important area to consider is that of the legislative and executive enactments of the individual Member States and whether such enactments can be held to be in contravention to the decisions of the E.C.J. in this field. This question was discussed before the Court in *Rutili v. Minister of Interior.*[26] This case concerned residence restrictions which had been placed upon an Italian national living and working in France whereby he was prohibited from residing in certain departments of France. This was justified by the French government as being in accordance with Article 48(3) the EC Treaty, which allows the Member States to limit the free movement of workers on the grounds of public policy, public security, or public health. The question therefore arose of whether the concept of "public policy" used as a justification for derogating from the fundamental principles of equality of treatment and free movement of workers could be unilaterally determined by a Member State without the control and supervision of the institutions of the EC, a contention which the Court was not inclined to accept. The Court also went on to endorse the view that the limitations on the right of Member States (being found in Community law) to restrict the freedom of entry, residence, and movement within their territory of Community nationals are a specific manifestation of the general principles contained in the ECHR. The Court said: "no restrictions in the interests of national security or public safety shall be placed on those rights other than such as are necessary for the protection of those interests in a democratic society."[27]

It would be incorrect, however, to assume from the above case that the ECHR forms part of the substance of EC law. In *The State v. Watson & Belman,* the Advocate General specifically repudiated this notion and argued that the basis of the decision in the *Rutili* case did not contain any substantive reference to the provisions of the ECHR themselves, but rather a reference to the general principles of which they are a specific expression. The Advocate General went on to argue that

> the extra Community instruments under which those states have undertaken international obligations in order to ensure better protection of those rights can, *without any question of their being incorporated as such in the Community order,* be used to establish principles which are common to the States themselves.[28]

Following from these judicial pronouncements, the other Community institutions have seen fit to endorse the view that fundamental human rights and the protection thereof are part of the objectives of the Community. In April 1977 a joint declaration was issued by the European Parliament, the Council, and the Commission, the contents of which read:

> 1. The European Parliament, the Council and the Commission stress the prime importance they attach to the protection of fundamental rights as derived in particular from the constitutions of the member States and the European Convention for the Protection of Human Rights and Fundamental Freedoms.
> 2. In the exercise of their powers and in pursuance of the aims of the European Communities they respect and will continue to respect these rights.[29]

In the same year a Resolution was passed by the European Parliament on the "Granting of Special Rights to Community Citizens." The Resolution called upon the Commission of the European Communities to facilitate an agreement between the Member States under which (a) the European Convention on Human Rights of 4 November 1950 and subsequent Protocols; (b) the International Covenant on Civil and Political Rights, adopted by the United Nations General Assembly on December 1966; and (c) the civil and political rights provided for in the constitutions and laws of the Member States would be regarded as integral parts of the treaties establishing the Communities.[30]

The above statements, while they might be indications of the development of Community thinking in this area, do not in any way alter the validity of the Advocate General's statement in *The State v. Watson & Belman.* Indeed, in *Confédération Française Democratique du Travail (CFDT) v. The European Communities,* the European Commission of Human Rights declared as inadmissible a complaint by the plaintiff (a French trade union) on the ground that the European Communities were not a party to the ECHR. The fact that the CFDT was not designated by the Council of the European Communities as a representative organization for the purpose of the Consultative Committee of ECSC was not something that the European Commission of Human Rights had jurisdiction to discuss.[31]

Moreover, while one might glibly talk about the accession of the Community to the ECHR, considerable legal problems will arise, not least being the probability that such a move could lead to jurisdictional disputes between the European Court of Justice at Luxembourg and the European Commission and Court of Human Rights at Strasbourg.[32] Furthermore, while it might be supposed that this problem could be solved by transferring the jurisdiction to one or other of the institutions concerned, or even creating a new hybrid body, the fact remains that not all the signatories to the ECHR are members of the EC. Additionally, one has the problem that while the ECHR grants the right of individual petition, this right has to be separately agreed to by the country concerned.

Since France was tardy in its acceptance of the right of individual petition (this had to await the election of President Mitterrand), the problem could have arisen of a French national being able to embark on litigation before the E.C.J. and making reliance on the Articles of the ECHR as having been incorporated into the Community legal order, while at the same time being denied such a right at Strasbourg.

While what has been dealt with so far has been the attempt of the E.C.J. and the other Community institutions to deal with the protection of fundamental human rights within the Community, there is also the subsidiary problem of the impact of the Community's philosophy on the courts of the Member States. It is of course not possible to analyze the effect of the Community's thinking on all the individual states; therefore, in the case of brevity and interest, the case of the United Kingdom will be examined. The UK is of particular importance in view of the fact that this state has the rare distinction among the members of the Community of having no written constitution and also no Bill of Rights protecting the individual citizen.

Under UK constitutional law, the power to enter into a treaty resides with the Crown and, as such, a Treaty is not part of the UK domestic law until the relevant legislation is passed by the Parliament at Westminister. In *Blackburn v. A-G*, the plaintiff sought to question the validity of the signing of the Treaty of Rome by Her Majesty's Government, as in so doing the government would be forever surrendering the sovereignty of Parliament. This was not an argument the Court was prepared to accept, as they maintained that they would refuse to take notice of this treaty (or indeed any treaty) unless and until the terms of the treaty were embodied in laws enacted by Parliament and then only to the extent that Parliament told them.[33] A similar outlook was expressed by the Courts in the earlier case of *Cheney v. Conn* in which a UK taxpayer sought to question his income tax assessments on the basis that a proportion of his income tax was used for the construction of nuclear weapons. Such weapons of war he contended were, among other things, contrary to the Geneva Conventions. To this segment of this submission, the Court replied by reiterating the well-known principles that treaties which are part of international law do not form part of UK law unless the legislature expressly makes them so, and therefore the court would not discuss the merits of his argument.[34]

It was a result of this constitutional rule that the UK Parliament passed the European Communities Act (ECA) of 1972 and gave domestic effect to the Treaty of Rome. Thus all acts of the Community either past or future have been or will be incorporated into the United Kingdom legal system, and this rule applies to both primary Community law which derives from the Treaty and secondary Community law which originates from Community legislation or from the jurisprudence of the Court of Justice. In addition, the Act also stipulates that any question as to the meaning or effect of the treaties is to be treated as a question of Community law and, if not referred to the E.C.J., is to be dealt with by the UK courts in accordance with the principles laid down by the European Court itself. Thus an entirely new factor was introduced into the UK legal and political system whereby the courts and Parliament were to be subject to outside constraints and enactments.

The situation is not, however, as straightforward as one might suppose. The incorporation of the Treaty of Rome into UK law has presented the UK Courts with the problem of how to give effect to the "human rights" articles of the Treaty of Rome, and, in particular, what might happen if they conflict with an Act of Parliament passed *subsequently* to the 1972 ECA.

Under traditional British legal thinking, Parliament cannot bind its successors as to form and content of future legislation, and since the ECA (according to the traditional approach) is an Act of Parliament like any other Act of Parliament, then its terms can be expressly or impliedly repealed. On the other hand, if Parliament were to pass subsequent legislation which overrode the Treaty provisions, then the organization and functioning of the EC would come under considerable strain and the doctrine of supremacy of Community law would be challenged.

In this context the Article which has presented most problems to the courts is Article 119, dealing with the principles of equal pay for equal work. In *Shields v. E. Coomes (Holdings) Ltd.*, Lord Denning M.R. took a decidedly unconventional approach to the issues surrounding Article 119. In the course of his judgment, the Master of the Rolls quoted Section 2(i) of the European Communities Act of 1972 and said that legal effect was to be given, among other rights and obligations, to those contained in Article 119. He then went on to deal with the hypothesis of Parliament passing a statute which was inconsistent with Article 119: "As, for instance, if the Equal Pay Act gave the right of equal pay only to unmarried women, I should have thought that a married woman could bring an action in the High Court to enforce the right to equal pay given to her by Article 119."[35]

Such an attack upon legal orthodoxy did not pass unnoticed, and in *Macarthys Ltd. v. Smith*, Lord Denning made further pronouncements upon this problem. If it should happen, the Master of the Rolls argued, that UK legislation is inconsistent with Community law as a result of defective draftsmanship, then the Courts were under a duty to give effect to Community law. The authority for this proposition, he reasoned, was to be found in the ECA. He cautioned, however, that if Parliament expressly passed an act "with the intention of repudiating the Treaty or any provision in it . . . and said so in express terms," then he maintained it was the duty of the Courts to follow the wishes of Parliament.[36] Lord Denning did not, though, envisage such a situation.

While the above might help throw some light upon some of the constitutional issues thrown up by the UK's membership in the EC, the situation upon the UK's ratification of the ECHR in March 1951 was quite different. The ECHR was not incorporated into municipal law by an Act of Parliament, and consequently it had no binding force before the UK courts. Or, such at least was the theoretical position—the reality has been somewhat more complicated. The most audacious approach to this problem was again taken by Lord Denning in *Birdi's* case in which he went so far as to say that if an Act of Parliament did not conform to the Convention then he might be inclined to hold it invalid! A statement which he retracted (wisely, it is submitted) in *R. v. Home Secretary ex p. Bhajan Sing.* He did, however, in the latter case give expression to the hope that no Act of Parliament would ever be contrary to the Convention.[37]

Following from these developments there were other judicial pronouncements upon the exact impact and effect of the Convention in UK domestic law. In one particular case, Lord Scarman felt moved to express the notion that it was the duty of the courts "so long as they do not defy or disregard clear unequivocal provisons" to interpret statutes in a way which promotes rather than undermines the rights set forth in the Convention.[38] In order, however, to counter any confusion which may have arisen as to the exact standing of the Convention in municipal law, Lord Denning again set forth his views in *R. v. Chief Immigration Office, Heathrow Airport ex p. Bibi:*

> The position as I understand it is, if there is ambiguity in our statutes or uncertainty in our law, then these courts can look to the Convention as an aid to clear up ambiguity and uncertainty . . . furthermore when Parliament is enacting a statute or the Secretary of State is framing rules, the courts will *assume* that they had regard to the provisions of the Convention and intended to make the enactment accord with the Convention will interpret them accordingly.[39]

But Lord Denning then went on to reiterate the traditionally accepted view that the Convention was not part of UK law and could not be regarded as such until incoporated by an Act of Parliament. Moreover, in *Malone v. Metropolitan Police Commissioner*, the Court was of the opinion that as the Convention was a treaty it was not a justiciable issue as to whether the Convention has been breached.[40]

In view of the failure of the UK Parliament to enact the ECHR as part of its domestic law, it would seem that the UK is destined to retain its almost distinctive constitutional characteristic of having no fundamental rights guaranteed by law and enforced by the courts. A possible solution to this problem might appear if the individual and human rights articles of the Treaty of Rome are continued to be given force by the courts of the UK in a conscientious manner. Although this would not prevent an express statutory repeal of the relevant provisions of the Treaty, it would provide some greater protection for the individual citizen than that which existed prior to the UK's membership of the EC. Moreover, under the terms of Section 3 of ECA, the UK courts are obliged to take judicial notice of Community law and the jurisprudence of the European Court. Thus by making intelligent use of the "human rights cases" of the E.C.J. and its comments concerning the ECHR, the ECHR might at last begin to play a significant role as part of the UK domestic law. One should be aware, though, that the ECHR could not be invoked in this manner in situations which are beyond the scope of EC activities.[41]

In conclusion, then, one might look over the last twenty-plus years since the founding of the EC and tentatively hold that an organization which set out primarily, though not exclusively, as an economic experiment, and whose Court reflected this view, has felt confident enough to pronounce upon other issues and objectives within the Community. The E.C.J., by making the first cautious steps toward establishing a "human rights philosophy" as part of its jurisprudential arsenal, has helped in the development of the final goal of the Community; that of political union and perhaps with it a European Bill of Rights.

NOTES

1. HMG White Paper, 1967 (Cmnd. 3301, paragraph 25).

2. M. Hilf, "The Protection of Fundamental Rights in the Community," in Francis G. Jacobs, ed., *European Law and the Individual* (Amsterdam: North Holland, 1976), p. 147.

3. *Costa v. ENEL, Common Market Law Reports* (1964) C.M.L.R. 425 at p. 455. Moreover, in this same case and in an earlier one, it was stated that Community law was applicable both to states and to their nationals and Community law "not only imposes obligations on individuals but also confers on their legal rights." See *Van Gend en Loos* (1963), C.M.L.R. 105 at p. 129.

4. *Administrazione delle Finanze Dello Stato v. Simmenthal SpA* (no. 2), (1978) 3 C.M.L.R. 263 at p. 283.

5. For a modern day formulation of what can be categorized as a "human right," see the *UN Charter; UN Universal Declaration of Human Rights; European Convention on the Prevention and Punishment of the Crime of Genocide; UN International Convention on the Elimination of all Forms of Racial Discrimination; UN International Convention on Economic, Social, and Cultural Rights; UN International Covenant on Civil and Political Rights.*

6. See *Costa v. ENEL; Van Gend en Loos; Administrazione dello Finanze Dello Stato v. Simmenthal* (no. 2) above.

7. Article 3(c) of the Treaty states the necessity for this proviso in order that the purposes of the Community can be achieved.

8. This theme is mentioned elsewhere in the Treaty: Article 51 relates to restrictions on freedom of establishment of nationals of a member state; the Treaty places in separate categories "workers" or wage/salary earners (Articles 48-51) and the self-employed who come under provisions relating to the right of establishment (Articles 52-57); Article 51 makes provision for social security for migrant workers and their

dependents; and Article 135 deals with freedom of movement of workers from certain overseas countries and territories.

9. *Van Duyn v. Home Office,* (1975) 1 C.M.L.R. 1; *R. v. Bouchereau, Weekly Law Report* (1978) 2 W.L.R. 250.

10. Article 3(i) of EC Directive 64/221 provides: "Measures taken on grounds of public policy or of public security shall be based exclusively on the personal conduct of the individual concerned."

11. *Van Duyn v. Home Office,* (1975) 1 C.M.L.R. 1 at p. 17.

12. *R. v. Bouchereau,* (1978) 2 W.L.R. 250 at p. 276.

13. (1976) 2 C.M.L.R. 98.

14. Ibid., p. 125.

15. (1978) 3 C.M.L.R. 312.

16. *Re The European Elections Act,* (1980) 1 C.M.L.R. 497.

17. See, for example, *Sgarlata v. EC Commission,* (1966) C.M.L.R. 314 at p. 324.

18. (1970) C.M.L.R. 112 at p. 119.

19. *Internationale Handelsgesellschaft,* (1972) 2 C.M.L.R. 255 at p. 283.

20. Ibid.

21. (1974) 2 C.M.L.R. 338 at p. 354.

22. Some countries which have ratified the ECHR are not members of the EC (i.e., Austria, Cyprus, Iceland, Malta, Norway, Sweden, Switzerland, and Turkey).

23. (1976) 2 C.M.L.R. 708.

24. Article 9(2) of the European Convention on Human Rights reads: "Freedom to manifest one's religion or belief shall be subject only to such limitations as are prescribed by law and are necessary in a democratic society in the interests of public safety, for the protection of public order, health or morals, or for the protection of the rights and freedom of others."

25. (1980) 3 C.M.L.R. 64.

26. (1976) 1 C.M.L.R. 140.

27. *Ibid.,* p. 155.

28. (1976) 2 C.M.L.R. 552 at p. 564.

29. *Official Journal* (of the European Community), 1977 C103/1.

30. As cited in *Human Rights Review* 3 (1978): pp. 66-68.

31. (1979) 2 C.M.L.R. 229 at p. 233. The C.F.D.T. argued that such an omission was a violation of Articles 11, 13, and 14 of the ECHR.

32. See Hilf, "The Protection of Fundamental Rights in the Community," *loc. cit.*

33. See *Blackburn v. A-G,* (1971) 1 W.L.R. 1037 at p. 1039. See also *Salomon v. Commissioners of Customs and Exise,* (1967) 2 Q.B. 166; *McWhirter v. A-G,* (1972) C.M.L.R. 882.

34. (1968) 1 W.L.R. 242 at p. 245.

35. (1978) 1 W.L.R. 1408 at p. 1415.

36. (1979) 3 C.M.L.R. 44 at p. 47.

37. *Birdi v. Secretary of State for Home Affairs,* Bar Library Transcript, No. 67B of 1975 (February 11, 1975); (1975) 3 W.L.R. 225 at p. 231.

38. *R. v. Home Secretary ex. p. Phansopkar,* (1975) 3 W.L.R. 322 at p. 339.

39. (1976) 1 W.L.R. 979 at p. 984.

40. (1979) 2 W.L.R. 701 at p. 709.

41. See *Surjit Kaur v. Lord Advocate,* (1980) 3 C.M.L.R. 79; *Allgemeine Gold und Silberscheideanstalt v. The Commissioners of Customs and Exise,* (1978) 2 C.M.L.R. 292.

J.-Albert Verreydt 11

THE EVOLUTION OF THE EUROPEAN PHARMACEUTICAL PROFESSION

What is "Pharmacy"? The 1969 edition of the Larousse encyclopedia provided the following description: "a science whose subject is the preparation of medicines." The 1975 edition, however, simply describes it as "a place where medicines are sold." Larousse's changing descriptions only confirmed, after some delay of course, that an important aspect of the pharmacist's traditional activity – the actual preparation of medicines – has now been taken over by industrial concerns.

The activity of the pharmacist has changed progressively and now consists, in large part, of just selling medicine that has been prepared by other people in other places. The individual pharmacist thus has taken on the characteristics of a tradesman: many even refer to the profession now as "retail pharmacy" in order to distinguish it from the wholesalers of medicines and pharmaceutical products. Unfortunately, and this point is discussed below, the perception of the profession as a simple trade can lead to some errors. But nonetheless, the shift in the manufacturing of pharmaceutical products – away from the individual pharmacist and toward industry – has been an important catalyst in the general transformation of the pharmaceutical profession.

An additional factor in the evolution of the pharmacist's activities has been the introduction and development of the various social security and health insurance systems across Europe. These systems have greatly affected the professional and economic relationships between the pharmacist and the public.[1]

Translated from the French by Leon Hurwitz.

EXTERNAL INFLUENCES

The Pharmaceutical Industry

Created from the individual pharmacist's workbench in the 1800s, the pharmaceutical industry evolved rapidly into major corporations with a high degree of technical expertise in synthetic chemistry. The vast advances made by medical and pharmaceutical research provided dazzling benefits for the maintenance of public health and the general standard of living. But since this particular area of industrial activity was—and still is—so closely linked to the public interest, the national governmental authorities were obliged to institute certain legislative controls and restrictions.

The (sometimes) conflicting national legislation, in turn, necessitated that the European Community (EC) institutions issue various directives concerning pharmacological, toxicological, and analytical controls; the marketing of pharmaceutical products; and the periodic inspection of the laboratory facilities and the manufacturing plants. The obvious first task was to reach an agreement on a "European" definition of medicine. In a 1965 Directive, the EC Council of Ministers issued the following statement:

> Article 1. It is understood that the following terms are to mean:
>
> 1. Pharmaceutical product: Any medicine prepared in advance and marketed under a trade or brand name;
>
> 2. Medicine: Any substance or compound alleged to possess curative and/or preventive properties with regard to human and/or animal illnesses. Any substance or compound which can be administered to humans or animals with the goal of establishing a medical diagnosis or to restore, correct, ameliorate or modify an organic function in humans or animals is also considered as a medicine;
>
> 3. Substance: Any material, whatever its origin, such as
>
> human: human blood and products derived from human blood, human secretions, human organs and products derived from such organs . . .;
>
> animal: micro-organisms, entire animals, parts of organs, animal secretions, toxins, substances obtained by extraction, animal blood and products derived from animal blood . . .;
>
> vegetable: micro-organisms, plants, parts of plants, vegetable secretions, substances obtained by extraction . . .;
>
> chemical: basic elements, natural chemical materials, chemical products derived from synthesis.[2]

It is not necessary at this point to describe the entire history of the European pharmaceutical industry, but some comments are offered on the effects that the industry's development has had on the pharmacy profession. At the EC level, the sections of the Rome Treaty that deal with the free circulation of goods and the attainment of a common market are also applicable to the manufacture and sale of medicines across the EC, and in 1975 several Council Directives addressed this issue.[3]

The EC is now without a doubt an industrial and commercial entity and the competition among firms can have a direct and immediate impact on the economy of each country. When the EC is considered, one must take into account the relative share of the pharmaceutical market held by the domestic industry, other EC countries, other European but non-EC countries (mainly Switzerland), and, above all, the United States. United States firms have captured approximately 33 percent of the EC market; other European but non-EC firms have about 17 percent—the remaining 50 percent of the market is shared by domestic/other EC-country-based pharmaceutical firms. Table 11.1, "The Pharmaceutical Industry in Italy, the United Kingdom, and France," contains some figures for three of the larger EC countries. As Table 11.1 indicates, US firms have captured over a third of the British market although the comparative figures for Italy and France are much lower.

The repercussions of this market division fall upon the individual pharmacists: the profits made for dispensing the drugs are usually calculated as a percentage of the sales price. This price, if not fixed by the government, is fixed by the manufacturer. The inescapable consequence of this is that the pharmacy profession more and more resembles a retail trade. It will be shown below that there are other conclusions to be reached from such a situation, but their are many pharmacists who see themselves in such light: "I might as well act like a tradesman since most people take me for one." The American-style drugstore has found many devotees in Europe.

Social Security

The European social security systems began in the nineteenth century through private initiatives, and under the aspect of a health insurance system risk-sharing would also allow cost sharing. The general principle followed was that "insurance does not eliminate risk nor does it eliminate danger—it shares it; it changes the incidence of the loss from the individual to the collectivity and, consequently, substitutes scope for intensity."[4]

In most of the EC countries, the private sector has been taken over by the public governmental sector. Social "insurance" has now become social "security," substituting the political slogan of "the right to health" for the "sharing of the risk." This evolution influences the activities of the pharmacy profession in the sense that the national social security systems must maintain the financial integrity and status of the system. This control and/or influence exerts constant pressure or the income of all health professionals—doctors, dentists, pharmacists, health auxilliaries, and paramedics. The relation between the public and the pharmacist is also influenced by the bureaucratic and economic organization of the social security systems' funding process.

Table 11.2, "Selected Data on the European Pharmaceutical Profession," summarizes the economic situation of the retail pharmacy in Western

TABLE 11.1

THE PHARMACEUTICAL INDUSTRY IN ITALY, THE UNITED KINGDOM, AND FRANCE

		EC	Outside EC	USA
Italy	Number of Firms	35	10	29
	% of Market	69	12	19
United Kingdom	Number of Firms	11	6	24
	% of market	44.4	9.1	36.5
France	Number of Firms	43	15	32
	% of market	73.3	9.1	17.6

Source: Report of the EFPTA (1980).

TABLE 11.2

SELECTED DATA ON THE EUROPEAN PHARMACEUTICAL PROFESSION (1981), EC AND NON-EC

Country	Area (km^2)	Number of Pharmacies	Area per Pharmacy (km^2)	Population (millions)	People per Pharmacy	% of People Under Soc. Sec.	Pharm. Cost (% of GNP)	Tot. Health Cost (% of GNP)
Belgium	30,507	5,134	5.94	10.00	1,948	99	1.50	19.50
Denmark	43,000	318	135.20	5.00	16,352	94	0.68	11.10
Germany	248,000	15.366	16.13	62.00	4,035	96	1.40	17.00
France	551,500	19,441	28.41	55.00	2,829	100	1.70	19.00
Greece	133,00	4,300	30.93	7.00	2,209	100	1.10	60.00
Ireland	70,300	1.149	61.18	3.30	2,872	100	--	--
Italy	301,200	14,000	21.50	56.00	4,000	97	1.90	36.00
Luxem.	2,600	71	36.60	0.38	5,352	100	1.03	15.00
Nether.	33,491	1,050	32.32	14.00	13,333	70	0.80	12.00
UK	244,000	10,610	23.00	56.00	5,278	100	0.75	13.80
Austria	84,000	807	104.00	7.40	9,500	--	--	--
Findland	337,000	666	506.00	5.00	7,000	--	--	--
Norway	324,000	284	1,136.80	3.90	14,500	--	--	--
Portugal	92,000	1,956	47.00	11.00	4,500	--	--	--
Spain	507,000	15,000	33.80	34.00	2,785	74	1.40	--
Sweden	450,000	600	750.00	12.00	14,000	100	--	--
Switzer.	41,295	1,200	34.40	6.30	5,500	--	--	--

Source: Secretariat Europeen des Pharmacies.

Europe, both for EC and non-EC countries. One of the more interesting columns in Table 11.2 is the one which contains the number of people per pharmacy: it ranges from a low of 1,948 in Belgium to a high of 16, 352 in Denmark. It is obvious that the availability of pharmacies across Europe varies widely, and, consequently, so does the economic returns for the pharmacists.

INTERNAL INFLUENCES

The Conditions of Access

The traditional training of a pharmacist—with the emphasis on the preparation of medicines—had to adapt itself to this evolution. One of the main reasons is that the danger presented by the very specific industrial pharmaceuticals is often more toxic than with the naturally occuring product. The pharmacist must now master pharmaceutical chemistry and the biological interactions of these specific products.

No longer a "preparer," the pharmacist now has become an "advisor" and a "dispenser" and is obviously incapable of memorizing the entire modern therapeutic arsenal and the proper dose of each individual drug. Moreover, the pharmacist must consider the public interest in countering the effects of the industry's advertising. The pharmaceutical industry has succeeded in doing something that was unheard of in the last century—the advertising of drugs. Despite the strict surveillance by governmental authorities and the outright prohibition of certain types of medicine, the ads still have as their overriding goal the sale of medicine. Too many ads are all-too-obvious attempts to create the need rather than to address a specific situation. The pharmacist should intervene at this stage and try to prevent, as much as possible, drug abuse and drug dependency.

In sum, instead of limiting the pharmacist's knowledge to the simple preparation of medicines, the training and education should be oriented toward the actual therapeutic actions of the drug, their side effects, and, perhaps most important, their effect on human behavior. The traditional mode of training has now been expanded to include the psychological side effects of medicines. Table 11.3, "Areas and Hours of Study in European Pharmacy," contains some summary figures for the hours of study devoted to the various areas within the pharmacy curriculum.

The Rome Treaty

The principle objective of the European Community is to achieve among the member states the full and free circulation of people, goods, and capital. The Rome Treaty (Articles 53-58) anticipates the right of establishment for the liberal (self-employed) professions. As of the time of writing, however,

TABLE 11.3

AREAS AND HOURS OF STUDY IN EUROPEAN PHARMACY (1981)

	Belguim	Denmark	France	Germany	Ireland	Italy	Greece	Nether.	Spain	Switzer.
Chemistry	1360	1480	794	1220	490	1040	1760	1970	915	1550
Botany	380	230	286	230	410	140	1800	340	410	620
Human Biology	295	195	387	482	295	300	360	295	245	225
Physics/Math	356	278	189	64	240	170	420	360	300	340
Pharmacology	185	295	213	385	335	160	360	572	180	220
Microbiology	50	110	185	32	62	60	30	86	300	130
Total	2,626	2,588	2,054	2,413	1,832	1,870	4,730	3,623	2,350	3,085

Source: *Bulletin* de l'Ordre des Pharmaciens de France (November 1980).

TABLE 11.4

LENGTH OF TRAINING FOR PHARMACISTS

Country	University (years)	Training Stage (months)	Total (Years)
Belgium	4.5	6	5.0
Denmark	4.0	12	5.0
Germany	3.5	12	4.5
France	4.5	6	5.0
Greece	4.0	12	5.0
Ireland	4.0	12	5.0
Italy	3.5-5	6	4.5-5.5
Luxembourg	4.5	6	5.0
Netherlands	3+3	12	6.5-7
United Kingdom			
England & Wales	3+A Level	12	1+4
Scotland & N. Ireland	4.0	12	5.0
Austria	4.0	12	5.0
Finland	2+4	6 (Included)	6.0
Spain	5.0	(Included)	5.0
Norway	4.0	12	5.0
Portugal	5.0	(Included)	5.0
Switzerland	4-5	12	5-6
Sweden	4-5	12	5-6

Source: Groupement Pharmaceutique de la C. E. E., Rapport de la Groupe de Travail academique (1978).

the only professionals that have yet to receive "European" status are self-employed physicians; pharmacists have yet to benefit from the free-circulation clause. But the European pharmacy profession is approaching a relatively standardized curriculum across Europe. Table 11.4, "Length of Training for Pharmacists," shows that there is little discrepancy in the amount of years required before certification is earned.

A recent EC Directive[5] has dealt with this curriculum, but in order to avoid as much as possible upsetting national traditions, the Directive was limited to coordination: a program of minimum study of at least five years after which a professional training stage of six to twelve months was required. The Directive defined the course of study's general content and listed the required areas of study, but did not fix a specific duration within any area:

The member states condition the award or issuance of diplomas, certificates, and/or other titles upon the following minimum requirements:

1. The education and training leading to the receipt of a diploma or certificate guarantees

A. Sufficient knowledge of the raw materials used in pharmacy, of medicines, chemical products, and naturally occuring products including micro-organisms and viruses;

B. Sufficient knowledge of pharmaceutical technology and the chemical and biological nature of medicines;

C. Sufficient knowledge of the effects of medicines and drugs as well as the proper use of such drugs; and

D. Sufficient knowledge about the practice of the pharmacy profession. . . .

3. The education and training should include both theoretical and practical training in at least biology, botany, experimental physics, chemistry (general, organic, inorganic, analytical), biochemistry, microbiology, anatomy, physiology, toxicology, pharmaceutical technology, deontology, and legislative guidelines. The relative amount of time devoted to theory and practice, for each of the above, should retain sufficient importance for theory in order to maintain the program's "academic character."[6]

The same Directive also was concerned with some coordination of the areas of pharmacist activity after the receipt of the diploma. Here again the EC was faced with national traditions and diversity—industrial manufacturing, laboratory research, hospitals, the retail pharmacy—and thus the EC opted to first identify some general directions rather than to attempt a more determined coordination. The coordinated areas are as follows:

1. The Member States will require the recipients of a diploma, certificate or other university title in pharmacy to meet the conditions in Article 2 and to be skilled in the activities mentioned in paragraph 2 and except for certain exceptions, will require an additional training stage or equal professional experience.

2. The activities referred to in paragraph 1 are
- basic research in pharmacology;
- manufacturing and the quality control of medicines;
- stocking, storage, and the distribution of medicines at the wholesale levels;
- the preparation and dispensing of drugs and medicines at the retail level;
- activities within hospital pharmacies;
- the accumulation and dissemination of scientific information for the medical and pharmaceutical professions.[7]

It should be noted that the various directives do not anticipate a standardization of the curriculum nor the complete coordination of all the pharmacy-related activities across the EC member states. This hesitancy is the consequence of the very real differences that have evolved within the profession in each member state. Some of these very real differences can be summarized as follows: in several countries the pharmacist is the only medical specialist in the entire manufacturing-to-sale process; in other countries, the pharmaceutical industry developed without close contacts with pharmacists. In the former group of countries, there exists what is termed a "pharmacist's monopoly" while in the latter group, a pharmacist is required only at the point of sale of the consumer.

It is obvious to all that a more rational coordination must be achieved in the future, but too much coordination too fast will lead to turmoil in many member states. The directives also respect the differences in national cultures and traditions and, additionally, respect the differences which exist from university to university within the same country.

The Conditions of Practice

Formerly, it was unthinkable within the liberal professions that the individual would not be the owner of the business or practice. In pharmacy, the growth of the pharmaceutical industry changed both the image and reality of the pharmacist: the individual pharmacist is now more often than not the "seller," and the management and ownership of the concern lies elsewhere. In several countries, the law does not require that the property belong to the registered pharmacist and many pharmacies are now controlled by absentee owners.

The commercial conception of "ready-to-use" applied to medicines has led in certain countries to a break in the traditional monopoly of dispensing drugs. The sale of non-prescription drugs/over-the-counter products has been authorized in many places other than a pharmacy, especially in areas where there was an insufficient number of pharmacies. This maldistribution of pharmacies has also led to physicians themselves dispensing drugs in rural areas. In order to enlarge the points of access, certain national legislation organized a geographical distribution of pharmacies. This distribution is generally expressed in terms of number of people per pharmacy and it is sometimes accompanied by a minimal distance between pharmacies.

PROSPECTS

The essential role of the pharmacist in any society always has been and should remain the delivery of pharmaceutical care. This mission includes several diverse areas of activity. In the area of medicine, the pharmacist must guarantee the quality and the safety of the product during all stages of the process: conception, manufacturing, inspection, delivery, and sale. At the retail level, the pharmacist has a role of a health educator and should provide advice to the public.

As a medical specialist, the pharmacist should provide to physicians, the ill, and to any other person who wishes, his advice and counsel on the composition of drugs as well as information on their side effects. He should also make explicit to his patients all the possible interactions between certain drugs as well as information on proper diet and other treatment. Finally, the pharmacist should cooperate with other health specialists in organizing and publicizing anti-drug, -tobacco, and -alcohol campaigns. The pharmacist should also join the fight against drug abuse and drug dependency.

An equitable geographical distribution of pharmacies is needed because this will guarantee everyone easy access to quality pharmaceutical care. The pharmacy is *not* a trade; to the contrary, the pharmacist must sometimes refuse a sale in certain situations. The pharmacist's independence must be guaranteed by appropriate legislation and his actions must be governed by an appropriate code of ethics.

NOTES

1. Abel Smith and Alan Maynard, *L'Organisation, le financement et le coût des soins de Santé dans la C. E.* (Brussels: Ec Commission, 1978).
2. European Community. Council of Ministers, *Journal Official* 22 (9 February 1965).
3. Directives 318/75 and 319/75, *Journal Official* 22 (9 June 1975).
4. P. Richard, *Theorie mathematique des assurances* (Paris: Hachette, 1969), p. 2.
5. Directive 35/81, *Journal Officiel.*
6. Ibid.
7. Ibid.

BIBLIOGRAPHICAL ESSAY

The literature on European integration has grown in quantity and sophistication just as EC integration itself has grown in the postwar period. This brief bibliographical essay traces the development of the European integrative process. The origins of the EC can be seen, of course, in events which far predate 1945 – the Roman Empire, the Holy Roman Empire, Christiandom of the Middle Ages, the writings of various philosophers – but space does not allow a full recapitulation. One can perhaps say that the origins of the EC began in the interwar period when Benelux was established – a customs union among Belgium, the Netherlands, and Luxembourg (Alan Valentine, "Benelux: Pilot Plan of Economic Union," *The Yale Review* 44, no. 1 (September 1954). In 1946, Winston S. Churchill, in a speech at Zurich, urged Franco-German reconciliation within "a kind of United States of Europe" (Winston S. Churchill, *The Sinews of Peace: Postwar Speeches*, London: Cassel and Co., 1948).

One year later, in 1947, U.S. Secretary of State George C. Marshall offered a massive injection of U.S. economic aid for a collective European Recovery Program (ERP), and in 1948, the Organization for European Economic Cooperation (OEEC, later called OECD) was established for the joint administration of Marshall Plan aid (Hans O. Schmidtt, *The Path to European Union: From the Marshall Plan to the Common Market*, Baton Rouge: Louisiana State University Press, 1962). Cooperation in the military field increased with the 1948 Brussels Pact, a collective security agreement among France, the United Kingdom, and Benelux (Arnold J. Zurcher, *The Struggle to Unite Europe: 1940-1958*, New York: New York University Press, 1958) and in 1949 with the establishment of NATO (Lord Ismay, *NATO: The First Five Years, 1949-1954*, Paris: NATO, 1955). The Council of Europe, strengthening European-wide cooperation in several areas and establishing some intergovernmental bodies, was also created in 1949 (A. H. Robertson *The Council of Europe: Its Structure, Functions and Achievement*, London: Stevens and Sons, 1961).

In May 1950, French Foreign Minister Robert Schuman proposed placing Europe's coal and steel economies under a common European authority. In April 1951, the treaty establishing the European Coal and Steel Community (ECSC) was signed in Paris by France, Germany, Italy, and the Benelux countries. The ECSC's executive body, the High Authority, began functioning in August 1952, with Jean Monnet as first president, and in 1953 the ECSC had established a common market for coal, iron ore, scrap, and steel (William Diebold, Jr., *The Schuman Plan: A Study in*

Economic Cooperation, 1950-1959, New York: Praeger, 1959; Louis Lister, *Europe's Coal and Steel Community*, New York: Twentieth Century Fund, 1960).

A further attempt to integrate along military lines was the European Defense Community (EDC), but this failed in 1954 (Clarence C. Walton: "Background for the European Defense Community," *Political Science Quarterly 68*, no. 1, March 1953; Hamilton Fish Armstrong, "Postscript to the EDC," *Foreign Affairs* 33, no. 1, October 1954. The Western European Union (WEU) was established in 1955, and the six countries of the ECSC began talks aimed at the possible enlargement of the functional areas of integration (Tibor Scitovsky, *Economic Theory and Western European Integration*, Stanford, Calif.: Stanford University Press, 1958). The Messina Conference was held in 1955, with the foreign ministers of the six deciding on further economic integration as the basis for future political unity (Comité Intergouvernmental crée par la Conférence de Messine, *Rapport des chefs de délégations aux ministres des affaires étrangères*, Brussels, 1956). In 1956, at the Venice Conference, the six foreign ministers authorized a subsequent conference to draft a treaty expanding European integration (Ernst B. Haas, *The Uniting of Europe: Political, Social and Economic Forces, 1950-1957*, Stanford, Calif.: Stanford University Press, 1961).

The Treaty of Rome, creating the European Economic Community (EEC) and the European Atomic Energy Commission (Euratom), was signed in Rome in March 1957 (*Treaty Establishing The European Economic Community, Rome, 25 March 1957*, London: HMSO, 1973). The treaties went into force on January 1, 1958; Euratom's first president was Etienne Hirsch, and EEC Commission's first president was Walter Hallstein (Walter Hallstein, *United Europe: Challenge and Opportunity*, Cambridge, Mass.: Harvard University Press, 1962; and his *Europe in the Making*, New York: W. W. Norton, 1972). The Rome treaties established the governing institutions and organizations of the EEC: the Council of Ministers, a Court of Justice, the Commission, and a Parliament which, until direct popular elections in June 1979, was chosen by and from the six national Parliaments (David Coombes, *Politics and Bureaucracy in the European Community: A Portrait of the Commission of the EEC*, London: George Allen and Unwin, 1970; Sir Barnett Cocks, *The European Parliament: Structure, Procedure and Practice*, London: HMSO, n.d.).

Western Europe was now split into two main economic areas: the Six of the EEC and the Seven of the European Free Trade Association (EFTA), created in 1960 by the United Kingdom, Norway, Denmark, Sweden, Austria, Switzerland, and Portugal (Emile Benoit, *Europe at Sixes and Sevens: The Common Market, The Free Trade Association and the United States*, New York: Columbia University Press, 1961). In late 1961 and early 1962, Denmark, Ireland, Norway, and the United Kingdom opened negotiations aimed at joining the EEC, but on January 14, 1963, French President Charles deGaulle declared that the UK was "not ready" for Community membership. DeGaulle thus exercised a de facto veto, and shortly thereafter negotiations between the UK—and the other three—and the Community were broken off (Miriam Camps, *Britain and the European Community, 1955-1963*, Princeton, N.J.: Princeton University Press, 1964).

In June 1964, the first Yaoundé Convention entered into force, associating seventeen African states and Madagascar with the Community. In July 1965, the Council of Ministers failed to reach an agreement on financing a common farm policy. The French boycott of the Council of Ministers began a seven-month crisis, but in January 1966, the foreign ministers agreed to resume full Community activity (John

Newhouse, *Collision in Brussels: The Common Market Crisis of 30 June 1965,* New York: W. W. Norton, 1967). In February 1967, the Community agreed to introduce the VAT turnover tax in all six countries (K.V. Antal, "Harmonisation of Turnover Taxes in the Common Market," *Common Market Law Review 1,* no. 1, June 1963; T. M. Rybczynski, *The Value Added Tax: The UK Position and the European Experience,* Oxford: Basil Blackwell, 1969). In July 1967, all Community executive institutions were merged, and the organization became known as the European Community (EC). For the second time, Britain, Ireland, and Denmark opened negotiations for EC membership, but in November 1967, deGaulle "objected" to Britain's entry, and in late 1967 negotiations broke off once again.

A common external tariff (CET) and a full customs union were achieved in July 1968, and the Community was able to remove the last remaining restrictions on the free movement of workers as well as the last remaining national obstacles to Member States' workers in employment, pay, and other conditions. Yaoundé II was signed in 1969, and the December 1969 Hague Summit of the EC foreign ministers agreed to complete, enlarge, and strengthen the EC. The UK, Denmark, Norway, and Ireland opened negotiations to enter the EC for the third time, and with the resignation of Charles deGaulle, entry was assured. The Norwegians rejected by a national referendum their country's entry in 1972, but on January 1, 1973, the United Kingdom, Ireland, and Denmark entered, enlarging the EC to nine members (Uwe Kitzinger, *Diplomacy and Persuasion: How Britain Joined the Common Market,* London: Thames and Hudson, 1973).

The period 1973-79 saw the EC solidify the base of economic and political integration by formulating common policies in regard to EC functional areas as well as with external relations. Some of these policies, however, were not very successful (Robert J. Lieber, *Oil and the Middle East War: Europe in the Energy Crisis,* Cambridge, Mass.: Harvard Center for International Affairs, 1976). Some policies were reasonably more successful (William F. Averyt, Jr., *Agropolitics in the European Community,* New York: Praeger, 1977; Bernard Bonnici, *Condition de Circulation et d'Etablissement des Médicins dans la CEE,* Paris: Editions Médicales et Universitaires, 1978; Frans A. M. Alting von Geusau, *The External Relations of the European Community,* Westmead, England: D.C. Heath / Saxon House, 1974; Ph. Petit-Laurent, *Les Fondements politiques des engagements de la Communauté Européenne dans la Méditerranée,* Paris: Presses Universitaires de France, 1976; James Caporaso, *The Structure and Function of European Integration,* Pacific Palisades, Calif.: Goodyear, 1974; Helene Wallace, William Wallace, and Carole Webb, *Policy-Making in the European Communities,* London: John Wiley and Sons, 1973; and Roger Williams, *European Technology: The Politics of Collaboration,* New York: John Wiley and Sons, 1973).

Some recent developments point toward an increased process of integration and harmonization of public policy: the European Monetary System (EMS) was established in 1979; Greece signed the Accession Treaty with a five-year transition period before becoming the tenth EC member; direct popular elections for the enlarged European Parliament were held in June 1979 (Michael Palmer, *The European Parliament,* Oxford: Pergamon Press, 1981); and Spain and Portugal are negotiating their entry into the EC. For current literature, one is advised to see the *Journal of Common Market Studies; West European Politics; International Organization; World Politics; International Studies Quarterly; Common Market Law Review;* and the *Official Journal* of the European Communities.

INDEX

CONTRIBUTORS

WERNER J. FELD (Referendar [Law], University of Berlin; Ph.D., political science, Tulane University) is professor and chair, Department of Political Science, University of New Orleans.

ROY GIBSON (Wadham College, Oxford University; London School of Economics) served as the European Space Agency's first Director-General (1975-1980). He is currently a consultant in aerospace and defense fields.

JOHN GOORMAGHTIGH (J.D., Brussels University) is Secretary-General, European Science Foundation, Strasbourg (France).

RODGER M. GOVEA (Ph.D., political science, Syracuse University) is assistant professor, Department of Political Science, Cleveland State University.

LEON HURWITZ (Ph.D., political science, Syracuse University) is professor, Department of Political Science, Cleveland State University.

HARMEN LEHMENT (Ph.D., economics, University of Kiel) is a research associate, Institute für Weltwirtschaft, University of Kiel (West Germany).

JONATHAN M. MILLER (L.L.M., University of London, London School of Economics) is lecturer in law, Polytechnic of Central London, London (United Kingdom).

JOSEPH RALLO (J.D., Western New England College; Ph.D., political science, Syracuse University) is an Assistant Professor in International Politics at the U.S. Air Force Academy in Colorado Springs, Colorado.

J.-ALBERT VERREYDT (Dr. Sc. Ph., University of Louvain) is Secretary-General, Pharmaceutical Group of the European Community, Brussels, Belgium.

DAVID M. WOOD (Ph.D., political science, University of Illinois) is professor, Department of Political Science, University of Missouri at Columbia.

ABOUT THE EDITOR

LEON HURWITZ is professor of political science at Cleveland State University in Cleveland, Ohio. He has published numerous articles in journals such as *Comparative Politics* and *Journal of Common Market Studies*. His previous books include *Introduction to Politics: Traditionalism to Postbehavioralism* (Nelson-Hall, 1979); *Contemporary Perspectives on European Integration: Attitudes, Non-Governmental Behavior, and Collective Decision Making* (Greenwood Press, 1980); *The State as Defendant: Governmental Accountability and the Redress of Individual Grievances* (Greenwood Press, 1981); and, with Werner J. Feld and Robert S. Jordan, *International Organizations* (Praeger, 1983).